Racial Ambiguity in
Asian American Culture

Asian American Studies Today

This series publishes scholarship on cutting-edge themes and issues, including broadly based histories of both long-standing and more recent immigrant populations; focused investigations of ethnic enclaves and understudied subgroups; and examinations of relationships among various cultural, regional, and socioeconomic communities. Of particular interest are subject areas in need of further critical inquiry, including transnationalism, globalization, homeland polity, and other pertinent topics.

Series Editor: Huping Ling, Truman State University

Jennifer Ann Ho, *Racial Ambiguity in Asian American Culture*

Jun Okada, *Making Asian American Film and Video: History, Institutions, Movements*

David S. Roh, Betsy Huang, and Greta A. Niu, *Techno-Orientalism: Imagining Asia in Speculative Fiction, History, and Media*

Racial Ambiguity in Asian American Culture

JENNIFER ANN HO

RUTGERS UNIVERSITY PRESS

NEW BRUNSWICK, NEW JERSEY, AND LONDON

Library of Congress Cataloging-in-Publication Data

Ho, Jennifer Ann, 1970–

Racial ambiguity in Asian American culture / Jennifer Ann Ho.

pages cm. — (Asian American studies today)

Includes bibliographical references and index.

ISBN 978–0–8135–7070–9 (hardcover : alk. paper) — ISBN 978–0–8135–7069–3 (pbk. : alk. paper) — ISBN 978–0–8135–7071–6 (e-book (web pdf))

1. American literature—Asian American authors—History and criticism. 2. Asian Americans in popular culture. 3. Asian Americans—Race identity. 4. Racially mixed people—Race identity—United States. I. Title.

PS153.A84H585 2015

810.9'895—dc23

2014035922

A British Cataloging-in-Publication record for this book is available from the British Library.

Visit our website: http://rutgerspress.rutgers.edu

Manufactured in the United States of America

For my Uncle Frank

He was the first person to talk to me about race and racism. He was the first person who made me care about social justice. I think he would have been proud of this book, because in so many ways it is a product of the many lessons he taught me.

CONTENTS

Acknowledgments   ix

Introduction: Ambiguous Americans   1

1   From Enemy Alien to Assimilating American:
Yoshiko deLeon and the Mixed-Marriage
Policy of the Japanese American Incarceration   22

2   Antisentimental Loss: Stories of
Transracial/Transnational Asian American
Adult Adoptees in the Blogosphere   44

3   Cablinasian Dreams, Amerasian Realities:
Transcending Race in the Twenty-First Century
and Other Myths Broken by Tiger Woods   71

4   Ambiguous Movements and Mobile
Subjectivity: Passing in between Autobiography
and Fiction with Paisley Rekdal and Ruth Ozeki   96

5   Transgressive Texts and Ambiguous Authors:
Racial Ambiguity in Asian American Literature   123

Coda   Ending with Origins: My Own Racial Ambiguity   148

Notes   153
Bibliography   189
Index   207

ACKNOWLEDGMENTS

This book began during a cocktail party conversation I had with John Jackson, who asked me what I was working on. Sometimes big things can start from casual questions and conversations. So I first want to thank the many people in my life with whom I've had the good fortune to be in conversation throughout my academic career: teachers, students, staff members, friends, and family. Those who have served as particularly helpful interlocutors at my home institution of the University of North Carolina (UNC) Chapel Hill include the English department chair who hired me, James Thompson, and my current department chair, Beverly Taylor, who helped to shepherd me through tenure; English and Comparative Literature colleagues who make me grateful for having such a nurturing academic home, Neel Ahuja, Maria deGuzman, Darryl Gless, Laura Halperin, Jordynn Jack, Heidi Kim, Jamie Rosenthal, Matthew Taylor, and especially to Minrose Gwin and Ruth Salvaggio, who have been extraordinary mentors to me; and to Jane Danielwicz and John McGowan, who have become my Chapel Hill family. I have been inspired by so many colleagues at UNC Chapel Hill, North Carolina State, Duke University, and others in the Research Triangle, among them John Begeny, Donna Bickford, Dan Cobb, Elizabeth Dickinson, Kathleen Kearns, Adriane Lentz-Smith, Laurie Maffly-Kipp, Tim Marr, Eric Muller, Dennis Mumby, Mai Nguyen, Michelle Robinson, Mark Sheftall, Julia Woods, Priscilla Wald, whose Americanist Speaker series allowed me a place to work through the ideas in this book, and Joy Kasson, who is my role model of the kind of respected and generous scholar I aspire to be one day. I am particularly appreciative of the incredible loyalty and friendship of Ariana Vigil, Rebecca Walsh, and John Charles Williamson, who read and commented on various parts of this book—they mean the world to me.

I need to thank the Institute of Arts and Humanities (IAH), especially the dedicated and hard-working staff, for the fellowship semesters (Fall 2008 and Fall 2012) that one graduate student has called "a spa for your mind." My cohorts both semesters, faculty colleagues in the College of Arts and Sciences, pushed my writing and thinking in deep and meaningful ways. I am especially grateful to the donors who supported my two fellowships at the IAH, Dr. J. McNeely Dubose and Mr. Max Chapman; their endowments and my participation at the IAH were integral to the completion of this book.

I have been lucky to have met so many scholars whose work and example motivate me to do the work that I do. Elizabeth Ammons, Frederick Aldama, Shelley Fisher Fishkin, and Jim Phelan were people whose scholarship first impressed me and then whose generosity as people impressed me even more. Leah Anderson, James Donahue, Shaun Morgan, and Janine Utell form my core accountability group; they have kept me honest about my work schedule for the last two years, and they remind me that you can be smart and funny and humane. To my colleagues in Asian American studies, I owe a huge debt of gratitude, particularly those I've developed such meaningful friendships with over the years, sustained during the annual meeting of the Association of Asian American Studies (AAAS): Crystal Anderson, Leslie Bow, Tina Chen, Floyd Cheung, Sylvia Chong, Elena Creef, Catherine Fung, Jennifer Hayashida, Robert Ku, Jim Lee, Josephine Lee, Anita Mannur, Sean Metzger, JoAnna Poblete, Cathy Schlund-Vials, Paul Spickard, Scott Wong, Grace Yoo, Timothy Yu, and Helen Zia. My deepest regard, admiration, and affection will always be for Betsy Huang, Sue Kim, Paul Lai, and Stephen Sohn—you kept me sane and reality checked me so many times, I can't imagine being in this profession without you.

This book wouldn't have seen the light of day were it not for the leadership of Huping Ling, who helmed the series "Asian American Studies Today" and the expert guidance of Katie Keeran—to them and the other staff members of Rutgers University Press I can only say that working with you has been a privilege and a pleasure. I am especially grateful to the two external reviewers whose suggestions have truly made this a better book. I also want to thank the bloggers in chapter 2, who allowed me to quote freely from their websites, and to the artist, iona rozeal brown, who graciously granted permission to use one of the images from her "a3" series as the cover for this book. To the Dorr family, especially Pat, Trish, Jack, and Alex, chapter 1 could not have been written without the stories you shared about Yoshiko deLeon and your generosity through these many years. Thank you.

Although my various academic communities have sustained my intellectual pursuits, my friends and family have given me sustenance, both literal and emotional, throughout the decade that it has taken this book to come to fruition. Sheri Alterman, Jason Chow, Seth Craigo-Snell, Shannon Craigo-Snell, Elysa Engelman, Eydie Harridge, Beth Houghton, Shaun Lopez, Tania Salazar, Paul Schmitz, and Karen Seto are friends who feel like family. Thanks go to my extended families, both Ho and Yap, whose support now and over the years has given me a strong sense of belonging. I am particularly grateful to a set of cousins whom I am lucky enough to claim as close friends: Greg Alger, Jeanine Chan, Soerha Chang, Eileen Ho, Craig Hosang, Andrew Yap, and Wayne Yap. I am also fortunate that my nuclear family, Yola, Tony, and Chris Ho, have always given me the unconditional love that has enabled me to be the person I am. And to the Grady family, I truly appreciate how you've welcomed me with open arms and heart.

I reserve my sincerest gratitude for my husband, Matthew James Grady, who is the best partner I could ever imagine (one might call him a unicorn). I don't have adequate words to express what I owe to you. It sounds cliché, but I truly feel that being with you has made me a better person. I hope I get to continue acknowledging how much I love you as long as I am able to write.

Racial Ambiguity in
Asian American Culture

Introduction

Ambiguous Americans

What Are You?: Race and the State of Asian America

At the beginning of *My Year of Meats*, the novelist Ruth Ozeki includes the following encounter between her protagonist, Jane Takagi-Little, a half-white–half-Japanese American documentary filmmaker, and an unnamed white American World War II veteran:

> "Where are you from, anyway?" he asked, squinting his bitter blue eyes at me.
>
> "New York," I answered.
>
> He shook his head and glared and wiggled a crooked finger inches from my face. "No, I mean where were you *born?*"
>
> "Quam, Minnesota," I said.
>
> "No, no . . . *What* are you?" He whined with frustration.
>
> And in a voice that was low, but shivering with demented pride, I told him, "*I . . . am . . . a . . . fucking . . . AMERICAN!*" [italics in original]

As the scene from Ozeki's novel indicates, the question "What are you?" affirms the alienation (or alien nation) of Asians in America—as enigmatically spaced, placed, and raced within the topography and taxonomy of American cultural identities. Jane's fierce assertion of her US nationality signals not simple jingoism but a reminder to the veteran that Asian Americans belong in the United States as *American* citizens; they have just as much claim on America as anyone else. Yet the veteran's inability to locate Jane, perhaps exacerbated by her biraciality, speaks to the indeterminacy of Asian Americans, their racial ambiguity.[1]

Asian Americans become a palimpsestic screen on which the anxieties and desires of the country are projected, as literary critic Leslie Bow asserts: "Asian

Americans are already situated as the national in-between; they do not merely triangulate relations between citizen/noncitizen or black/white, they invoke cultural anxiety as American but not quite; as middle class—almost; as minority but not one of 'those' minorities; as like us but not really."[2] Moreover, Asian Americans experience an ambiguity different from other raced groups, and those identifying as mixed race Asian American feel a different type of ambiguity from both their mixed non–Asian American peers as well as their monoracial peers, whether they be Asian American, black, white, or any other point on the racial pentagram.[3] Though we may be able to say that because race is a fiction, there is no substantive difference between a monoracial and multiracial Asian American, the types of experiences, on the whole, that monoracial subjects face versus their multiracial peers does suggest, once again, that lived reality and abstract theory face a divide that can only be addressed through recording and interpreting the stories told by multiracial Asian Americans alongside those told by monoracial Asian Americans. "In spite of the current tendency to celebrate and even romanticize multiculturalism," writes cultural critic Elena Tajima Creef, "there is a genuine dilemma of where one may place a hybrid body that does not fit into any one simple place on a white American map."[4]

What we need is a theory that can speak to issues of race and ambiguity for Asian Americans, monoracial and multiracial alike, and the scholar-artist-activist Kip Fulbeck has attempted to create such a theorizing of the body by observing and visually recording the ambiguity of multiracial Asian Americans. Fulbeck, who identifies as mixed heritage Asian American himself, created a project whereby he photographed sundry people who identified as *hapa* (mixed race Asians) and then had them answer the question, "What are you?"[5] The subjects' images and their answers formed both a traveling art exhibit as well as a book, *Part Asian*100% Hapa*. All of the participants were photographed naked from the shoulders up, their pictures encompassing the entire right-hand page, with the left-facing page listing their self-identified ethnicities and the answer to the question "What are you?" None of the subjects has any other identifying marks: no names, birthdates, or places of residence accompany these images. Reading each answer and looking at each portrait creates an effect that simultaneously makes all the images blur, yet their answers give them a distinction that makes each one unique in their communal identification as hapa. To flip through quickly or to thoughtfully contemplate this work is to experience the ambiguity of seeing each person as both an individual and part of a collective, a condition that perhaps mirrors that of any other racial group, yet for the subjects of Fulbeck's work it allows each person to claim a subjectivity so often denied to them within the zero-sum game of identity politics. For example, one person who lists African American and Japanese as his ethnicities writes, "I am

100% Black and 100% Japanese."[6] For this man, the answer to "What are you?" cannot be contained by the logic of mathematics but instead must reside in a seemingly paradoxical realm in which one can be both wholly black and wholly Japanese.

Indeed, racially ambiguous subjects and stories resist reinscription into narrow understandings of race and serve as counternarratives to official and hegemonic discourses. For example, Chinese American rapper Jin's debut album *The Rest Is History* pays tribute to multiple ethnic histories and contributions (like the song "Senorita") and defies easy ethnic categorization in its syncretic union of Asian American and African American culture. *The Rest Is History* self-consciously plays with Asian stereotypes (in the interlude "Chinese Beats" Jin denounces the Orientalized music that his producers believe signifies Chinese culture), challenging its listeners not to draw simple conclusions about Jin's artistic abilities or his ethnic identity while simultaneously paying homage to the tradition of African American rap (particularly in its guest appearances by impresarios Kanye West and Wyclef Jean). In "Learn Chinese," Jin urges listeners to reconsider their fetishization of Asian culture and to understand Asian Americans as exceeding the stereotypes placed on them by the dominant society: "The days of the pork fried rice and the chicken wings coming to your house by me is over." The album's sampling of Das EFX and James Brown, as well as performances by Ayeesha, exhibits its debt to African American culture (not to mention that Wyclef Jean cowrote Jin's most acclaimed Asian American thematic song, "Learn Chinese").

Jin and his debut album resist normative racial formation because the ambiguity of *The Rest Is History* forces listeners to think about Asian Americans within a different cultural context. For example, listeners must challenge their assumptions about what a rapper looks like, the kind of music associated with hip-hop artists, and the ability of Asian Americans to enter into meaningful working relationships and dialogue with African American peers, which subsequently counters the discourse of Asian American and African American hostility that the Red Apple Boycott, Latasha Harlins, and the aftermath of the Los Angeles uprising perpetuated.[7] To label *The Rest Is History* or Jin as simply Asian American or African American or even Afro-Asian does not address the ways in which both album and artist exceed these racial monikers through the myriad samplings of multiple ethnic signs and signifiers.[8] The ambiguity of Jin and *The Rest Is History* does not reside in one's inability to identify discrete ethnic signs or the work's ethnic hybridity; rather, ambiguity marks both artist and album because the sum of their ethnic and racial codings cannot be adequately totaled through a single interpretation or label. They exceed ethnic expectations and, hence, become racially ambiguous. However, this ambiguity is not rendered as a hodge-podge of indeterminate meanings; instead, *The Rest Is History*, through both its individual selections, like "Learn Chinese" as well as the album as a whole, produces a legible narrative of pride: pride that crosses ancestral borders as well as pride of craftsmanship in producing a hip-hop album that illustrates the relationship among Jin, his various African American collaborators, and his Chinese and Asian American communities.

We often believe that one's body, through its perceived genetic material and its phenotypic surface, is bounded and bonded to a specific geographic location or particular context, even when there is contrary evidence. In the Ozeki excerpt, the veteran's insistence on asking Jane a series of questions whose purpose is to elicit her ethnic heritage is one such example; her response to his initial query "Where are you from?" does not satisfy his desire to link her racially marked and ambiguously figured Asian body to a locale that is commensurate with his idea of where Asian bodies should be located. Similarly, both Fulbeck and Jin, through their respective artistic endeavors, defy genetic (in Fulbeck's case) and categorical (in Jin's case) definitions that would reify singularity and absolutism. Fulbeck's photographic subjects are not reducible to a single race or ethnicity, and may, in fact, reject the locales and contexts others prescribe for them. Jin, too, through his syncretism, asserts hybridity and multiplicity that subverts our ideas of musical categorization. What these three examples—a fictional character's fierce declaration of her US nationality, Fulbeck's mixed race Asian heritage project, and Jin's rap album—all have in common is an assertion that they are more than the sum of their ethnic parts. This excess, in turn, produces racial ambiguity—one whose stakes for Asian Americans are important in allowing people to traverse boundaries of geography, genetics, and genre, particularly because Asians in America have historically been forced into narrow confines, ghettoized spatially and symbolically in US society.

Racial Ambiguity in Asian American Culture, as the title suggests, is primarily concerned with examining ambiguity in various modes of cultural production created predominantly by and about Asian Americans,[9] particularly mixed race and mixed heritage Asian Americans, in the late twentieth and early twenty-first century.[10] I argue that ambiguity, specifically racial ambiguity, is the only truly productive lens through which to view race because race itself is so slippery. Only ambiguity accepts the full truth of race in its continuously changing permutations across time and space; it is a concept created to uphold a system of inequity, one in which certain races are subject to oppression by others. Yet the various categories and meanings ascribed to race have not remained static. Understanding how ambiguity manifests through assorted cultural forms to produce knowledge by and about race helps to remind us of the constant power of race to transform itself due to its protean quality—it is inherently unstable and cannot be fixed. Interpreting race through the perspective of ambiguity allows us to see the institutions that uphold not only the category of race but also the system of racism that race undergirds, institutions of labor, marriage, and education to name just a few. Although we understand race to be a social construct and know it to be fluid, in our day-to-day lives, in public policy and practices, and even among academics and activists, we continue to use a language of race that presumes the steadfast coherency of racial identities and to treat race as if it were immutable—as if one's racial identity maps neatly onto an unchanging set of behaviors, values, and ideals that can tell us something about who this person is, by virtue of which racial category she or he identifies or can be slotted into.

Racial ambiguity denaturalizes the process of racialization and makes transparent the power structures that underlie racial classification. Applying this concept to Asian American cultural productions troubles our understandings of race, racism, and racialization, a troubling that is productive and generative. Asian American subjects (both agents as well as modes of analysis) are ideological constructions that unmoor the concept of race from any fixed and finite field. Understanding Asian Americans as racially ambiguous (particularly acknowledging mixed race Asian Americans as such) allows for a more nuanced understanding of not only the position of this particular racial group in the United States (a position that is different and distinct from other racial minorities and the white majority) but also the way that race has developed as a political system of power and oppression, one that continually hierarchizes people and communities through the privileging of whiteness.

This book traces racial ambiguity specifically through contemporary Asian American culture as a productive analytic (a way of scrutinizing objects), hermeneutics (a way of interpreting objects), and epistemology (a way of knowing objects). Racial ambiguity resists both the rhetoric of colorblindness as well as essentialism—it defies notions of singular authenticity and normative constructions of racialization for Asian Americans. Indeed, the topics in each chapter challenge racial prescriptions and meanings while simultaneously adding new perspectives and knowledge about the category "Asian American." The racially ambiguous Asian American subjects of this book reveal the role of state interventions in racial classifications, ones predicated not only on ethnic ancestry but gender and reproductive abilities (chapter 1), narratives of genetic inheritance and social construction that affect family formations and racial identifications (chapter 2), our investments in the body and the narratives that bind bodies to specific locales and scripts (chapter 3), the permeability of generic categories and racial categories (chapter 4), and the political meanings that adhere to questions of authorship and canon formation (chapter 5).[11] Taken as a whole, *Racial Ambiguity in Asian American Culture* scrutinizes the various axes of belonging and authenticity of Asian American affiliation, examining the eruptions of different anomalous configurations of Asian American representation.

Although I engage a variety of discourses in my analysis of Asian American cultural forms, one goal of this book is to theorize Asian American issues by looking at popular as well as academic forms of culture produced by and about Asian Americans. In other words, my theorizing derives from the observation that feminist scholar Barbara Christian has made: "People of color have always theorized—but in forms quite different from the Western form of abstract logic. And I am inclined to say that our theorizing . . . is often in narrative forms, in the stories we create, in riddles and proverbs, in the play with language."[12] Taking these words to heart, *Racial Ambiguity in Asian American Culture* focuses on stories (including oral histories and those found in new media) and looks at more popular forms of culture in order to demonstrate that to theorize about race does not require that we employ "high" literary theory and philosophy. Christian's "play of language" as a form of theory appears in the blogs written by transracial/transnational Asian American adoptees as evidence of an organic intellectualism. For these adult adoptees, who are the subjects of chapter 2, the Internet acts as the primary venue for them to literally write themselves into being and negotiate the racial ambiguity of their Asian-ethnic first mothers, their adoptive white families, and their chosen adult identities as adoptees who both embrace and feel alienation with the term "Asian American" and who oppose the sentimental narrative and official discourse of adoption through producing an antisentimental counternarrative that resists closure. Similarly, Tiger Woods's invention of a racial category, "Cablinasian," unique to his person (the topic of chapter 3) seems an especially apt example of playing with language as a way of theorizing about race. Although he was mocked by those in both liberal and conservative quarters for his moniker (with those on the right seeing Cablinasian to be an extreme pandering to hyper-political correctness and those on the left castigating Woods for not claiming racial pride as a person of color), Woods's personalized racial category affirms the imaginative possibilities of people creating a language of their own through which to enact their racially ambiguous subjectivity.

Racial Ambiguity in Asian American Culture insists on the power of narrative, whether in popular culture or in literature, as critical to Asian American epistemology. Noted narratologist Gerald Prince, in *Dictionary of Narratology*, states that narrative "also functions as a particular mode of knowledge. It does not simply mirror what happens: it explores and devises what can happen. It does not merely represent changes of state; it constitutes and interprets them as signifying parts of signifying wholes."[13] Narratives are not simply representations of our reality; narratives embody and generate knowledge. In the case of ambiguous narratives, while ambiguity, racial or otherwise, can often connote incoherency, there is, in fact, a cogency to specific forms of racially ambiguous Asian American narratives, one that allows for legibility and legitimacy rather than obscurity. Interpreting Asian American narratives through the lens of racial ambiguity allows Asian Americans who do not fit into standard histories of immigration and racialization to have themselves legitimated instead of mired in questions of authenticity and the ersatz; their stories make legible (interpretable) their status as Asian Americans, albeit racially ambiguous Asian Americans.

As a form of what Michel Foucault calls "subjugated knowledges," Asian American narratives that are understood as racially ambiguous represent an archive "that were present in the functional and systemic ensembles, but which were masked."[14] For Foucault, these subjugated knowledges "have been disqualified as nonconceptual knowledges, as insufficiently elaborated knowledges: naïve knowledges, hierarchically inferior knowledges, knowledges that are below the required level of erudition or scientificity."[15] While she does not use the same terminology as Foucault, Gloria Anzaldúa, in writing about the primacy of a new mestiza consciousness, similarly asserts the importance of unearthing knowledges and stories embedded within experiences that have not been part of mainstream discourse, ones that have been dismissed and disqualified. "The new *mestiza* copes by developing a tolerance for contradictions, a tolerance for ambiguity," asserts Anzaldúa. "Not only does she sustain contradictions, she turns the ambivalence into something else."[16] The "something else" that Anzaldúa refers to is knowledge derived through the active generation of culture and narratives: "I am participating in the creation of yet another culture, a new story to explain the world and our participation in it."[17] *Racial Ambiguity in Asian American Culture* strives to unearth these subjugated knowledges and to uncover the narratives that have been shrouded in contradiction and ambivalence—to unmask that which was previously masked and to demonstrate that the knowledge produced by these narratives is not naïve nor inferior but greatly adds to our understanding of Asian American culture and racialization.

As the allusions to Foucault and Anzaldúa indicate, this book is indebted to many critics who have shaped my understanding of the intellectual genealogy of the phrase "racial ambiguity" and, concomitantly, convinced me that racial ambiguity is a key term in Asian American epistemology. For example, I investigate racial ambiguity rather than national, ethnic, or cultural ambiguity because I am most centrally interested in race as a manifestation of racism and am invested in thinking about racial ambiguity as an antiracist theory. Postcolonial critic Paul Gilroy maintains that race is a byproduct of racism and not its natural essence, which has guided my own analysis about racial formation and institutional racism. Writing in the introduction to *Postcolonial Melancholia*, Gilroy proclaims that

> if the historical anomaly represented by archaic racial division does, contrary to expectations, remain legally or morally open, if it is still somewhere "on hold" and therefore a muted part of the history of our present, the discomforting events to which these discussions refer are most likely to be recovered or remembered in the name of the same racial, ethnic, and national absolutes and particularities that I intend to call into question. "Race" would then become an eternal cause of racism rather than what it is for me—its complex, unstable product.[18]

Understanding race as the "unstable product" of racism illuminates the power dynamics in which social categories are always already entangled. Each chapter examines racial ambiguity—the primary thematic of this book—and reveals the structures of oppression that undergird notions of race and, thus, the ways in which racially dubious Asian American cultural subjects work around and through the strictures of racism.

Although *Racial Ambiguity* contains shades of poststructural investments, allusions to philosophers and academics who have interrogated the nature of ontology and epistemology, it is to my colleagues who are actively engaged in Asian American knowledge production that this book owes the greatest intellectual debt.[19] I want this book to be part of a rich ongoing conversation about Asian American knowledge production that stimulates other scholars and students to see racial ambiguity as a key term for understanding how Asian American culture, and those who create and are shaped by this culture, simultaneously and continually assert and subvert what it means to be Asian American. I, along with countless critics, have benefited from the forceful insights of Lisa Lowe, whose *Immigrant Acts: On Asian American Cultural Politics* remains a foundational text in Asian American studies (not to mention American and ethnic studies). Her theorization of the trio of terms heterogeneity, hybridity, and multiplicity underpins my own conceptualizations of racial ambiguity and Asian American culture, particularly in my insistence on a pluralistic interpretation of racial formation and cultural production. Kandice Chuh's call for "conceiving Asian American studies as a *subjectless discourse*" [emphasis in original] motivates my own desire to decouple the term "Asian American" from an overreliance on the visual traps of the body and essentialist notions of blood and ancestry.[20] Similarly, Leslie Bow's articulation of "racial interstitiality" and "racial indeterminancy" in *Partly Colored: Asian Americans and Racial Anomaly in the Segregated South* influences my own understanding of the often anomalous position of Asian Americans along the supposed color line of US race relations.

As Bow astutely observes, "Anomaly is a productive site for understanding the investments that underlie a given system of relations: what is unaccommodated becomes a site of contested interpretation."[21]

Certainly contested interpretation informs a body of innovative mixed race scholarship, and these scholarly perspectives have shaped my own interest in engaging with multiracial Asian American subjects and stories.[22] Paul Spickard, Teresa Kay-Williams, Maria Root, Wei Ming Dariotis, Laura Kina, and many others have been working on mixed race Asian American studies for the past decade (or more) and have contributed to such break-out anthologies as *We Are a People: Narrative and Multiplicity in Constructing Ethnic Identity* (Spickard and Burroughs, 2000), *The Sum of Our Parts: Mixed Heritage Asian Americans* (Valverde, 2001), *Mixing It Up: Multiracial Subject* (Zack, 2004), and *War Baby/Love Child: Asian American Art* (Kina and Dariotis, 2013). These edited collections give voice to the multiple and diverse nature of multiracial issues and about mixed Asian issues as well. Furthermore, several scholars who address the histories, social lives, experiences, and writings of mixed race Asian Americans have noted the struggles they have had to gain recognition within academic settings, let alone within US society. *Amerasia Journal's* Spring 1997 "No Passing Zone," a volume dedicated to multiracial issues, includes an introduction by guest editors Velina Hasu Houston and Teresa K. Williams in which they declare "that resistance and non-acceptance still rear their ugly heads in the mainland Asian American context, particularly when the Asian-descent multiracials in question are of African and/or Latino ancestries."[23]

As the *Amerasia* contributors and other scholars of mixed Asian Americans attest, the field has not always been open to the emergent discourse of multiracial subjects and has often subsumed the complexity of mixed heritage scholarship under the monoracial designation of "Asian American." To combat this invisibility and marginalization, scholars attempt to stake a claim for multiracial issues within the field by asserting the need to be inclusive of multiracial issues within varied communities and cultural productions.[24] They are also joining forces with other mixed heritage scholars in creating Critical Mixed Race Studies, an academic collective that has sponsored biennial conferences and fostered rich conversations among a multidisciplinary group of academics, artists, and activists.[25] By making visible the marginalized and invisible presence of mixed race Asian Americans and by moving that discourse away from the margins and toward the center of scholarship, mixed Asian American research validates the importance of instituting ambiguity into our understandings of racial formation.

Racial Ambiguity in Asian American Culture contributes to this movement of reorienting multiracial Asian American scholarship as integral to Asian

American studies. Framing this study under the organizing principle of racial ambiguity, I show how the distinctions we make about Asian Americans blur the concerns of multiracial and monoracial alike. Furthermore, I respond to the concerns of mixed race scholars by using the methodological tools of Critical Mixed Race studies to conceptualize racial ambiguity in Asian American culture; rather than being the material that becomes subsumed to monoracial concerns, the hybrid, the indeterminate, and the anomalous are foregrounded as paramount to Asian American epistemology. By highlighting the ambiguity that coheres around racial formation, this study advocates resistance to normalizing and essentializing discourses in order to understand and undermine race and racism. Mindful of literary critic Viet Thanh Nguyen's warning not to read resistance or its binary compliment, accommodation, in a simplistic manner within Asian American literature or culture, my work engages in "ideological heterogeneity"—a perspective that takes into account the uneven and multiply informed political and power dimensions within Asian American culture, specifically, and US society overall.[26] Multivocal and multiple perspectives—voices that are sometimes contradictory and in tension with each other—inform my scholarship; hence, *Racial Ambiguity* claims that Asian American cultural products undermine singular prescriptions and insist on pluralistic and multiple interpretations.

The Ambiguity of Race and Asian Americans

As numerous researchers have pointed out, there is no biological basis in race; people within a racial category exhibit more diversity, genetically speaking, than those between racial groups.[27] It has become cliché to say that our contemporary understanding of race is a social construction, an illusion perpetrated in the sixteenth century by European colonial nation-states for purposes of acquiring power through slavery and imperialism. In "Is There a Neo-Racism?" Etienne Balibar dismiss the idea of race in one sentence: "It is granted from the outset that races do not constitute isolable biological units and that in reality there are no 'human races,'" and continues to observe that "the behavior of individuals and their 'aptitudes' cannot be explained in terms of their blood or even their genes, but are the result of their belonging to historical cultures."[28] Yet understanding race as a de-essentialized quality does not make it disappear; as Michael Omi and Howard Winant point out, acknowledging race as a social construction does not solve issues of racism or the ways in which race has become entrenched in the socioeconomic realities of people living in the United States.[29] Indeed, the imaginary construction of race does not mean that it is not a potent abstraction that affects real people's lives. For instance, another powerful social construct, currency, has wide ranging material, consequences—ones that are most deeply felt precisely when a nation no longer believes in the power of its currency during times of economic and political turmoil. Although a hundred-dollar bill can be said to be simply a piece of paper, as a society we believe that it is not simply a piece of paper—it has a value in excess of its materiality. Similarly, while we could argue that race is simply a matter of melanin, the reality is that the value we ascribe to race exceeds the surface of the skin.

One of the goals of this book is to question the notion of race—to probe how all racial identities, whether mono- or multi-, are inherently ambiguous because race is inherently a suspect category—one that derives its power precisely because of its continuous and consistent mutability. At different points in time it has been linked to national origin, blood, and phenotype—sometimes all three at once.[30] To talk about racism in the United States depends on region as much as time period; the experiences of Chinese laborers in the nineteenth century were not the same as those of African Americans in the antebellum South, even though both were targets of white supremacist institutions. Moreover, one cannot talk about US racism in the same ways that one talks about Chinese racism (the targeting of Uighur minorities in western China or the marginalization of indigenous populations in Tibet and Taiwan); both are predicated on power, but each has its own distinct history of oppression and institutionalized prejudice linked to an ethnic-national minority.

The other conundrum with race, as previously mentioned, is that because nearly all scholars of race and ethnicity agree that there is no biological basis to race and that race is a social construct, the entire category is illusory. Thus, as a scientific phenomenon, we cannot talk about raced identities let alone mixed race identities because neither is "real." "Since there are no races in current biological understanding," asserts scholar Naomi Zack, "there can be no mixed races."[31] Yet the experiences of people who identify as multiracial are different from those of monoracial people, so the conundrum becomes, as researchers SanSan Kwan and Kenneth Speirs profess, that "even to talk about a concept of mixed race is itself to reify racial categories, with mixed race being simply a combination of various separable but stable classifications. The concept of mixed race, we must recognize, carries the danger of reinscribing monoracial paradigms."[32]

How do we talk about race or mixed race issues if by doing so we only further reinforce the category of "race"? The alternative, to ignore race and to believe that its fictive qualities will allow it to disappear, is neither feasible nor realistic; ignoring a problem does not make it go away. But perhaps we can perceive race for what it is: ambiguous. Ambiguous in the sense of being open to multiple interpretations. Ambiguous in the sense of being read differently by different people. Ambiguous in the sense that we cannot fix or stabilize race. To recognize race is to recognize ambiguity—a terrain that most of us are not comfortable with, because to acknowledge ambiguity is to acknowledge a complexity that does not allow for easy answers or predictable outcomes.

Ambiguity most centrally marks Asian Americans because they have been variously and multiply interpreted: they are neither wholly accepted into white privilege nor fully subjected to institutional discrimination. An analysis of Asian Americans as racially ambiguous is productive and generative because the ways that Asian Americans have been racialized in the United States have rendered them as particularly ambiguous within US society because of their geographic, ethnic, linguistic, and cultural diversity, their relatively recent status as a racial group, and their place within US racial politics. The 2010 US Census lists twenty-four Asian-ethnic groups (with a twenty-fifth category for "Asian-Other"), with Chinese, Filipino, and Asian Indians as the three most numerous Asian ethnicities found within the United States. A number of academics and activists have admitted the imperfections of "Asian American" as a category because it condenses ethnic and national groups into an amorphous lump, flattening their differences into a geographical continent that neither recognizes the long histories of varying ethnicities nor the transnational nature of much Asian American life. Furthermore, they believe that using "Asian American" as the principle term of identity subordinates class, gender, sexuality, regional, linguistic, and other "differences" in favor of a unifying racial embrace.[33] The sheer diversity of the Asian American populace renders them an ambiguous racial category, yet this ambiguity is further heightened because the entire category "Asian American" is a relatively recent phenomenon, created out of a desire to engender a phrase and a field of study that would affirm the place of Asians in American culture and social life and that would dispel the idea of Asians as a foreign presence, temporary sojourners, or the exotic objects that the term "Oriental" conjures up. Although a variety of people we would now label as "Asian American" have lived in this country for almost two centuries, the term "Asian American" did not come into standard use until after 1968, when it became a rallying cry for claiming space at the metaphoric national table at which a rich and contentious conversation on race was being held.[34]

Indeed, where Asian Americans are placed at this metaphoric table contributes to their ambiguous status. They vacillate between being conceived, by some, as sell-outs who achieve honorary whiteness at the expense of their browner and blacker minority peers or forever foreign aliens subject to the same forms of racism and jingoism as any other US racial minority.[35] As historian Gary Okihiro has famously and rhetorically queried: "Is yellow black or white?"[36] At different points in US history Asians in America have been metaphorically darkened and likened to African Americans, subject to similar vilification based on hatred and fear.[37] Certainly the lynching of Chinese laborers in numerous western mining towns in the late nineteenth century is reminiscent of African American lynching in the South.[38] Anti-miscegenation laws were aimed as much at Asian Americans as at African Americans in the first half of the twentieth century, with the same racist theories of eugenics and the dilution of whiteness directed at both the "Yellow Peril" Oriental figure and the menacing black man.[39] Yet in more recent times, Asian Americans have been held up as the "model minority," touted for their academic achievement and economic success. This discourse was designed to place Asian Americans into a privileged minority position while subjugating other racial groups, notably African Americans and Latinos, by negative comparison, during a time when civil rights agitation and affirmative action policies were making headway in national politics.[40]

Admittedly, when Asian Americans have been used as intermediaries in sundry issues—like college admissions, the achievement gap, and affirmative action programs—they have been aligned with white Americans in a state of relative privilege over African Americans, Latinos, and American Indians. Programs designed to correct for systematic racial disparities, particularly in the realm of education, often use the phrase "underrepresented minority" in order to exclude Asian Americans from these programs in the belief that they do not need additional help with acculturation to systems of higher education, linguistic adaptation to English, or acknowledgment of their historic disenfranchisement from institutions of knowledge. Asian Americans have been aligned with whites in their ostensible ability to pass into a privileged state, with Latinos in their shared sense of being mistaken as perpetually foreign and non-native/ non-English-speaking, with American Indians in their multiple ancestral-linguistic affiliations as well as overlapping indigenous interests, and with African Americans in their irrefutable difference from a white American racial normativity.[41] However, Asian Americans ultimately exist in their own racial-political category, ambivalently figured as sometimes privileged and sometimes oppressed, but often and generally invisible and forgotten from the public sphere.

Although it may seem that I am arguing for "Asian American" to be seen as a suspect category, I do not believe it is any more or less suspect than any other racial category, only that it is suspect in a way unique to itself (as other racial categories also are found similarly unreliable and inconsistent in ways unique to them). Yet despite these critiques, the term "Asian American" has been a powerful organizing force and an important conceptual category. We do not live in a postracial society, because racial disparities and inequities still exist, and, as noted previously, eliminating the category of race will not diminish the institution of racism that it undergirds. We need the category Asian American as a tool that helps us to consider the way that race operates for people with ancestral roots in Asia. The rubric "Asian American" allows us to consider a shared history of oppression and discrimination, most notably marked by the ways that various Asian-ethnic groups were transformed into aliens ineligible for citizenship and as Yellow Peril foreigners who threatened the white sanctity of the United States. Asian Americans are no more nor less ambiguous than any other racial group because all racial categories contain their own sets of inconsistencies and anomalies; however, Asian American ambiguity should be understood as unique not in the sense that it is more ambiguous, only in the sense that it is differently ambiguous. There is a distinction to the manner in which Asian American ambiguity is represented, figured, and interpreted in US society, which makes Asian American, as a conceptual and organizing category, a significant analytical instrument.

Furthermore, the category Asian American arose not only from a desire to shed the exoticizing label "Oriental," but out of an activist and academic agenda of prioritizing the study of Asians in America within colleges and universities; in other words, the embrace of Asian American as a category also led to the emergence of the discipline of Asian American studies. This field of study, with its roots in pan-ethnic coalition, cross-racial alliances, and transnational social justice, attempted to make a space for itself in American higher education at a time when Asians were perpetually figured in stereotypic terms: racist portraits showed slant-eyed, buck-toothed Viet Cong enemies, exotic geisha girls, and Chinese laundrymen and restaurant workers. The first Asian American studies classes, which began as ethnic studies courses at San Francisco State College (now San Francisco State University) and the University of California-Berkeley, addressed the long-ignored history of Asians in America as well as the damaging representations of Asian Americans in popular culture and US society. Asian American studies in this sociohistoric context allowed for a multiplicity of voices to claim America, not in a strictly assimilationist manner but as a way of signaling the demarginalization of Asian Americans in US public discourse.[42]

It is often within Asian American scholarship that the most fervent critiques of the term "Asian American" appear. One could say that Asian American studies developed out of a desire for ambiguity, as a way to allow Asians in America to be multiply interpreted and to be read in a richer, more complex manner that moved beyond caricature and stereotype. Although initially Asian American activists and academics appeared to desire a united vision for Yellow Pride akin to that of the Black Power movement, the heterogeneous, hybrid, and multiple realities of Asian American Studies as a multi- and interdisciplinary study of disparate peoples from a wide variety of Asian and Pacific Islander backgrounds coming together over two centuries has meant a plurality of voices and a further indeterminancy of whom the label and definition Asian American refers to.[43] Today, the field of Asian American studies includes disciplines such as literary studies, cultural studies, ethnic studies, history, political science, art history, film studies, communication studies, economics, music, performance studies, drama, women studies, queer studies, urban studies, public policy, legal studies, public health, and a host of other fields commonly found in most US universities and colleges.[44] And the scholarship emerging out of this field also encompasses a wide array of perspectives, methodologies, and archives—ones that continually challenge any monolithic sense of a singular Asian American point of view or orientation.[45]

Asian American studies is an ambiguous field because it questions itself within (and without) its scholarship and expands to meet the changing social and political atmosphere of our world, which makes an analysis of racial ambiguity as applied to Asian American subjects especially dynamic. Though Asian American studies was initially figured to be a shorthand for Chinese, Japanese, and Korean American studies (with a glancing nod at Filipino Americans), the field has consistently interrogated the hegemonic placement of East Asian Americans as subjects and producers of Asian American epistemology.[46] The rise of Southeast Asian, South Asian, Pacific Islander, and now West Asian American studies within the larger discipline illustrates the field's attempt to contend with the diversity and multiplicity of the term "Asian American." Most important, as the allusion to "West Asian" signals, Asian American studies attempts to make sense of the current political turmoil, post-9/11, that has reignited the discourse of yellow peril once again. The people who consider themselves to be engaged with Asian American knowledge production continually push the boundaries of who is included in the category Asian American and what the term "Asian American" means. Additionally, scholars in the academy question the efficacy of establishing Asian American studies; some fear that institutionalizing Asian American studies could result in its subversive edge being filed away when it enters the bureaucratic machinery of a university system. Yet most scholars also believe that championing Asian American studies in our university and college systems will further the knowledge production of Asian Americans, an epistemological value of paramount importance. Others, like Timothy Yu, rhetorically wonder whether Asian American studies has "failed," given the continual misunderstandings and fallacies that the general American public holds about Asian Americans.[47]

Although those inside Asian American studies may see the ambiguity of this field—the way that it is open to multiple interpretations and understandings—scholars in other fields within the ivory tower of academia also perceive its indeterminate position, but for different reasons. For many, Asian American studies does not register as a field because of ignorance, even within academic institutions, over the term "Asian American" and the place of Asians in America. Others consider Asian American studies an unnecessary field of study because of the model minority rhetoric that fosters the belief that Asian Americans are not an oppressed group and therefore are unworthy of additional scrutiny or analyses.[48] And there are those who fail to see any difference between Asian American studies and Asian studies. I continue to encounter colleagues across the nation who ask me whether it is challenging for me to conduct research when I am not fluent in an Asian language or who worry about the difficulty of my finding translated novels for my courses in Asian American literature.[49] Asian American studies, like the population it researches, is not understood very clearly or legibly by those within and without higher education—a further reinforcement that the knowledge produced about Asian Americans is ambiguously figured within both US social relations and American academic institutions.

The Archive and Methodology of *Racial Ambiguity*

My understanding of "archive" derives from critic Brent Hayes Edwards's definition, which articulates its importance within cultural frameworks. He uses the term "in the sense not so much of a site or mode of preservation of a national, institutional, or individual past, but instead of a 'generative system': in other words, a discursive system that governs the possibilities, forms, appearance, and regularity of particular statements, objects, and practices."[50] Similarly, I believe that the archive I amass in this book is a generative system that provokes and promotes debate within American and cultural studies discourses. By looking at the exceptions to Japanese American internment during World War II (the subject of chapter 1) my scholarship takes an existing archive, the documents related to World War II and the Japanese American Incarceration, and illustrates how an underreported piece of history, the Mixed-Marriage Policy of 1942, can be unearthed from these files and reframed to provide a new narrative for understanding this critical period of US history.

Moreover, one of the reasons that I employ a cultural studies perspective is to affirm the multiplicity of knowledges that Americans both produce and consume. Part of the archive for *Racial Ambiguity* results from the rise of technology in the late twentieth century and from the different forms of new media that are part and parcel of cultural production in the first decades of the twenty-first century. An attention to new media, particularly to blogs (the subject of chapter 2) as a source of knowledge dissemination as well as identity making is vital in our current digital age. Critics like Geert Lovink and Lisa Nakamura address both the power and limitations of new media to transform society and change social attitudes and values while pondering the liberating potential of the Internet to move beyond race because "the Net is as racist as the societies that it stems from."[51] Yet despite or perhaps because of these limitations, Nakamura believes that "it is crucial that scholarship assess these practices to evaluate the Internet as a popular environment for representations of identity. Visual culture provides a powerful methodology for parsing gender and racial and ethnic identity in these digital signifying practices that became so prominent at the turn of the century."[52] Our knowledge is formed from multiple sources, not simply the site of the classroom or the textbook. We are living in a twenty-first-century age of digital technology—where information speeds around in cyberspace, and young adults are more media literate than the people producing the scholarship they are consuming in their courses. Scholars, particularly ones invested in issues of race and culture, have a responsibility to meet their students on the terrain they are familiar with and to acknowledge the role of technology in producing knowledge and culture, for we are all producers and consumers of both and therefore must become familiar with the role of new media in our research.

However, as much as I am indebted to the methodology and philosophy of cultural studies and as much as I believe that we must turn our attention to interpreting the sites of knowledge that new media has produced, my own training in literary interpretation and close reading also announces itself in this book, particularly through my examinations of contemporary Asian American literature and questions of canonization in the field of Asian American literature (the subjects of chapters 4 and 5). Very early in my literary training a mentor at my undergraduate institution told a classroom of students looking at Asian American women's literature that one of the things she found lacking among younger scholars was an attention to close reading techniques. Far from a formalist, my mentor was a politicized advocate for Asian American studies. However, she was also a poet and writer who believed formalist techniques should be incorporated into analyses of Asian American literature. In a similar vein, literary critic Daniel Kim makes a very compelling and cogent argument for the attentive close readings in his own work *Writing Manhood in Black and Yellow: Ralph Ellison, Frank Chin, and the Literary Politics of Identity* by arguing not for a return to formalism and the conservative ethos that this phrase implies but rather a hermeneutics "that addresses the cultural specificity of literary objects and subjects."[53] "I am not advocating a return to a moribund notion of aesthetic culture that sees it as cleansed of political and historical matters," writes Kim, "more simply and more modestly, I am asserting the need for literary critics to engage in the disciplined study of the specific kinds of political interventions that writers attempt to make through the act of writing literature."[54] I take Kim's call for a return to close reading seriously and explicate various "texts," be they actual bodies or literary bodies, because the tools of my training in literary criticism and analysis are ones I rely on to illuminate the ambiguity of various Asian American subjects.

Racial Ambiguity in Asian American Culture refutes color-blind rhetorics affiliated with specific Asian Americans who are racially ambiguous. It examines assimilation by tracing the story of a Japanese American woman who evaded incarceration during World War II through her marriage to a non-Japanese man. It looks at the concept of honorary whiteness through the blogs of transracial and transnational Asian adoptees in the United States. It scrutinizes how a celebrity figure, Tiger Woods, transcends race. And it considers the performance and presentation of racial identities in Asian American literature as well as issues of authorship and authenticity surrounding this literature. These subjects have important aspects in common yet also raise separate questions. People in inter- or intraracial relationships, adoptees, Tiger Woods, mixed race Asian American authors, and Asian American literature are all part of either popular culture or our common knowledge base, and they are often associated with a language of color blindness. Yet these figures and topics are racially ambiguous Asian Americans who resist interpellation into a singular definition of Asian American authenticity; chronicling and analyzing their stories reveals their defiance of color-blind rhetorics.

Chapter 1 opens with an examination of the theme of racial ambiguity for Japanese American nisei Yoshiko Nakamura deLeon, following her journey during World War II from an enemy alien to an assimilating American, albeit one who resisted American acculturation through adoption of her husband's Filipino ethnicity instead of the predominant white-Anglo culture. Drawing on official military records, historical accounts of the internment, and the unique family narrative of deLeon, this chapter charts the rationale and implementation of the Mixed-Marriage Program, concluding with the ambiguous effects of this policy on the deLeon family. Assimilation guided the Mixed-Marriage Program; hence, this chapter demonstrates how the military's conception of assimilation was predicated on the paradoxical belief that racial identity was both immutable and flexible, thereby allowing Japanese Americans to be coded as either assimilable or unassimilable depending on their marital, gender, and reproductive status. Analyzing the language of the Mixed-Marriage Policy documents, as well as its lingering effects on the deLeon family, exposes the inherent instability of race as a category as well as its efficient persistence as a mark of difference, one used all too often in times of crisis to demarcate lines of threat and security. The ambiguity in deLeon's life and exemption from incarceration refutes the idea that assimilation was a simple matter of national identity accessible to all regardless of race and ethnicity.

Chapter 2 continues to explore the relationship between racial and national identity by looking at the racial identity formation of US adoptees from Asian nations and the ways that their racial ambiguity complicates the honorary white status conferred on them through their location within white adoptive US families. This chapter focuses on narratives about adult Asian American adoptees, with a particular emphasis on bloggers from Korean, Taiwanese, and Vietnamese backgrounds. Many of these blogs express outrage and frustration as well as sadness and confusion, but most of all, these bloggers create both an identity and a body of knowledge that is self-consciously Asian and American, one that encompasses the inherent indeterminacy of being transracial/transnational Asian American adult adoptees. Understanding these blogs as a continual negotiation of racial ambiguity allows us to see that the puzzle of race lies in its paradoxical persistence as both essentialist myth and social construction. These blogs (and bloggers) produce counternarratives by rejecting the standard sentimental narrative of adoption, reminding their audiences that like the medium that they participate in, there is no closure to their stories; their lives do not wrap up neatly in tidy endings. As racially ambiguous subjects, these adoptees resist being defined solely through either the whiteness of their families or the Asianness of their ancestries.

Chapter 3 extends the interrogation of color-blind rhetorics with an investigation of how Tiger Woods, one of the most famous mixed race Asian Americans, fails to transcend race (and hence racism), despite the language of exceptionalism that surrounds him. Woods is often referred to as a monoracial African American but never as a monoracial Asian American; thus, he is racially ambiguous precisely because of the persistence of the one-drop rule of hypodescent in defining racial identities as well as the occlusion and illegibility of his Asian heritage to the general American public.[55] This illegibility of his Asian heritage speaks to the manner in which Asians in America are similarly ambiguously figured: as not truly American because of their perceived inability to assimilate and as model minorities who have not suffered from discrimination and thus are honorary whites. To think of Woods as racially ambiguous is to reject the notion that his exceptional status allows him to transcend race. To view Woods as racially ambiguous allows us to interpret him through alternate stories that are embedded within his family's (and the US nation's) history: the American war in Viet Nam and the Amerasian children produced through that war.[56] Understanding Tiger Woods as a racially ambiguous subject places mixed race Asian Americans, particularly black Amerasians, into a legible space with respect to Asian American communities and US society. Woods's assertion of his racial ambiguity, through his refusal to be interpellated as monoracial, reinforces the fictiveness of race as a singular category of authenticity that can be clearly coded on the body.

Chapter 4 analyzes passing as a trope denoting movement instead of imposture as a more apt metaphor for mixed race identity in Paisley Rekdal's *The Night My Mother Met Bruce Lee* and Ruth Ozeki's *My Year of Meats*. The racial ambiguity inherent in the concept of racial passing has typically taken the form of passing from a state of abjection to a state of privilege—a form of racial impersonation. Rekdal and Ozeki are contemporary Asian American writers who embody hybridity in their writing as well as in their actual bodies—both mixed race writers depict biracial Asian American white women who come of age in the post-civil rights era and who pass for what they are rather than for what they are not: they pass, at various times, as white and they pass as Asian because they are both white and Asian. Creating mobile subjectivities for their narrators, each work moves back and forth—through genre, through identities, through countries—crossing borders of form and content. As passing stories, neither entirely fictional nor entirely factual, neither fully Asian nor not Asian, Rekdal's and Ozeki's works use the trope of passing as movement to expound on their respective preoccupations with the ambiguity of their racial identities as mixed race Asian Americans. I investigate this strategy for resistance to notions of authenticity and read Rekdal's and Ozeki's works as a type of theorizing about racial identity formation that promotes a richer understanding of multiracial subjectivity.

Chapter 5 asks two canon-related questions: How do we define Asian American literature and which bodies matter more—the body of fiction or the body of the writer? In other words, what counts as Asian American literature? All of the authors in this chapter write transgressive texts: works with protagonists of a different racial identity from their authors. Concentrating on novels by Sigrid Nunez and Cristina Garcia that trouble a simplistic correspondence between the ethnicity of the writer and the literature she creates, I scrutinize the language of authenticity that circulates around ethnic literature, a language that masks an anxiety about legitimacy and authority in contemporary American literature and the academy. Because transgressive texts prove that race is a social construction, allowing such texts into the canon of Asian American literature is one of the most antiracist actions that we can take as literary critics. If authenticity does not reside solely in and through one's body, then writing an Asian American novel is not the exclusive purview of those who identify as Asian American, which means that Asian American literature is a flexible and racially ambiguous category. To consider which texts qualify as Asian American literature is to interrogate the place of this archive in the academy and the place of literary critics and professors as gatekeepers of racial knowledge production.

I conclude this book with a coda that reflects on more intimate associations of Asian American racial ambiguity, namely that of my maternal family and our ethnic and cultural connections to Jamaica. My identification as Chinese Jamaican and my family's history, which is also a history of the Chinese diaspora in the twentieth century, are centrally marked by racial ambiguity.

Taken as a whole, this book critically appraises the cultural productions surrounding anomalous Asian Americans, notions of mixed heritage issues, and multiracial Asian Americans in order to place Asian Americans within the conversation about race—to make visible the presence of Asian Americans within the longer history of US American life and the larger society of US American culture. To use ambiguity as a lens through which to analyze Asian Americans is to recognize the complexity of race and the complications of "Asian American" existing as a nascent political, cultural category. As applied to contemporary culture, racial ambiguity highlights the diverse means by which Asian Americans resist finite constructions of themselves within US society. Thus, racial ambiguity troubles any easy conception of what it means to be Asian American by revealing the polymorphous nature of culture as productive of an ongoing engagement with race.

In closing this introduction, I profess that it is not enough for us to say that race is a social construction, and we certainly cannot claim an essentializing belief in racial identities. Therefore, interpreting culture through ambiguity becomes one of the only means of truly seeing race for what it is: an open signifier and overdetermined mirror of the widely held assumption that race is an absolute, knowable, quantifiable substance. Race is an abstraction that we treat as concrete material; it reflects our desires, fears, anxieties, hopes, and queries about humanity. Seeing race as ambiguous puts us one step closer toward an antiracist theory and praxis, one that figures ambiguity as a potential antidote to racism. Racist discourses are predicated on binary constructions and fixity. Racial ambiguity undermines and destabilizes race—and only by destabilizing categories of race can we begin to dismantle the powerful structures of racism.

1

From Enemy Alien to Assimilating American

Yoshiko deLeon and the Mixed-Marriage Policy of the Japanese American Incarceration

Yoshiko Tanaka Nakamura deLeon led an exceptional life. Her Japanese immigrant mother divorced her alcoholic husband at the turn-of-the-century at a time when divorce was unheard of and in a cultural climate that made female enfranchisement nearly impossible, and she moved with her daughter to the Central Coast of California after remarrying another Japanese immigrant farmer. Yoshiko herself also transgressed propriety and Japanese cultural norms by marrying her Filipino immigrant husband, Gabriel deLeon, a man who initially sold vegetables out of a truck upon his arrival to the United States and who built up his fortunes and his political clout to become the first Filipino–Asian American mayor of a US city—Arroyo Grande, California. However, what makes Yoshiko's life story truly exceptional is that she was one of ninety women of Japanese ancestry living in Military Zone I who evaded incarceration during World War II through the auspices of the Mixed-Marriage Policy of 1942—the military-sponsored program that allowed for "certain persons of Japanese ancestry" to be exempted from imprisonment in US concentration camps during World War II.[1]

The Mixed-Marriage Policy of 1942 was an exemption program that allowed for a total of 568 people of Japanese ancestry (predominantly women and children) to live within the restricted zone of the United States—the West Coast—and to escape incarceration.[2] But more specifically, it was an assimilation policy; one of its stated goals was to allow mixed race (or in the language of the policy, "mixed-blood") children of Japanese women and non-Japanese men a chance to live a "normal" lifestyle outside of the contaminating cultural influence of the Japanese community detained in American concentration camps, a belief stated clearly by General John deWitt, one of the architects of both the Japanese American incarceration as well as the Mixed-Marriage Program: "The policy was designed to afford an opportunity for mixed-blood children, the product of mixed-marriages, who had previously been raised in a non-Japanese environment, to continue their development under conditions as nearly normal as feasible."[3] To qualify for exemption under the Mixed-Marriage Program you had to be a Japanese or Japanese American woman married to a non-Japanese man with unemancipated children.

Few people knew of the Mixed-Marriage Program during World War II, and among contemporary scholarship on the incarceration there is only a single essay dedicated to this phenomenon by historian Paul Spickard, with brief commentary in works by Tetsuden Kashima and Klancy Clark deNevers.[4] Indeed, conventional wisdom among most Asian American scholars avers that all people of Japanese descent living on the West Coast during World War II were incarcerated.[5] The Mixed-Marriage Program remains an under-recorded exception to incarceration among nearly all secondary sources. This is an unfortunate lacuna because the policy exposes important implications about the basis for incarceration and the ambiguity of race as a category. The entire rationale for incarceration was predicated on the myth of "military necessity": the threat of a fifth column element embedded in the Japanese American communities of Hawaii and the West Coast.[6] Believing the Japanese to be, inherently, more foreign and less trustworthy than their Euro-American counterparts, the architects of the incarceration connected a Japanese essence with disloyalty. However, the exceptions to incarceration under the Mixed-Marriage Program prove that loyalty and assimilation could be engineered, as Spickard notes: "The criteria for choosing these groups [for exemption] had little to do with individual loyalties. Rather the groups were chosen by racial and gender attributes."[7] These exemptions under the Mixed-Marriage Policy betray the absolute fixity of racial difference and the concomitant "military threat" that Japanese people embodied (and upon which the incarceration was based). If the US government could arbitrarily decide that certain types of Japanese were suitable for assimilation and qualified for exemption based on exterior factors of marriage and children, then the idea of race as an immutable, essential, inheritable category is undermined by the Mixed-Marriage Program's attempt to socially engineer "appropriate" racial and national identities. In other words, assimilation becomes a form of racial ambiguity in this period as implemented through the Mixed-Marriage Policy and as evidenced in the life story of Yoshiko deLeon.

As a twenty-three-year-old nisei married to a non-Japanese man, Yoshiko deLeon, along with her three-year-old son Martin, qualified for exemption on October 6, 1942.[8] A conversation with my college roommate twenty-five years earlier began my investigation into Yoshiko's exceptional status, because deLeon was her maternal grandmother. Family lore, as recounted by my roommate, asserted that Yoshiko was kept out of the camps by her Filipino husband, a man of considerable charisma and influence. My roommate did not have more details other than the fact that her grandmother had never been incarcerated, whereas the rest of my roommate's extended family—great-grandparents, great-aunts, and great-uncles—had spent the duration of World War II in Poston, Arizona.[9] This story was fascinating but also a bit unimaginable because everything I had read in my collegiate Asian American studies classes had led me to believe that there were no exceptions to incarceration for Japanese Americans. Yet on March 8, 2005, at the National Archives in College Park, Maryland, I found the document that proved if not fully explained Yoshiko deLeon's exemption.[10]

Yoshiko deLeon's tale is part and yet apart from the official record of mass removal and incarceration of Japanese Americans.[11] Her life was exceptional in multiple ways: in her family of origin, in her decision to marry a man outside of her ethnic community, and in her embrace of her husband's cultural affiliations over her own. Yet Yoshiko deLeon could never assimilate completely, whether into American, Japanese, or Filipino cultures. Her multiple border crossings marked her as ambiguous, particularly in an age when race was purportedly believed to be an essential category and identities were, seemingly, fixed. In many ways deLeon and her story of non-incarceration is an ambiguous narrative that cuts against the grain of the threat of military necessity, the government's belief in assimilation, as well as standard narratives of Japanese American incarceration during World War II.

Drawing on official military records, historical accounts of the incarceration, and the unique family narrative of Yoshiko deLeon, this chapter charts the rationale and implementation of the Mixed-Marriage Program, concluding with the ambiguous effects of this policy on the deLeon family.[12] Assimilation guided the Mixed-Marriage Program; hence, this chapter demonstrates how the military's conception of assimilation was predicated on the paradoxical belief that racial identity was both immutable and flexible, thereby allowing Japanese Americans to be coded as either assimilable or unassimilable depending on their marital, gender, and reproductive status.[13] Analyzing the language of the Mixed-Marriage Policy documents, as well as its lingering effects on the deLeon family, reveals the inherent instability of race as well as its efficient persistence as a mark of difference, one used all too often in times of crisis to demarcate lines of threat and security. Conceptually, if one could be exempt from incarceration, as the select cases of women and mixed race children demonstrate, then one could be neither an alien nor non-alien in the language of Executive Order 9066, since both alien and non-alien Japanese were subject to incarceration during World War II.[14] Exemption discursively created another category of Japanese Americans, who, according to the Mixed-Marriage Policy of 1942, could only be rendered as racially ambiguous since their ability to evade incarceration rested on the government's interpretation of both their racial and national identities, which were often conflated to be one and the same. Women like Yoshiko deLeon who qualified under the Mixed-Marriage Policy of 1942 were ambiguously figured as not quite Japanese and hence almost white, nearly American.

Japanese American Incarceration and Exemption: The Mixed-Marriage Policy of 1942

On February 19, 1942, President Franklin Delano Roosevelt signed Executive Order 9066, the presidential decree that led to the mass removal and incarceration of any persons of Japanese ancestry, whether American citizen or not, living on the West Coast of the United States. The atmosphere of fear, anxiety, and xenophobia that permeated the United States, and especially the West Coast, during this time period, cannot be overstated. Rumors of Japanese espionage and treachery abounded, while pressure for the US government to address the threat of enemy alien saboteurs mounted. Thus Executive Order 9066 was, ostensibly, designed to identify and target people potentially hostile to US military interests.[15]

Although approximately 120,000 Japanese and Japanese Americans were subjected to incarceration in US concentration camps during World War II, the executive order made no mention of race or geography. Instead, President Roosevelt allowed for the secretary of war (Henry Stimson) and various military commanders (most notably Lieut. Gen. John DeWitt and Col. Karl Bendetsen) "to prescribe military areas in such places and of such extent as he or the appropriate Military Commander may determine, from which any or all persons may be excluded, and with respect to which, the right of any person to enter, remain in, or leave shall be subject to whatever restriction the Secretary of War or the appropriate Military Commander may impose in his discretion."[16] In effect, Executive Order 9066 nullified the constitutional rights of every person living in the United States, although in practice the military designated only the West Coast region as military areas and solely targeted people of Japanese ancestry. As historian Roger Daniels observes, "The words Japanese or Japanese Americans never appear in the order; but it was they, and they alone, who felt its sting."[17]

As Daniel notes, although the language of the order never referred to race, numerous scholars have shown that President Roosevelt and his advisors had only one ethnic group in mind when they signed the order. In a memorandum to President Roosevelt the day after he signed Executive Order 9066, Attorney General Francis Biddle confirmed the legality of the order in excluding citizens based on their ethnic heritage: "These powers are broad enough to permit them to exclude any particular individual from military areas. They could also evacuate groups of persons based on a reasonable classification. The order is not limited to aliens but includes citizens so that it can be exercised with respect to Japanese, irrespective of their citizenship."[18] This correspondence makes clear not only the designated group targeted within Executive Order 9066 but also that the mass removal of both Japanese aliens and Japanese American citizens was always part of the original thinking of Executive Order 9066—one completely in keeping with the popular anti-Japanese sentiment of the majority of US Americans as well as those within the Roosevelt administration.[19]

Yet despite the popularity or even the purported "military necessity" of incarcerating Japanese and Japanese Americans, the Western Defense Command (WDC) and West Coast Civil Authority (WCCA) were immediately presented with a problem: how Japanese did one have to be to qualify for imprisonment?[20] According to *The Final Report: Japanese Evacuation from the West Coast 1942*, the official government and military record documenting the Japanese American incarceration, if you were one-sixteenth Japanese, if you had a great-great-grandparent who was Japanese, you were incarcerated, even if no one else in your family tree was Japanese.[21] However, in the wake of Executive Order 9066, the WDC became inundated with appeals: letters from senators, priests, student organizations, sheriffs, and attorneys all inquired after exemptions on the grounds of religion, infirmity, veteran class, and, most notably, mixed race and mixed marriage status.

In one such letter, dated March 27, 1942, Seattle attorney Austin Griffiths asked whether Japanese American women married to Chinese American and Filipino American men could be exempted.[22] Replying to this request, Lieut. Col. William A. Boekel stated that "no exemption from evacuation in favor of Japanese of the whole or part blood" regardless of their spouse's status, could be granted.[23] In another letter, addressed on March 30, 1942, Contra Costa County deputy sheriff Ralph Harrison inquired after several different cases for possible exemption: pregnant Japanese women in their last trimester, Japanese parents of a US soldier, a Japanese American World War I veteran who also happened to be of mixed Chinese and Japanese ancestry, and "a Japanese girl, American born and married to an American [*sic*] Husband" with "one young child."[24] Thomas A. Clark, chief of Civilian Coordination, answered point by point all of Deputy Sheriff Harrison's inquiries. Like Lieut. Col. Boekel, Clark's reply to Harrison confirmed that the military was not considering any types of exemptions—not for pregnancy, current service in the armed forces, veteran class, or mixed marriage/mixed race status.[25]

However, even in Clark's reply, the rationale for the Mixed-Marriage Policy was already formed; in both the case of the Chinese-Japanese American veteran as well as the Japanese American wife and her "Eurasian child," the possibility of exception that was briefly raised and then quickly terminated was based on their cultural upbringing or, in Clark's phrasing, a particular "way of life."[26] In the case of the veteran, Clark advised Harrison that the young man's affidavits declaring his loyalty and service to the United States in World War I "should be particularly keyed to the question as to whether the young man in his way of life is more American or Chinese than Japanese."[27] As for the family with the "Eurasian" child, Clark again emphasized that the daughter would be incarcerated "unless a petition can be presented similar to that discussed earlier, disclosing that the child has been brought up in the American way of life rather than the Japanese."[28] For both the veteran and the "Eurasian" child, of paramount concern was the environment in which the biracial person in question was raised—Japanese or not Japanese, or perhaps more important, was this a person who was more American than Japanese?

Another dilemma that Clark's reply raised was the issue of not only split heritage but split families. Continuing his explanation for the possible exemption of the "Eurasian" child, he noted that "the mother, of course, cannot be exempted from evacuation. The exemption of the child, if granted, would involve the splitting of the family. All things considered, it would probably be better to have the mother and child evacuated together."[29] Various letters inquiring after exemptions indicated that the composition of many interracial marriages troubled the ideology of whom the WDC should incarcerate and how to keep families together.[30] However, despite the concern of not wanting to fracture families, the WCCA adhered to the policy that no exemptions would be granted, regardless of the unique circumstances or influence of those petitioning for exceptional status.[31]

Yet by late May 1942, the WDC had changed its view on exemptions. The first formal mention of a Mixed-Marriage Policy allowing for exceptions to incarceration can be found in correspondence of the WCCA records as of May 23, 1942.[32] The earliest internal memorandum, dated July 12, 1942, outlined the exemption of families based on interracial marriage status; the only families who would be both exempted from incarceration and allowed to remain in the restricted military area were "families composed of a Caucasian husband who is a citizen of the United States, a Japanese wife, and mixed blood children."[33] Initially, the WCCA's bias was for families with a "white" lifestyle, emblemized by a Caucasian American head of household.[34] Yet Maj. Herman P. Goebel, the author of this memo, included a paragraph immediately following the four categories of exemption observing that "a policy respecting families composed of Filipino and Chinese husbands, Japanese wives and mixed blood children, is now under consideration. You will be advised relative thereto as soon as the policy has been established."[35] Although the initial conception for the Mixed-Marriage Policy was founded upon a white male–Japanese female model, the program was eventually expanded to include spouses other than Caucasian husbands under the rubric of "non-Japanese." Emphasizing loyalty, the wording of the official policy would eventually state that the husband of a Japanese woman must be a "United States citizen or citizen of a friendly nation."[36] On August 31, 1942, the Regasa family, composed of Matsuyo Regasa (Japanese and Hawaiian wife), Hugo Regasa (Filipino husband), and their teenage daughter Miyoko Regasa were allowed to leave the Tanforan assembly center, becoming the earliest recorded instance of a mixed marriage exemption.[37]

As the example of the Regasa family demonstrates, the language of the policy and the presumption of who was considered to be non-Japanese was predicated on an ethnic rather than racial paradigm. During the 1940s, Filipino and Chinese spouses were considered to be in a mixed marriage with Japanese women because the belief that ethnic groups retained nativistic ties to their ancestral homelands predominated in the public imagination. Indeed the whole concept of race as we currently understand it was not the manner in which people used the term "race" in the period leading up to World War II and throughout the duration of the war. Race, in this period, was aligned with heritage and national origin. A Chinese American and Filipino American were of two different races in the same way that two white Americans with ancestors from France and Germany, respectively, were also regarded as members of two different races.[38] Indeed, as sociologists Michael Omi and Howard Winant observe, race theory was essentially indistinguishable from ethnicity in the period leading up to and through World War II.[39] Researchers associated with the University of Chicago—the Chicago School of sociology—heralded a new kind of race theory that challenged the eugenicist and biological explanations of race by advancing "an insurgent theory which suggested that race was a social category . . . one of a number of determinants of ethnic group identity or ethnicity."[40]

In a time when race was considered a matter of distinct ethnic nationalism, popular culture of this era was careful to depict differences among assorted Asian racial groups, particularly because the Philippines and China were allies of the United States during World War II. Many Americans could not differentiate among Filipino, Chinese, Korean, and Japanese Americans. Although some people wore buttons that declared themselves to be a loyal Korean American or Chinese American—out of devotion to the United States as well as protection against mistaken ethnic identity—American popular culture also provided guides for average Americans to differentiate between "good" Asian-ethnic allies, like the Filipinos and the Chinese, versus the "bad" Japanese enemy aliens.[41] For example, an infamous *Life* magazine essay, "How to Tell Japs from the Chinese," contains two diagrammed photos explaining the phenotypical and physiological differences between Japanese and Chinese men. Side by side the head shots of the Chinese minister of economic affairs and Adm. Tojo of Japan were dissected for their tell-tale racial signs. Meant as a racial key for white Americans, the language of the article clearly links the genetic differences of the two races to their status as loyal ally or treacherous enemy: "Chinese wear the rational calm of tolerant realists. Japs, like General Tojo, show the humorless intensity of ruthless mystics."[42] Furthermore, the necessity for such a guide only affirms the racial ambiguity of these two East Asian ethnic groups, even while the essay attempts to decode the indeterminacy of each Asian ethnicity and define each man by discrete rather than ambiguous phenotypical traits.

The Politics of Assimilation

The extreme racial profiling that Japanese Americas suffered during World War II resulted from the belief that Japanese Americans were seen as enemy aliens rather than US citizens—their racial difference collapsed any distinction between themselves (American citizens) and those living in Japan (citizens of an Axis power). Even prior to World War II, Japanese Americans suffered from a barrage of anti-Japanese rhetoric, much of it coalescing around the issue of assimilation. According to Paul Spickard, white Americans throughout the first half of the twentieth century believed that "the Japanese were very un-American and 'unassimilable'— incapable of becoming good Americans."[43] In 1900, Mayor James Phelan of San Francisco declared that "the Chinese and Japanese are not bona fide citizens. They are not the stuff of which American citizens can be made. . . . Personally we have nothing against Japanese, but as they will not assimilate with us and their social life is so different from ours, let them keep at a respectful distance."[44] Similarly, anti-Japanese agitator V. S. McClatchy stated that "the Japanese are unassimilable and more dangerous as residents in this country. . . . With great pride of race, they have no idea of assimilating in the sense of amalgamation. They do not come here with any desire or any intent to lose their racial or national identity."[45] Of course Phelan, McClatchy, and many anti-Japanese proponents forgot that issei were categorized as aliens ineligible for citizenship and that their very distinctive Asian racial features would not allow them to assimilate like their European counterparts.[46] In 1922, issei Takao Ozawa petitioned for naturalization, taking his case all the way to the Supreme Court, where he was subsequently denied the right to become a US citizen because he was not Caucasian and therefore was not white.[47] As sociologist Wendy Ng explains, "Ozawa's case points out how the US judicial system clearly acknowledged racial classification in determining citizenship status. No matter how loyal or 'American' one professed to be, it was the racial category one belonged to that determined inclusion."[48]

Much like the rationale for denying Ozawa's right to naturalize, the WDC and WCCA, in crafting the exemption policy based on mixed marriage status, used "whiteness" as a key term and proxy for American culture and citizenship.

The more American (read white) the family atmosphere, the more likely exemption would be granted. Despite the focus on marriage in its title, the Mixed-Marriage Policy was actually a misnomer. The program was not concerned with exempting adults or with keeping married couples together. Instead, it focused on ensuring that mixed race Japanese children would have an opportunity to assimilate into an American, or in the language of the Mixed-Marriage Policy, "Caucasian" culture. Therefore, the question of whether Japanese American women and mixed race Japanese children could truly leave behind their Japaneseness and assimilate into Americanness became the cornerstone of the Mixed-Marriage Program—the rationale for whether or not families were excluded from incarceration. The WDC along with the WCCA determined who qualified for removal and incarceration based on who they believed could be assimilated into an American way of life, which they subsequently equated with a Caucasian way of life.[49] Therefore, a Japanese American who qualified for exemption would have to be seen as an ambiguous figure—someone with a flexible identity who could change, via assimilation, into a (somewhat) fully fledged American who was almost but not quite white.[50]

Although the WDC and WCCA do not define what an American way of life is within the documents related to the Mixed-Marriage Policy, in reading through the memos and correspondence of these files what emerges in the repeated and often tautological use of American and Caucasian is an adherence to principles and norms associated with US sensibilities, particularly during a time of war: being loyal to the United States, speaking English, practicing American behaviors, and associating with American or Caucasian people. Predominantly, American and Caucasian are defined by what they are not: Japanese. This means not speaking Japanese, not eating Japanese food, not practicing Japanese customs, and not mixing with Japanese people or taking an active role in the Japanese community. An American or Caucasian lifestyle erases all traces of the foreign Japanese element from the home. To assimilate into the United States and as an American in the mid-1940s meant adhering to Western European or white Anglo-Saxon Protestant values.

Although the idea of mandatory assimilation seems to be a retrograde and conservative ideal, during the early 1940s, assimilation theory, particularly as generated by the Chicago School, was understood as a progressive model based on race as a social construction rather than a biological fact. The eugenicist movements of the early twentieth century argued for white racial superiority and a belief that race was an immutable, essential genetic quality. These ideas were overthrown in the 1930s and 1940s by an insurgent model of race that attacked this paradigm and shifted the focus of race to questions of immigration and assimilation. No longer believing race to be a primordial fact, the Chicago

School of sociologists, led by Robert E. Park, developed theories that investigated the means by which various racial groups (understood in this time period to be synonymous with nationality and ethnic ancestry) assimilated at faster or slower rates, particularly relative to their immigration status and length of residence in the United States.[51] The prevailing sentiment was that assimilation was possible for all Americans of all racial backgrounds, as long as they were willing to embrace American (read white, Anglo-Saxon, Protestant) ideals, customs, and traditions and to give up their ethnic-nationalist practices and beliefs. The WDC and the WCCA, believing assimilation to be a progressive and positive goal, enacted the Mixed-Marriage Program to facilitate the erasure of Japanese ethnicity (understood by many during World War II to be a malignant foreign taint) in favor of the more ameliorative and positive American culture.

Indeed, the language used in rationalizing the policy speaks volumes about the racial assumptions of the day. *The Final Report* states that those who were exempted "were American-born, had been through American schools, had not developed Oriental thought patterns or been subjected to so-called Japanese cultures" and that "their sympathies were and would remain American."[52] And in the WDC report "Outline of Mixed-Marriage Policy," the most important criterion that the document listed as a necessary condition for exemption was that the "environment of family has been Caucasian and head of family is United States citizen or citizen of friendly nation."[53] The policy implies that if the head of household is not white but a member of a friendly nation, nonetheless the culture in the home should be Caucasian. The stress on the Caucasian environment of the home as the most salient factor in exemption further points to the elision of the term "white" with "American," reinforcing hegemonic notions of white superiority and a conflation of nationality with race.

As additional proof that assimilation rather than loyalty was at the heart of these exemptions, a letter from Gen. DeWitt to John McCloy, assistant secretary of war, discussed whether or not to amend the policy to include couples who did not have unemancipated children—to allow exemptions for interracial married couples who were either childless or who had adult children. Gen. DeWitt strongly opposed such an amendment. He believed that return to the restricted military area, that is, the West Coast, was not favorable for Japanese or Japanese Americans. He stated, quite bluntly, that "although certain individuals are prone to believe that persons of Japanese ancestry would be acceptable to the communities from which they were evacuated, I am convinced that this belief can be regarded only as wishful thinking."[54] DeWitt was convinced that an amendment to the act would encourage Japanese women to marry non-Japanese men solely for purposes of exemption, fearing that "it will pave the way for large numbers of Japanese women to return to the evacuated areas, and has no relation to the original objective of protecting mixed blood children and adults from a Japanese environment."[55] In yet another letter between DeWitt and McCloy, DeWitt stated that

> a mixed-marriage family which included unemancipated children has not been considered necessarily more loyal than a similar family which does not include mixed-blood children. The policy was designed to afford an opportunity for mixed blood children, the product of mixed-marriages, who had previously been raised in a non-Japanese environment, to continue their development under conditions as nearly normal as feasible. . . . Unlike their adult parents who inter-married and voluntarily accepted whatever social consequences ensued therefrom, mixed-blood children were in an unique situation. It was for them the policy was adopted.[56]

In both letters, DeWitt's rationale for the policy was clear: American assimilation of pre-adult children was of paramount importance. Life in the camps would entail an immersion in an entirely Japanese American environment. DeWitt's objective of "protecting" mixed blood children in order to raise them "under conditions as nearly normal as feasible" reveals a language that equates degeneracy and danger with Japanese culture. DeWitt believed that the policy was a benevolent intervention on behalf of these multiracial children. Furthermore, the program's emphasis on assimilating into an "American" lifestyle indicates that the Mixed-Marriage Policy's implicit aim was to connect correct values and attitudes with the correct racial group: a Caucasian lifestyle was affiliated with an upstanding American way of life, and a Japanese lifestyle was tantamount to being raised in a hostile environment. Additionally, DeWitt conflated Japanese with Japanese American, because he was unable to distinguish between Japanese as foreign enemy alien and Japanese American as native loyal citizen. For DeWitt, as for many others during World War II, the two—Japanese and Japanese American—remained indistinguishable, inherently unassimilable, and therefore un-American.

Assimilation was entirely at the heart of the Mixed-Marriage Program because issues of national loyalty or military threat were a secondary concern throughout the correspondence discussing the rationale and implementation of the policy. In a telephone transcript of a conversation between Col. Karl Bendetsen and Capt. John Hall of the WDC, Bendetsen asserted that "there have always been two bases for the policy from the beginning, there had to be two things in any case: Caucasian environment and an intelligence clearance."[57] His statement was in response to Hall's query about whether Theresa Takayashi, the Japanese-Caucasian wife of a nisei soldier, could return to Seattle where her white mother was still residing.[58] For Bendetsen, the woman's marriage to a

Japanese American man, along with the particular details of her parentage—her white mother married her Japanese immigrant father—nullified any Caucasian influence: "There is no indication of a Caucasian environment; there is an indication of just the reverse, because not only did the entirely white mother marry a Japanese, but so did the half Japanese daughter."[59]

When Hall countered Bendetsen by bringing up the issue of loyalty—that the Japanese American husband, by serving as part of the 442nd all-nisei regiment, had proven his patriotism to the United States—Bendetsen emphasized that the Mixed-Marriage Policy had never been a litmus test about loyalty but was, instead, a program to ensure the preservation of a Caucasian way of life: "The question is as to whether Japanese—purely Japanese persons—are or are not to be reintroduced into this area. This person is a Japanese, pure and simple; she's had a Japanese environment. Not only did her mother marry a Japanese, but so did she. . . . The mixed-marriage policy was not based on loyalty."[60] Furthermore, Bendetsen ended the conversation by elaborating on the real rationale behind the Mixed-Marriage Policy, namely the benefit for multiracial children: "Where families who are non-Japanese environment from the beginning, and because of Japanese blood would have been required to commingle with Japanese when they never had before, it was thought desirable to give them a chance to avoid that and continue the non-Japanese environment."[61] This family did not qualify for exemption because, for Bendetsen, the fact that both mother and daughter chose to marry Japanese men revoked their status as either white (in the case of Theresa Takayashi's mother) or mixed race women (Bendetsen refers to Theresa Takayashi as Japanese rather than acknowledging her bi-racial status); their racial identities were compromised through the taint of Japanese male miscegenation.[62]

Theresa Takayashi was denied exemption not only because the WDC (with Bendetsen as its arbiter) deemed her to be insufficiently white, but because her marriage to a Japanese American man disqualified her (and her children) because their household was deemed to be Japanese rather than American, a belief seemingly wholly predicated on Takayashi's decision to marry an American man of Japanese ancestry. As Takayashi's case demonstrates via the disdain shown to her white mother by Bendetsen, white women married to Japanese men were seen as race traitors—their white cultural influence nullified by their husbands' Japanese ethnicity.[63] When Hall quotes from Takayashi's letter of appeal, which states that "neither the children nor I speak a word of Japanese, being brought up in the purely American way," Bendetsen returns to the issue of interracial marriage and the link between male head of household with the culture of the home: "I still state that the mother, that is, the children's grandmother, married a Japanese; again, her daughter, the product of that marriage also married a Japanese. I don't see where you have found a Caucasian environment."[64]

Because it was the belief of the WDC that the male "head of household" determined the prevailing culture of the home, eligibility for exemption became just as much a matter of gender as race.[65] "There was a not-so-subtle sexism that went with the racism in this selection system," asserts Spickard. "The WDC assumed that males would dominate the culture and loyalties of their households."[66] For the architects of the Mixed-Marriage Policy, it was as equally inconceivable to imagine that a Japanese American, male or female, could produce an American culture in the home as it was to believe that women, of any racial or cultural background, could dominate or influence the ethnic identities and atmospheres of their children's home environment. A male head of household who was Japanese would produce a Japanese home, regardless of the race of his wife. Male Japanese–female non-Japanese mixed marriage families, therefore, did not qualify for exemption from incarceration. The best that such a family could hope for would be that the wife and her mixed race Japanese children would be allowed to reside either with the husband in the camps or to reside outside of the restricted zone, separated from her Japanese American husband.[67] Assimilation for the biracial children of a Japanese father and a white mother was impossible to conceive for the WDC; only multiracial children who had non-Japanese fathers could reliably be rehabilitated into an American way of life and therefore deserving of an existence free from "infectious Japanese thought."[68] As the language of the WDC and WCCA documents makes clear, assimilation was never a simple matter of adhering to American customs and practices. One's gender along with one's race determined one's ability to assimilate, reinforcing the idea that race has always been ambiguously figured and interpreted in US society.

For Bendetsen and his peers in the WDC and WCCA, it was inconceivable that women could influence, in any way, the culture of their homes, a confirmation of the misogynist and patriarchal attitudes that these architects of the Mixed-Marriage Policy held. A woman was a blank slate; only through her marriage to a man was her identity consolidated, which is why assimilation via the Mixed-Marriage Policy was predicated on racial ambiguity—the idea that a woman's race, and those of her children, is changeable based on marriage. Japanese American women eligible for exemption found themselves at the intersection of race, gender, and sexuality. Their legitimacy and legibility were framed, racially and sexually, through their reproductive powers and their unions with non-Japanese men. Yet as the next section will demonstrate, marriage to a non-Japanese man did not guarantee that an American or Caucasian culture would predominate in the home, particularly when that non-Japanese man is, himself, an Asian immigrant.

Yoshiko Tanaka Nakamura deLeon: An Exceptional Woman

Returning to the example of one specific exception to incarceration, Yoshiko Tanaka Nakamura deLeon's life reveals how the Mixed-Marriage Policy exemption, with its underlying intent to assimilate families into a more desirable "American" way of life, both succeeded and failed. Although Yoshiko was born and raised in a Japanese family, her decision to choose a spouse and an ethnic identity outside of the one she was born into becomes a very American decision—the ability to remake oneself in the crucible of the US melting pot.[69] Yet her story also uncovers the costs of such a choice and the question of whether it was freely made or a reaction to the anti-Japanese sentiments that proliferated during World War II.

Yoshiko Tanaka was born March 27, 1919, in Del Paso, a small farming community outside of Sacramento, California. Her mother, Eju Tanaka, an immigrant from Japan, married a farmer whose last name was Watanabe, also from the same prefecture as her family. However, this man adopted the name Tanaka upon his marriage to Eju because her family had no male heirs to carry on the family name.[70] Although I could not confirm the precise dates of their arrival to the United States, from the restrictions on immigration imposed by the 1924 Immigration Act as well as the birthdate of their daughter Yoshiko, the youngest of their four children, the couple (together or separately) had to have immigrated sometime between 1908 and 1919.[71] The marriage between Eju and Watanabe/Tanaka was neither happy nor secure. She divorced her husband on the grounds of dereliction (he had imbibed and gambled away the profits from their farming business), an act that was untraditional and unaccustomed for someone of her gender, culture, and time period. After the divorce, Watanabe/Tanaka took their three oldest children (two sons and a daughter) and returned to Japan. Eju would not see her oldest children again until after they were grown and had returned to Sacramento, many years later.

To underscore the unconventionality of Eju's situation, the divorce rate for Japanese families living in the United States in the first two decades of the twentieth century was only 1.6 percent.[72] By most accounts, the issei generation living in the United States in the first half of the twentieth century was marked by traditional gender roles and practices. As sociologist Evelyn Nakano Glenn notes, "Most issei women, of course, persevered even in the face of an unhappy marriage and an intolerable workload. Issei marriages were stable and long-lasting, if not harmonious."[73] Eju and her youngest (and now only) child Yoshiko stayed in Sacramento, where Eju found employment in a Japanese grocery store. It was here that she met and eventually married Heigo Nakamura, an issei widower with two sons. The newly blended Nakamura family would eventually grow to include three additional children, Bob, Masako, and Jim, as the family moved

south to Edna, a small farming town on the Central Coast of California located
outside San Luis Obispo.

Growing up in the rural town of Edna was hard on Yoshiko; all family members had to work to sustain the family. Masa, her youngest sister, recounts a story
of Yoshiko running away from their farm.[74] In Masa's words, their family was very
poor, and Yoshiko felt frustrated about the lack of opportunities available to her.
As a high school teenager she ran away in an attempt to escape her family's poverty and limited social atmosphere. Yoshiko was eventually discovered in Santa
Maria, the nearest large city close to Edna. Shortly after this incident, she started
a job in a Japanese grocery store. Mirroring her own mother's unique life, it was
while working in this store that Yoshiko met and eventually married Gabriel
deLeon, a Filipino immigrant and fellow employee.[75] Just as her own iconoclastic
mother had defied cultural and social expectations, so too did Yoshiko by crossing
the boundaries of race and nation through her marriage to a non-Japanese man.[76]

Eager to leave behind the poverty and lack of opportunities of her family
of origin, Yoshiko willingly embraced Gabriel's culture, even temporarily moving back to the Philippines with him. While in Manila she learned Tagalog and
became intimately acquainted with Filipino culture and customs. The Philippines
was also where their first son, Martin deLeon, was born in 1939.[77] The deLeons
returned the following year to the Nakamura farmstead in Edna, where Yoshiko
and Gabriel worked on the family farm along with the other Nakamura members
until the family was split apart with the advent of World War II and the beginning of the Japanese American incarceration. In the months leading up to their
eventual incarceration, the Nakamuras moved inland, hoping to escape imprisonment by removing themselves from the California coastline. The extended
Nakamura family, including Yoshiko and Martin deLeon, literally made camp
in a rural section of California close to the Sierra mountain range. For a period
of time, Yoshiko and Martin stayed with the Nakamuras in this makeshift habi-
tation until Gabriel came and brought his wife and son back to Edna; the rest
of the Nakamura family were consigned to Poston for the duration of the war. While
the Nakamuras endured incarceration in Arizona, Yoshiko and Gabriel raised their
son Martin in Edna, California, and had a second child, Patricia, during the war.

As one of only ninety women of Japanese descent exempted from incarceration and living in the restricted zone of the West Coast during World War II,
Yoshiko undoubtedly suffered from both isolation and discrimination. As
reported by Masa, who recalls only a few stories that Yoshiko shared about her
days during the war, the local sheriff would occasionally get phone calls warning
him of a "Jap on the loose." But because he was familiar with the deLeon family,
he knew that Yoshiko posed no security threat and even allowed her to break
curfew occasionally. Although the local sheriff might have been sympathetic

and understanding of her exceptional situation, Yoshiko faced discrimination from other community members. Her daughter, Patricia Dorr, remembers that her mother refused to set foot in a local movie house. When asked why she would not patronize the Farrell theater, Yoshiko intimated that she had suffered extreme discrimination by the theater owner during the war.[78]

Indeed, from the scant stories shared by Yoshiko's sister and daughter, it appears (and seems apparent) that the atmosphere in Edna as well as the Central Coast of California (and the entire nation) was distinctly anti-Japanese. Although Yoshiko disclosed few stories with any family members about her experiences in Edna during the war, first-person accounts of Japanese Americans returning to the West Coast after their years of incarceration attest to the anti-Japanese sentiment that prevailed throughout California, Oregon, and Washington State.[79] Describing the atmosphere of returning Japanese Americans to the Hood River area of Oregon after World War II, Ng affirms that "the hostility toward the Japanese did not subside. Vigilantes vandalized farm equipment, broke windows, and generally harassed Japanese in whatever way they could. . . . Japanese Americans were ostracized and prevented from entering many public places: movie theaters, restaurants, and stores."[80] One can only imagine the loneliness, fear, anxiety, disgrace, and anger that Yoshiko felt as the sole Japanese American in her community during a time when jingoism, xenophobia, and anti-Japanese sentiment were at their peak.

If the rationale of the Mixed-Marriage Policy was to ensure that an American or Caucasian way of life was the main home environment of the mixed heritage family, without the taint of Japanese cultural influence, then the policy had ambiguous results in the deLeon family. Yoshiko deLeon's husband, while not Japanese was also not Caucasian; therefore, the preservation of a white lifestyle was never realized in their culturally mixed Japanese-Filipino American home. Instead, Yoshiko fully adopted and embraced her husband's Filipino heritage: she spoke Tagalog, cooked Filipino food, wore traditional Filipino dresses, participated in Filipino community events, and, most important, raised her two children with a strong Filipino ethnic identity. In this way, Yoshiko and Gabriel deLeon resisted and indeed subverted the assimilationist goals of the Mixed-Marriage Policy; the atmosphere in their home preserved rather than erased all traces of Asian culture. Theirs was a home full of racial ambiguity that was not the same as the architects of the Mixed-Marriage Policy hoped for; the flexibility of Yoshiko's racial identity trended to Filipino rather than white, allowing her to assimilate as a racially ambiguous Asian American into a Filipino home and culture. In the language of the Mixed-Marriage Policy, the deLeon household emphasized a Filipino culture in the home (the culture of a nation friendly to the United States), but theirs was not one that promoted Caucasian culture, which means if American-ness is predicated on whiteness, then it is questionable as to how American the deLeon family would have been, according to the strictures of the Mixed-Marriage Program.

Although the Mixed-Marriage Policy may not have inculcated a Caucasian atmosphere in the deLeon family, its mission to prevent a Japanese influenced family did, in part, succeed. As both her daughter and sister attest, Yoshiko did not pass on any Japanese traditions to her children. Instead, both Martin and Patricia deLeon were raised with a strong sense of Filipino culture and pride and a stronger connection to their father's Filipino friends and family members. One story that illustrates the estrangement that Yoshiko's daughter, Pat, felt toward her Japanese heritage occurred over the topic of Japanese language acquisition. While in high school, Pat had asked Yoshiko to teach her Japanese; however, Yoshiko replied, "Oh why do you want to learn that for?"—an emblematic response because the mother did not pass on either Japanese language or customs to her children. The Asian-ethnic dishes and traditions that Pat learned from her mother were Filipino rather than Japanese. These are the ones that Pat has, in turn, taught to her own children. Pork adobo rather than mochi pounding became an annual winter tradition among the second- and third-generation deLeons.[81]

Moreover, Masa recalls that Yoshiko embraced the Filipino community and was, in turn, embraced by them, showing a preference for her adopted Filipino culture and community. Although Yoshiko's issei parents lived in the farmhouse adjacent to the deLeon's, their family's main social and family ties were with Gabriel's Filipino family and friends. It is this Filipino community that Yoshiko's daughter recalls when asked about spending time with extended family. Filipino aunts, uncles, and cousins dominated the deLeon family get-togethers, while the Japanese American Nakamuras, who had all relocated to Southern and Northern California, were visited during infrequent road trips.[82] Family, for the post–World War II deLeons, was largely a Filipino affair. Whether Yoshiko's privileging of a Filipino cultural identity, for herself and her children, derived from shame, survival, or sheer preference can only be speculated, because Yoshiko deLeon, a quiet woman to begin with, never explained this preference. Indeed, the story of her exemption may have been forgotten entirely were it not for her daughter and granddaughter's passing along her story in the brief form they knew—that Yoshiko deLeon, through the auspices of her Filipino immigrant husband, was somehow kept out of the camps.[83] This family tale, although incomplete, is true; Yoshiko escaped incarceration because of her marriage to a non-Japanese man and her multiracial children. And although this-mixed heritage family may not have fulfilled the WDC's goal of assimilating into a Caucasian way of life, their family did, in fact, assimilate into an American household—one uniquely if somewhat ambiguously Asian American.

The Legacy of the Mixed-Marriage Policy, the Japanese American Incarceration, and Yoshiko deLeon

Race as the barometer for inclusion, or in the case of Executive Order 9066, exclusion, is at the heart of both the incarceration as well as the exemptions of Japanese Americans during World War II. The mass removal and incarceration of Japanese Americans was a policy based on a racialized idea of threat and loyalty. Yet the very existence of an exemption policy defied the supposed "military necessity" of imprisoning every man, woman, and child of Japanese ancestry living in the restricted military zone. The WDC and WCCA's implementation of the entire removal, relocation, and exemption process was arbitrary and punitive in nature. The emphasis upon the kind of household that multiracial children were raised in suggests that the WDC and WCCA believed paradoxically that race was an immutable quality bound up in blood quantum and reducible to certain percentages, in exactly the same way that the one-drop rule was used throughout the South to maintain a color-line hierarchy, and that race was a malleable condition that could allow for a reinterpretation and redefinition of one's person depending on other intersectional identitarian factors, such as marital, gender, and reproductive status.

Furthermore, the purpose of the policy, "to afford an opportunity for mixed blood children, the product of mixed-marriages, who had previously been raised in a non-Japanese environment, to continue their development under conditions as nearly normal as feasible," implies that assimilation was possible based on a changeable and ambiguous racial identity and a correct cultural environment.[84] In other words, one could socially engineer an environment conducive to American assimilation. So long as one's development is "normal," that is, not Japanese and hence not foreign, one can overcome the taint of Japanese blood through rigorous Americanization, which also in the language of the War Relocation Authority (WRA) and WCCA seemed akin to whitewashing. Furthermore, according to the language of *The Final Report*, Japanese race was not a barrier to assimilation because ideal candidates for inclusion in the Mixed-Marriage Program were Japanese women who "were American-born, had been through American schools, had not developed Oriental thought patterns."[85] As long as one thought like an American one could be an American, regardless of one's Japanese ancestry. More important, as long as one could stop thinking like a Japanese person one had the possibility of becoming an American and thus could be almost but not quite white. The accident of one's Japanese race could be overcome through thought control. And if this is the case, then the idea that a Japanese American person's race made his or her loyalty to the United States questionable was a fallacy, a political construction used to justify incarceration predicated on racial prejudice instead of racial inassimilability. The Japanese

American incarceration was never meant to protect Japanese Americans from hordes of angry white mobs, nor was it to guard US borders from treacherous Japanese spies. The incarceration was a reaction to racial bigotry and fear—a common wartime reaction—to scapegoat a group of people who look like the enemy and therefore can symbolically stand in for the enemy. The exemption policy was similarly a reaction to bigotry and fear, except rather than scapegoating a group of people, the Mixed-Marriage Program created an exceptional category of immunity for select people who could be interpreted as non-enemy Japanese if they were no longer exposed to Japanese cultural and behavioral influences. If Japanese women who married non-Japanese men could be interpreted as betraying the Japanese race through their martial choices, then this meant that they, and their progeny, could be discursively figured into a category of non-Japanese enemy alien/non-alien—it means they could be rendered into ambiguous figures who were neither Japanese nor not Japanese, neither wholly American yet not wholly un-American either. By betraying Japan they could, potentially, be redefined as not disloyal to America.

The story of Yoshiko's exemption and the story of the Mixed-Marriage Policy illustrate the racial ideology that was emblematic of the US government and American society during World War II. The language used in the correspondence around this policy underscores the ways in which the bureaucrats, politicians, and military officers believed American society and culture should be—the kind of culture and society they wanted to create, maintain, and preserve through a program of assimilation into an American way of life, an assimilation predicated on the racial ambiguity of certain subjects based on gender and sexuality. Embedded in the assumptions of the WRA and WCCA is a hegemonic imperative—that culture and society can be regulated along subtle and not-so-subtle axes, through institutions as large as the US military or as intimate as marriage. Fundamentally, the Mixed-Marriage Program reveals the inherent ambiguity of race and assimilation: that race is never a fixed entity but is, instead, an unstable product of others' fears, desires, and anxieties, particularly when they intersect with assumptions about gender and sexuality. Race is open to multiple interpretations from various perspectives and thus ultimately flexible, fluid, and beyond the control of any single institution or individual.

The documents of the Mixed-Marriage Program speak volumes about the ideology of the policy makers—their beliefs surrounding race, gender, and sexuality and about preserving an American way of life in the face of wartime anxiety and fear. Ultimately the exemptions shed light on a way of thinking about race that predominated among the Roosevelt administration and among many American citizens during World War II: that Japanese Americans were considered noncitizens, expendable from a constitutional point of view.[86] But what the policy, the documents related to the Japanese American incarceration, and the subsequent redress and reparations movement can not tell us is how families were affected by this policy—specifically, the legacy of this policy on one particular family: the deLeons.

On December 1, 1965, Yoshiko deLeon died, suddenly, of a brain aneurysm, at the age of forty-six. No one could have anticipated her death, certainly not her only daughter Pat, who was twenty-one and pregnant with her first child at the time of her mother's passing. When asked about her mother, Pat does not recall stories of someone defined by racism or her wartime experiences. Instead, she remembers a sweet and gentle woman—characterized as generous, funny, and kind. Pat remembers the hard labor her parents performed on their family farm in Edna; their time was preoccupied with raising their family and maintaining their crops. Her parents did not dwell on the war years or share stories of discrimination with their children. In many ways, this is a theme that runs throughout the lives of the sansei and yonsei—the third and fourth generation of Japanese Americans whose parents and grandparents were incarcerated. There is a great silence and shame surrounding the incarceration; many who endured the hardships of World War II do not like to talk about their wartime experiences and prefer to concentrate on the present and future rather than return to memories of the past. It seems that even the condition of not being imprisoned rendered its own silence for Yoshiko, as she declined to share stories of her time during World War II with her siblings or children.

Yoshiko's exemption from incarceration was also an exemption from her Japanese-ness; she was literally kept away from her Japanese family members during their imprisonment in Poston and must have eschewed Japanese customs living in Edna with her husband given the atmosphere of anti-Japanese hysteria and xenophobia, a habit that seems to have continued in her postwar life. And though the exemption gave her immunity from incarceration, she could not have been immune to the mixed messages she received because of her exceptional status; that she was a different kind of Japanese American, a special kind but still subject to regulation by the state—allowed freedom because of her mixed race children and her non-Japanese husband but without these connections she would be like the rest of her Japanese family: an incarcerated enemy non-alien. Yet despite the government's attempts to engineer correct racial and national identities for her and her children, neither Yoshiko nor the second-generation deLeons assimilated into a Caucasian lifestyle. In their home they continued to eat rice and use chopsticks (especially when eating with Yoshiko's Japanese parents), and even though Yoshiko did not teach her children Japanese or pass along Japanese traditions, neither did she denigrate Japanese customs and culture, a particularly salient point considering her parents continued to live next door to them on their Edna farm. And perhaps most telling, of all the various names that Yoshiko Tanaka Nakamura deLeon changed into and discarded during her lifetime, her first name, Yoshiko, was one she never gave up.[87]

Interestingly both Martin (the son born before the war) and Pat (the daughter born during the war) continued their parents' tradition of marrying someone of a different race: Martin's wife MaryLou is Mexican American, and Pat's husband Dick is white. Looking deeper into the third generation of deLeons, Pat's only daughter, Trish, has also married interracially. Despite their marriage partners, both Yoshiko's daughter and granddaughter continue to identify as Japanese and Filipino American (and in Trish's case, as mixed race Asian–white American). Both also embrace a political Asian American identity because, as they have each noted, they recognize that they are part of a non-white minority group in the United States. Although both Pat and Trish acknowledge that they did not and do not suffer from the types of racial discrimination that Yoshiko did, they choose to identify with and honor the respective heritages of both Gabriel and Yoshiko. Indeed, Trish, as a member of the third generation, has a renewed interest in her ethnic ancestries. She has made trips to both Japan and the Philippines in order to meet extended family members and to learn more about these two Asian cultures. Perhaps most telling of all, Trish retains a connection to Yoshiko by carrying her grandmother's legacy as part of her own name: Patricia Yoshiko. Giving her daughter her mother's name was a conscious act by Pat to have part of her mother live on in her daughter and to instill an appreciation for their shared Japanese heritage. Trish, in turn, has bestowed this legacy onto the fourth generation—giving her own daughter the same middle name that she shares with her grandmother: Alex Yoshiko. So perhaps, in the end, despite its attempt to erase all traces of Japanese culture from the multiracial progeny of these interracial couples, the WDC and WCCA failed miserably. Although Pat may not have learned Japanese from her mother nor learned many Japanese customs from Yoshiko, she did retain an interest in her Japanese heritage and, most important, has very fond memories of spending time with her Japanese grandparents after school. Indeed, one memory in particular that Pat cherishes is learning to make a special family recipe, apple pie, from her Japanese immigrant grandmother, a recipe she has passed down to her own children. Yoshiko's legacy does live on in her grandchildren and great-grandchildren, through her name, through their continued interest in Japanese culture, and through the stories they share about her.

At the end of Toni Morrison's haunting novel about slavery, *Beloved*, Morrison writes, "This is not a story to pass on."[88] In similar fashion, this ambiguous statement proves aphoristic for Yoshiko deLeon, because the story of her exemption from incarceration and how she survived during World War II was not passed on to her family out of, perhaps, shame, neglect, or simply due to a need to forget the past and move on with her life. Yet hers is a story that we should not pass on; we need to record and acknowledge these exemptions as part of the complex, complicated, and ambiguous history of the Japanese American incarceration. Her story, as well as the story of Mixed-Marriage Policy, signals the racist (il)logic of the US concentration camps. This exceptional narrative ruptures the official government discourse of the "military necessity" of incarceration because Yoshiko, like the other exemptees, was neither a threat to national security nor a model for assimilation into a white American way of life. Furthermore, the story of Japanese American exemptions illuminates the inherent instability of race—that despite attempts by the US military and government to fix racial categories, even their prescriptions resulted in ambiguous decisions about whom to incarcerate and whom to exempt.

Ambiguity—of Yoshiko's status, of her mixed race Asian American progeny, or of the idea of Asian American assimilation—is an important act of resistance. The ambiguity demonstrated in Yoshiko's life and exemption and in the idea of Asian American assimilation, refutes simplistic notions of what it means to be an American and points to the fluid and flexible qualities of race to mutate over time and throughout political events. Despite the WDC and WCCA's ideals in implementing the Mixed-Marriage Program, Yoshiko deLeon and her children, grandchildren, and even great-grandchildren continue to live their lives identifying with their Japanese culture while also assimilating into an Asian American lifestyle—one that recognizes the indeterminacy and complexity of living with Asian ancestry in America. In many ways Yoshiko deLeon's life should be remembered not because she was an odd footnote in a disgraceful part of US history but because she was a woman who lived her life in the best and fullest way she knew: she married a man, had children with him, and loved them. Perhaps what we should remember from Yoshiko deLeon's life is not whether she assimilated as American, Japanese, Filipino, white, or Asian American; rather, we should recall that her very existence points to the small ways that individuals resisted through the prosaic acts of simply living their lives.

2

Antisentimental Loss

Stories of Transracial/Transnational Asian American Adult Adoptees in the Blogosphere

From Huckleberry Finn to Harry Potter, narratives about orphans fascinate and proliferate in popular culture, and in recent years, the figure of the adopted child has made its way into several films and television sitcoms, such as *Modern Family*, *Trophy Wife*, *Easy A*, *The Blind Side*, *Then She Found Me*, *Did You Hear about the Morgans?*, and the *Sex in the City* franchise (both the television series and the two films that followed). In the works listed, many of these adoptees are Asian children, who are used as plot points for a happy resolution to infertility or childlessness.[1] Furthermore, these cinematic Asian adoptees represent the hope of America to overcome its racist past and to embrace a multicultural future, particularly one that celebrates an assimilative and sentimentalized diversity wrought in the crucible of the white American family.[2] But what happens to these transracial and transnational adopted children when they develop into adults who begin to question who they are and how they came to be living in families that do not share their first language, ethnic background, or racial identity? Where is the voice of the adult Asian American adoptee, and why is there no cinematic version of the adult adoptee? Is he or she still a figure that can serve as the resolution for sentimental orphan narratives? What do they think about their adopted status as transracial and transnational adult adoptees, and what knowledge do they have to share for themselves as well as for adoptive parents and general American society? And are they, in fact, Asian, American, neither, or both?

This chapter examines adult Asian American adoptees as racially ambiguous subjects. Born in Asian nations and raised in white families, these transracial and transnational (hereafter abbreviated as TRA/TN) Asian American adoptees narrate their experiences in a variety of venues, through memoirs, personal essays, films, and most notably blogs. They describe their ambivalence with their racial and ethnic identities and the struggle to position themselves within white mainstream culture, Asian American culture, and the families in which they were raised. Additionally, this chapter looks at the ways in which adoptees from Asian countries use various forms of media to articulate their TRA/TN identities. The stories of adult adoptees express outrage and frustration as well as sadness and confusion, but most of all, they create both an identity and a body of knowledge that is self-consciously Asian and American, which thereby encompasses the inherent indeterminacy of being TRA/TN Asian American adult adoptees. These adoptees narrate their continual negotiation of racial ambiguity, which refutes the standard sentimental narrative of adoption, particularly that of the war-torn Asian orphan adoptee who is rescued by the bounty and generosity of white America. Jae Ran Kim, the blogger of *Harlow's Monkey*, one of the preeminent blog sites for TRA/TN adoptees, explains that she writes first and foremost for herself and for other adoptees as a way of making sense of her TRA/TN adoptee experience:

> I write this blog for you, my fellow adoptee. I hope that the information I write about—the quirky, the touching, the outrageous—in some way informs *your* journey. Since that day in 1999 when I saw myself reflected in another person who had shared so many experiences as me, I knew I was not alone. One of the biggest tragedies I think many of us adoptees face is that we are so isolated. Many of us have tried for so long to "fit in" with everyone else, that it's hard to recognize another adoptee. But I've come out of the closet as an outspoken TRA. And I want to find solidarity with others who have been informed by adoption.[3]

Kim relies on new media to create a community of people negotiating their racial ambiguity as Asian adult adoptees. When she writes about the moment in 1999 of seeing her life reflected in the experiences of another person who shares her background, her history, Kim speaks to the unspoken history of adoption in America, one that is more complex and nuanced than the sentimental stories of orphans and adoptees promoted in popular culture over the past two centuries.

Prior to the mid-nineteenth century, adoption in the United States occurred informally and was not tied to institutional mechanisms but handled between family or community members. Literary critic Carol Singley traces the many different kinship formations within Cotton Mather's colonial household, noting that Mather "was a step- and foster parent as well as a biological parent" whose nonbiogenetic family members came to the minister through "death, remarriage, or clerical calling."[4] According to the devoutly puritan Mather, adoption was part of his duty as a Christian: "Mather articulates a common sentiment in American literature: adoption is a form of child saving. By adopting others, one does God's work."[5] For Mather, adoption saved both lives and souls; his perspective contributed to the creation of a salvation that would become a driving force and rhetorical tool used in promoting transnational adoption in the mid-twentieth century.

As adoption developed into a contractual and legal issue, so too did the process become institutionalized and subject to professional regulation for all parties in the adoption triad: children eligible for adoption, relinquishing first parents, and prospective adoptive parents.[6] Ellen Herman's *Kinship by Design: A History of Adoption in the Modern United States* offers a trenchant examination of the way that adoption professionals attempted to engineer families in order to make non-consanguinous kinship more "real"—more like biogenetic families. Tracing the various developments in how parentless children were treated by the state and by society in general, Herman discusses how the ethos and paradigm of "matching" guided social workers, adoption professionals, and adoptive parents in their desire to create families as close to a "natural" or biological family as possible: red-headed children with green eyes were placed with red-headed families with green eyes.[7] Placing children and parents of differing races most vehemently defied the matching paradigm; transracial adoptions were unheard of until after World War II, and non-white children were often sent to institutions rather than adopted out.[8] The more a white child "looked" like she or he could have been the biogenetic child of a white couple, the more authentic the adopted family became, thus overcoming the stigma of non-consanguinous family structures that guided society's ideas about correct kinship throughout most of the twentieth century. According to historian Julie Berebitsky, "The matching of physical characteristics provided one way to minimize the difference [of non-consanguinous families] by making adoption invisible to outsiders . . . and reflected social workers' belief that adoptive families should be modeled as closely as possible on biological families."[9]

Additionally, proper matching ensured that a child would never need to know that he or she had been adopted. The conventional wisdom of this era believed that the stigma of adoption—the knowledge that one was unwanted or that one's mother had been involved in such sordid activities as having out-of-wedlock sex—was to be avoided at all costs. Adoptive parents were advised never to tell a child that he or she was adopted. The ethos of matching and of hiding the knowledge of one's adoption had the added effect of eliminating entirely the rights and identities of first families. "Matching made adoption real by making natal kin disappear, literally," writes Herman. "It meant that the original families of adoptees ceased to have any legal standing or social meaning at all."[10] Families receiving a child who looks just like them can pretend that the child is theirs and that there was never an originary mother; effectively, they can erase the entire prenatal history of their child and preserve the illusion that their family is just like any other biogenetic family. As E. Wayne Carp has written about in *Family Matters: Secrecy and Disclosure in the History of Adoption*, "Adoption records are sealed and access is denied to everyone," thus ensuring that adoptive families could keep the fact of adoption hidden from their children by erasing traces of their past.[11]

By the late 1960s, matching and the concomitant belief in hiding the adoptive status of one's child would no longer be the prevailing wisdom among adoption professionals. The social atmosphere of the modern civil rights movement, with an emphasis on racial equality and a tolerance for interracial sociability in education, in the workforce, and in one's intimate relationships, would also seep into the adoption world, as more white adoptive couples became open to including non-white children into their families. Although the controversial 1972 statement by the National Association of Black Social Workers (NABSW) decrying the placement of black children with white families is often credited as a factor in reducing the number of transracial placements, Herman notes that "the decline in whites adopting black children after 1972 may have had as much to do with stubborn private preferences among would-be parents as with organized protests or policies that erected barriers to placements that crossed the color line."[12] Certainly, as the next section examines, the number of white families adopting Asian children from overseas (from the late 1950s to our contemporary period) not only suggests that white families were and are willing to cross over certain segments of the color line, it also shows that some white parents believed that a TRA/TN adoption of an Asian child could be mitigated to the degree that the color line would simply cease to exist. Yet the ethos of "proper matching" that pervaded much of US adoption policy could still be seen, and felt, by the Asian adoptees who had to negotiate childhoods in white families. To once again quote blogger Jae Ran Kim: "Many of us have tried for so long to 'fit in' with everyone else"; the dilemma of fitting in, of their early struggles trying to match the race and culture of their white adoptive families, is part of the racial ambiguity that marks Asian adult adoptees.

Transnational and Transracial Adoption: Asian War Babies and the Racial Ambiguity of Asian American Adoptees

Asian transnational adoption as an institution began in the 1950s in the aftermath of the Korean War, when thousands of displaced and orphaned children created a humanitarian crisis.[13] Korean war babies were widely publicized in newspaper and magazine articles and advertisements, from the *Los Angeles*

Times to *McCall's* to *Ebony* magazine.[14] The advertisement in *Ebony* magazine was specifically designed to appeal to African American families because the children depicted in the magazine were black-Korean children. By targeting black couples as adoptive parents, the ideologies of both the one-drop rule and race matching were invoked: the proper parents for mixed race black-Asian children must be black families. Similarly, the number of mixed race white-Korean children in orphanages sparked the humanitarian interest in adopting children who seemingly had no place in Korean society. Herman describes the stories circulated in newspapers and magazines figuring Amerasian children—the product of unions between US servicemen and Korean women—as essentially unadoptable because of the stigma of their mixed race status: "Mass-circulation magazines reported that mixed-race children were cruelly stigmatized, subject to infanticide and slavery."[15] The racially ambiguous status of Asian adopted children was thus born out of the actual mixed race, racially ambiguous bodies of orphaned children in Korea. For many Americans of the post–Korean War era, Amerasian children and Korean war babies were essentially one and the same.

Just as the colonial puritan minister Cotton Mather felt called on by his religious principles to adopt children into his family as an act of charity and spiritual rescue, three centuries later the rhetoric of Christian salvation and humanitarian aid continued in the movement to adopt Korean children. In her groundbreaking work, *Adopted Territory: Transnational Korean Adoptees and the Politics of Belonging*, Eleana Kim notes that "the adoption of mixed-race Korean American children thus became another alternative for so-called childless couples, especially those motivated by Christian values."[16] One of these couples spurred by their evangelical values, Bertha and Harry Holt, were monumentally influential in promoting transnational adoption, a legacy that has made their name "virtually synonymous with overseas adoption and child welfare" and has spawned an international adoption industry that continues to this day.[17] Although the Holts were not the first nor only advocates for transnational adoption from Korea, as E. Kim asserts, "interest and demand for Korean war orphans exploded in the United States, especially after Holt's widely publicized adoption of eight children in 1955."[18] This publicity was arranged by the Christian evangelical organization World Vision, which, according to Laura Briggs and Diana Marre, "employed a publicist on their behalf, and photographers and journalists made their arrival into a media circus."[19] Images of the Holts with their eight adopted Korean children and six biogenetic children (making a total of sixteen for this nuclear family) were widely circulated throughout the United States and inspired many evangelical families to adopt children of their own.

Indeed, immediately following the adoption of the eight children, the Holt Adoption Agency was established in 1956 with the explicit aim of recovering children from Korea and placing them into Christian homes. As social worker, blogger, and Korean adoptee JaeRan Kim states, "The Holts believed that the only qualification prospective parents had to have was a personal belief in Jesus Christ."[20] Although the Holt Adoption Agency came under scrutiny by adoption professionals for their single criteria of placing children in evangelical Christian homes, forgoing home studies and proper vetting of adoptive parents, they very successfully linked a rhetoric of salvation and humanitarian rescue to the transnational adoption of Korean children.[21] White families who might normally have been wary of transracial adoption understood that it was their Christian duty to adopt and that through adoption white families could save abandoned Korean children, both literally and spiritually. Notes J. Kim: "I have at times believed my parents adopted me for the purpose of adding bonus points to their heavenly tally."[22]

The Holt Adoption Agency currently operates under the name Holt International Children's Services and still facilitates adoptions from Korea, as well as from nine other countries.[23] Most notably, Holt International helped organize Operation Babylift in 1975, an effort by various humanitarian organizations and the US government to evacuate nearly two thousand Vietnamese children (many Amerasian) out of Saigon on the eve of the US military pullout from Viet Nam. And Holt International also arranges adoptions between families in the United States and children in China, currently the largest sending nation of international adopted children, with just under five thousand children adopted into the United States per year.[24] Thus Holt International, along with other adoption agencies specializing in transnational adoption, continues the legacy begun from Bertha and Harry Holt's initial adoption of eight Korean Amerasian children by encouraging the transnational adoption of Asian children to America and facilitating the transracial family formation of Asian children in white families.

Transnational adoption from Asian nations exploded the ethos of race matching because the vast majority of families who participated in "intercountry" adoption (the term that was commonly used to describe transnational adoption in the mid-twentieth century) were white; therefore, not only was matching rendered superfluous, so too was the idea that one could keep secret the reality of an adopted child's status. As Herman observes, "Asian children placed in white families were the adoptees who made transracial adoption a conspicuous social issue for the first time."[25] The white families with visibly Asian children forced a reevaluation of adoption practices and a reconsideration of the American nuclear family as extending the boundaries of nonconsanguineous kinship and racial difference.

Yet the Asian American adoptee represents a particular kind of racial integration, one facilitated by the ability of the adoptee to be read as racially ambiguous and to achieve a type of honorary whiteness. Many white families looking to adopt were not comfortable with raising African American children because of their unease with racial difference, specifically with black Americans. In describing the reasons for a preference and increase in international over domestic adoption, sociologist Heather Jacobson observes that "the avoidance of older, (assumingly) troubled, black or biracial children and a privileging of healthy and (presumably) unencumbered white or Asian infants" influences white middle-class American parents to choose transnational adoption from Eastern Europe and Asia.[26] Another white adoptive father confesses to anthropologist Andrea Louie that when imagining what people will think about his future imaginary adopted children, he thinks of a "math major at some snooty ivy league school" when thinking of a Chinese adoptive girl answering the door to his home, whereas with a Latino son, "if it is a South American boy who answers the door, they think gardener, waiter, or something like that."[27] This father can more easily adapt the stereotypical associations of his future Chinese daughter (or actual Chinese daughter because he and his wife are one of the couples in Louie's study who do, indeed, adopt a Chinese girl) into his household than he can adapt to the stereotypes associated with Latino men. Furthermore, these stereotypes align with the model minority myth that plagues Asian Americans. Although the associations are seemingly positive—the idea that Chinese girls are good at math and high achieving in educational arenas—nonetheless the (il)logic of the model minority myth places Asian Americans in a hierarchy over and against other racial minorities, implicitly (or not so implicitly) maligning Latino, African American, and American Indians as not as smart or as successful and hence capable of only being a "gardener, waiter, or something like that"—the implied "like that" meaning a job that requires little to no education and without respectable social status. Louie affirms that this couple "was guided in part by the positive US stereotypes of Chinese girls versus negative ones of South American boys" in rationalizing why they chose to adopt from China.[28] Using terminology from Pierre Bourdieu's notion of "habitus," one can see that Asian girls become another type of commodity signaling the cultural capital of white bourgeoisie or middle-class families.[29]

The intersection of race and gender becomes another contributing factor in the racial ambiguity of Asian American adoptees.[30] Ethnographer Kristi Brian observes that "since 1955, the gender ratio of adoptees from Korea has been approximately 58 percent female," confirming the statistic that girls are placed for adoption at a higher rate than boys.[31] In the contemporary case of China, where the one-child policy along with adherence to traditional Confucian family systems in rural areas makes having a boy the primary concern for families, girls have become synonymous with the phrase "Chinese adoption."[32] As cultural anthropologist Toby Alice Volkman states, "Until the wave of Chinese adoptions there had never been another cohort of transnational, transracial adoptees that arrived in the United States in such large numbers, in so few years, of roughly the same age and largely the same gender."[33] Sociologist Sara Dorow writes explicitly about the ways in which gender and our conceptions of Asian female sexuality play into the desirability of adopting Chinese girls. Discussing the "flexible racialization of Asian subjects in the American imaginary,"[34] Dorow notes that "in a context in which 95 percent of adoptees are girls" it is paramount to ask "questions of how racialized desire might intersect with the construction of Asian *female* bodies" [emphasis in original].[35] Additionally, scholars such as Yen Le Espiritu, Judy Yung, and Rosalind Chou have amply documented the sexed, gendered, and racialized identities of Asian women in America, an intersectionality that allows them to be valued as sexualized objects of white masculinist desire, thereby making it easier to imagine Asian American female bodies incorporated into the social fabric of the United States and into white family structures.[36] Certainly the history of interracial marriages between white men (traditionally white US military men) and Asian women (initially as war brides) and the current rate of interracial marriages between Asian American women and white men attests to a certain comfort level if not familiarity with the picture of a mixed race family formation that includes an Asian female body, as Jacobson affirms: "The adoption of Asian children by white parents is facilitated by the fact that acceptance of Asian/white interracial families has increased."[37] An Asian female child adopted into a white nuclear family, therefore, seems not to challenge norms of racial difference and discomfort in the way that transracial adoption of African American children clearly do.[38] "Chinese children were in some instances desirable because they could be imagined as neither white nor black," asserts Dorow, "interesting without being so different that they would not 'fit in.'"[39]

The racial ambiguity of Asian American adoptees allows them to become blank slates for the projections of white adoptive parents, seemingly without the historical baggage of race that is the legacy of white supremacy in the United States. One Vietnamese American adult adoptee, Rachel Quy Collier, affirms the idea of the parentless child as tabula rasa when she writes, "The Orphan is the unknown Other, a blank page. An adopted child can be appropriated, assimilated, made into the image and likeness of her parents and society. She is given a (new) name, language, religion, cosmology, worldview; she is, in a sense, colonized—for her own good, out of love."[40] Although it may seem impossible for the Asian American adult adoptee to fully assimilate into white American culture, David Eng, in *The Feelings of Kinship: Queer Liberalism and the Racialization of Intimacy*, theorizes about a new form of racial passing "which is less about the concealment of difference than about our collective refusal to acknowledge it."[41] Such passing reinforces the notion of a "neoliberal multiculturalism under which race only ever appears as disappearing, a racial politics that acknowledges difference only to dismiss its importance."[42] The Asian American adult adoptee can pass as white and achieve honorary whiteness in a neoliberal and colorblind American melting pot because her race does not matter; all that matters is that she is, as Collier notes, "colonized—for her own good, out of love," and the love and culture of her adoptive family will form the basis of her new American identity.

The example that Eng uses in his study to support the "new passing" of "the acknowledgment and dismissal of difference" comes from scenes in Deann Borshay Liem's trailblazing documentary *First Person Plural*.[43] Borshay Liem, a Korean American adult adoptee (hereafter abbreviated to KAD), interviews her siblings, Duncan and Denise, about being adopted into their family. Both siblings deny noticing any differences and, in fact, go so far as to create familial similarities between the adopted Borshay Liem and their white family, with Duncan asserting that "you don't have the family eyes, but you've got the family smile" and Denise claiming that "people would see us or whatever and they'd say 'Is that your sister? You guys look just alike.'"[44] Both siblings also tell Borshay Liem that her racial difference does not matter to them—with Duncan emphatically saying, "Color and look doesn't make any difference" and Denise claiming that she doesn't think of Borshay Liem as Korean—she just thinks of her as her sister.

White adoptive parents of Chinese children echo the language of honorary whiteness and colorblindness in how they view their children's identities. One mother in Louie's study of Chinese adopted children says that "she thought that her daughter would become Irish American like she and her husband."[45] Similarly an adoptive father interviewed by Dorow states clearly his intentions for his adopted daughter: "To know she's American first, and that's her heritage."[46] Certain white adoptive parents seem to view their Asian adopted children as malleable and flexible; their natal ancestry is simply the backdrop on which they can mold, anew, their American identities, and their racial difference is rendered ambiguous—it can be acknowledged and then discarded as unimportant because, as the father states, "she's American first."

Moreover, the emphasis on minimizing difference, particularly the racial and ethnic difference between Asian adoptees and their white adoptive families, reinforces the idea of achieving the kind of "natural" family structure that earlier adoption advocates had striven for through the practice of matching. In other words, matching children to families was as much about minimizing difference as it was about creating seamless physical similarities within the adoptive family. Minimizing differences allowed the illusion of an adoptive family as equivalent to a biogenetic family. Thus, ignoring the racial differences of an adopted Asian child allows the family to feel that they all belong to one another, that they're all the same, and hence that their family is "real."

However, from the first-person accounts of TRA/TN Asian American adult adoptees, the sense of internalizing the ethos of colorblindness, of being seen as racially flexible and ambiguous subjects, has resulted in a cognitive dissonance between what these Asian American adult adoptees believed themselves to be and tried to adapt to while growing up—namely being white—versus the reality of the image that stared back at them from the mirror—being Asian American. Jane Jeong Trenka, in her trenchant and moving memoir, *The Language of Blood*, describes how she checked white on her college applications because

> I didn't want to be Korean. Korea was a place that couldn't be talked about at home; it made other children leer at me in school. Korea was the reason my face was mutated, why my glasses wouldn't quite stay on my nose, why it was hard to find clothes that fit. It was the reason some children weren't allowed to play with me, some felt justified in calling me a chink or a rice-picker, and adults didn't feel compelled to defend me. . . . I checked "white" because I was culturally white.[47]

Trenka's childhood experiences with racial difference and racism prove the lie of colorblindness and passing that adoptive parents of Asian adoptees want to believe, that their children achieve honorary white status and that these Asian American adoptees can be raised believing themselves to be American, despite the fact that the term "American" has always signaled white normativity for full enfranchisement and citizenship, particularly given the history of immigration and naturalization restrictions that Asians have faced in the United States.

Trenka desired whiteness, was raised as a culturally white American, and rejected her Korean racial difference in an effort to assimilate into her white midwestern family. Yet the description of glasses not fitting and racist epithets that she suffered from as a child become the ambiguous terrain on which her racial status as a TRA/TN is formed, as E. Kim affirms: "Adopted Koreans experience a misfit identification with the dominant white mainstream as well as with dominant ways of being Korean or Korean American, and this alienation structures their senses of national, ethnic, and familial belonging."[48] KADs and other adult adoptees of Asian ancestry cannot seamlessly meld into their white adoptive families; most do not have access to their ethnic national first families, and many find no common ground with Asian American non-adoptees who are raised in Asian-ethnic cultures seemingly commensurate with their Asian ethnic and racial subjectivities. Furthermore, Asian American adult adoptees become racially ambiguous subjects because of the ways in which their white adoptive families ignore their ethnic-national histories in favor of asserting a white American ethos of colorblind assimilation and because they have internalized the experiences of living as honorary white subjects who nonetheless recognize their racial difference from their white adoptive families as they mature into adulthood. These Asian American adult adoptees negotiate their racially ambiguous status through a rejection of sentimental tropes and narratives common within adoption stories, which is the subject of the following segment.

Rescuing Discarded Children: The Sentimental Story of Adoption

Although today many white American families who adopt children from Asia may not be propelled to do so out of Christian charity in the way that adoptive families in the 1950s were, the language of humanitarian aid and rescue continues to permeate the discourse and rationale for why white couples choose Asian children for adoption. Rescuing and saving a poor parentless child characterizes many orphan narratives. In *Adopting America: Childhood, Kinship, and National Identity in Literature*, Carol J. Singley opens her work by stating, "American literature abounds with orphaned, homeless, destitute, or neglected children."[49] I would expand on Singley by noting that American popular culture abounds with parentless children. Shirley Temple's career flourished by playing variations on the orphan everyone loved and wanted to adopt in *Little Miss Marker*, *Bright Eyes*, *Curly Top*, *Stowaway*, *Captain January*, *Heidi*, *Rebecca of Sunnybrook Farm*, *Little Miss Broadway*, *The Little Princess*, and *Susannah of the Mounties*.[50] Broadway musicals *Oliver!* and *Annie* were so successful that film versions were made.[51] Prominent orphans make up the rank and file of many superhero narratives, most notably Batman, Spiderman, and Superman. And in our contemporary period, the most lucrative children's book series and film franchise features an orphan at its center: Harry Potter. Although Harry Potter may be British in origin (by dint of the character's and author's nationality), his ubiquitous presence in American popular culture (as well as the Florida theme park The Wizarding World of Harry Potter) points to the significance of the series for US readers and moviegoers.

Our fascination with orphan narratives stems from the sentiment and sympathy that the parentless figure evokes in readers and audiences. Arguing for the prevalence of juvenile homeless characters in American literature, Singley observes, "Disrupted biological families and elective family units are a defining feature of American literature, in a way that is strikingly absent in other national literatures."[52] Orphans are figures of mystery and intrigue. They are romantic characters who have suffered unspeakable loss and tragedy and therefore are most deserving (and in want) of love and kindness from generous adoptive parents and legal guardians.

This narrative theme of rescue and salvation is one that also inspires affect and sentiment; saving a child is among the most moving and affect-ful of images. The adoption narrative is almost always a sentimental narrative, at least it has been rendered as such in American public discourse and popular culture over the past two centuries. A standard plot in sentimental adoption narratives features a parentless child who is reluctantly taken in by a curmudgeonly adult who is eventually won over through the winsome goodness of the orphan, transforming into a loving parent, particularly when there is a threat of losing the child to another party.[53] In the sentimental adoption narrative, both the adopted child and adoptive parent(s) have their lives changed forever, always for the better and always with much emotion and shedding of tears. Readers' sympathies are evoked through the display of sentiment on the part of the characters and the sentimentality of the rescued orphan narrative, particularly the parentless child who is capable of healing the emotional wounds of his or her adoptive family.[54]

These themes—salvation, healing, and sentiment—can be found in several narratives written about (but not by) TRA/TN Asian adoptees, including Ann Hood's contemporary American novel *The Red Thread*. Hood's title comes from a Chinese proverb that believes that an invisible red thread connects you to the people you are destined to meet, and Hood provides a longer and more maudlin explanation as the epigraph to her novel:

> There exists a silken red thread of destiny. It is said that this magical cord may tangle or stretch but never break. When a child is born, that invisible red thread connects the child's soul to all the people—past, present, and future—who will play a part in that child's life. Over time, that thread shortens and tightens, bringing closer and closer those people who are fated to be together.[55]

Although the red thread concept has been used to describe the fated nature of romantic liaisons, in recent decades the Chinese adoptive community has appropriated it to describe the connection between adopted couples in the United States and their adopted Chinese daughters, as Jacobson confirms: "The China-adoptive community, for example, has adapted the Chinese legend of the red thread (one traditional version has a thread connecting destined lovers) to read specifically about and narrate the international adoption experience, with the thread now connecting newborn Chinese infants with their destined international-adoptive parents."[56] The red thread story lends a sense of predestination to these transnational and transracial adoptions—a belief that fate preordained the union between adoptive families in the United States and baby girls in China—a notion that reinforces the sentimental nature of Hood's narrative through the connection it makes to the empathy and sympathy that the adoption triad facilitates, at least between adoptive parents and their adopted children.

The evocation of sympathy and empathy are particularly important in sentimental narratives of adoption because they provide catharsis for readers and audience members. Literary critic Markman Ellis observes that "it has often seemed that tears most obviously characterize the sentimental novel's conspicuous display of emotion,"[57] and literary scholar Michael Bell further emphasizes that "'sentimental' has become the crucial term for discriminating *within* the realm of feeling" [emphasis in original].[58] Nowhere is the scene of sympathy, affect, and tears more harrowing and emotional than in the moment of contact when adoptive parents receive their adopted children. In Hood's novel, the anxiety and emotion is largely channeled through the perspective of Maya Lange, the grieving mother and adoption agency director who, right before she receives her adopted infant daughter, wonders, "Could she feel it twice? Could she love this baby, this stranger?"[59] The answer, as one could easily predict in this sentimental novel (as in most sentimental novels about adoption), is a resounding yes, confirmed in the last paragraph of the narrative when Hood returns to the red thread legend, affirming that it is destiny and fate that binds the middle-class, middle-aged white American mother Maya to her Chinese baby daughter: "Maya almost saw it, that red thread, tangled and curved, connecting each baby to their mother. She blinked. The red thread glimmered and then slowly disappeared. No matter how knotted or tangled it became, at the end of it was the child you were meant to have."[60] As in other orphan narratives, the adoptive parent's healing comes in the guise of the parentless child she holds in her arms, one that Hood romanticizes through the reappropriated story of the red thread. Yet by returning to the red thread theme, Hood's novel diminishes and obscures the complicated machinations of state institutions and the reality of privilege and oppression that allows for these transnational adoptions to occur in the first place.

Although Hood's novel is careful not to emphasize a language of salvation, other contemporary narratives of TRA/TN Asian adoption evoke the sentimental trope or the theme of humanitarian aid and rescue, even while explicitly denouncing it. In the National Geographic documentary *China's Lost Girls*, host Lisa Ling follows one Atlanta, Georgia, couple, the Halls, and their eldest adopted daughter, Marissa, who have returned to China to adopt a second daughter. The family travels to the orphanage where Marissa stayed and where, we are told, hundreds of abandoned children reside. Denise Hall says that some of these children were there at the orphanage when they first came to adopt Marissa and that she cannot wait to get her daughter away from the orphanage. Although earlier in the documentary Denise had been clear about how she was grateful to the foster parents who took care of Marissa and that she rejects the narrative that posits her and her husband as aid workers, in this scene her acute anxiety over thinking that her daughter could have remained in China in an orphanage is palpable. Her belief that she has rescued her from tragedy—being left behind in a Chinese orphanage—is announced in her statement that she wants to take her away as quickly as she can. The documentary frames this scene for maximum pathos, showing the older Chinese children playing in a bare-bones playground and having the orphanage director tell Lisa Ling that there are up to three hundred children who reside in the orphanage; many will most likely remain there until they reach adulthood. Audience members are clearly meant to be moved by this scene, to sympathize with the hundreds of children in this anonymous facility as well as the thousands in orphanages throughout China. We are meant to see transnational adoption as a benign intervention that is necessary to prevent these abandoned children, a majority of whom are girls, from languishing in state run institutions, bereft of loving homes and parents. In other words, the National Geographic documentary, Hood's novel, and other narratives of TRA/TN adoption use sentiment and affect as a means to elicit sympathy for the baby girls abandoned in China and to view the adoptive families as necessary intercessors in helping to rid the world's suffering.

What It Means to Be an Asian American Adult Adoptee: Blogging Your Truth and Countering the Sentimental and Static Portrait of Transnational/Transracial Adoption

Although the prevailing genre that has encapsulated the story of adoption, be it domestic, transnational, same race, or transracial, has been the sentimental narrative of evoking affect for maximum sympathetic effect, there are other adoption stories that are challenging the trope of humanitarian aid. The majority of adoption narratives, whether fictional or autobiographical, are told from the point of view of adoptive parents, yet stories are beginning to be told by adoptees as a counternarrative to a variety of themes often found in adoption stories: rescue and relief, love conquering all obstacles and a force for color-blindness, and race either as nonexistent or a factor that can be absorbed by a neoliberal multicultural rhetoric of inclusiveness. And the perfect medium for this counternarrative that resists the sentimentality of traditional adoption narratives is the blog. Asian American adult adoptees who blog create a community of voices that seek to usurp the dominant salvation theme that has been shadowing them throughout their lives. Blogs do not exist in a vacuum: they are connected to other blogs, and they form a network and a community. Adult adoptee bloggers create both a community and a discourse through their blogs, a narratological corrective to the simplistic and romanticized portraits of themselves promulgated in popular culture.[61]

Blogs differ from other mediums because of their interactive nature. They are not static entities that just sit on the screen. They contain links to other websites and blogs, and they engage with people through the comment section. Bloggers who share similar interests, ideals, or ideologies will find their way to one another's blogs and will post comments on blogs that share their visions and perspectives (or for those who are contrarian, they will engage in polemical debates with those who hold opposite views). Through the links to one another's blogs and to other websites, as well as the running dialogue on the comment threads, blogs create not only a hub of interactivity but a communal space for people to gather, as Aaron Barlow emphasizes: "*Community*, that is what lies at the heart of the blog" [emphasis in original].[62] Community is also what lies at the heart of the identities of adult adoptee bloggers, and community is the means by which they create their own stories that challenge the traditional sentimental narratives of adoption through an embrace of racial ambiguity.

Indeed, community is one of the primary reasons that JaeRan Kim, the aforementioned blogger of *Harlow's Monkey*, began her blog. She wanted to create a community of fellow adoptees, particularly those who share her experiences as a racial minority growing up in a white Christian family in the Midwest during a time when the ethos among adoption professionals was to treat adopted kids of color as if they were just like their nuclear family—to treat them as if they were white. From 2006 to 2010, the years in which Kim was actively producing content for *Harlow's Monkey*, she amassed a loyal and consistent readership, many of whom left their own reactions to her posts or to other's observations in lively comment threads. Several of these commenters were also fellow bloggers, and a large number of them also identified as TRA/TN adoptees.

I first found my way to *Harlow's Monkey* through the blog of another KAD, Sang-Shil of *Land of the Not-So-Calm*. Sang-Shil (her blogging pseudonym) had been leaving comments on my blog, *Mixed Race America*, and from there I had followed her back to *Land of the Not-So-Calm*. While reading and leaving comments on her blog, I realized that there was a community of TRA/TN bloggers, with the strongest contingent being KADs. I begin with this personal anecdote because as Barlow states, "To effectively 'know' the blogs, one must participate in them—at least to the level of commenting. One does not have to become a real blogger, but experiencing the interactive aspect of the blogs is essential to knowing the blogosphere at all."[63] Certainly my knowledge as a blogger has deepened my understanding of how blogs work as well as the cultural attitudes and etiquette among bloggers, especially those who write about issues of race.[64] My interest in the racially ambiguous status of adult adoptees began through blogging—through noticing a community of commenters who also happened to be a community of bloggers. I realized that this community could exist only online; in many ways, like the genre that supports their community, adult adoptees are born from the Internet.

In the 1970s and 1980s, when a great number of adoptees from Korea were being raised as the "only one"—the only Asian American, the only Korean American, the only adopted person, the only person of color—in their small, often midwestern, towns, they would not have been able to find one another so easily or to realize that there were other adoptees with similar experiences, questions, anxieties, and frustrations. Beside the ethos referred to earlier of raising children of color as white children, the geographic distances would have prevented adoptees from finding and meeting one another on a regular basis. There were camps and other meet-up groups for adoptees, but they were sporadic and, given the ages of the adoptees, dependent on adoptive families for maintenance and/or simple logistics of travel. With the rise of Internet technology, space and time have shrunk, and adoptees can find others simply by going to Google.[65] Particularly with the practice of blogging, for which a Live Journal, WordPress, or Blogger account is free, being able to locate both information and a community of other adoptees was no longer prohibitive in cost, distance, or time.[66] Eleana Kim confirms the importance of new media technology to adoptee identity: "The Internet transformed what were relatively autonomous local and regional groups into a self-conscious network of individuals and groups and provided virtual spaces for the production and performance of Korean adoptee personhood."[67] The many adoptee communities and organizations that exist are now able to link to one another, virtually and in real time, through conferences and meet-ups. Attending conferences, particularly large international conferences, are still cost prohibitive for a great number of adoptees, but through various online sources like "Internet chat rooms, electronic mailing lists, blogs, social networking sites, video streaming, and the like" adoptees can participate in ongoing identity formation work as well as community building.[68] According to the editors of *Race in Cyberspace*, "Cyberspace can provide a powerful coalition building and progressive medium for 'minorities' separated from each other by distance and other factors."[69] Furthermore, blogs, especially those generated and consumed by adult adoptees, become important hubs by which to create and disseminate information. These blogs become sites of knowledge and resources for adoptees, exceeding boundaries of geography and nation-state. In these blogs, adult adoptees produce knowledge by and about themselves without the filter of their adoptive families or adoption professionals—they form a community cyberspace for themselves.

Certainly the five blogs I examine in this chapter exist as community cyberspaces for adult adoptees to talk about themselves and to forge networks with others of similar backgrounds. These blogs include *Harlow's Monkey* (written by JaeRan Kim),[70] *Heart, Mind and Seoul* (written by Paula O.),[71] *Jane's Blog: Bitter Angry Ajumma* (written by Jane Jeong Trenka),[72] *Ethnically Incorrect Daughter* (written by Sumeia Williams, who goes by the handle "Sume"),[73] and *The Original Heping*[74] (written by Mei-Ling).[75] Both JaeRan and Jane write under the names that they are known by in their professional lives.[76] The other bloggers employ either pseudonyms or abbreviations of their full names (for example, using only their first name and not their last). None of the bloggers use their adoptive families' names, choosing married surnames or reclaiming names from their first families and/or original ethnic nationalities. Writing about the formation of a Korean adoptee identity, Sunny Jo claims that one of the steps in establishing one's adoptee identity "has been to embrace Korean names" noting that "some have legally reverted back to their birth names, while others use Korean names in their e-mail addresses and computer IDs."[77] Using a blogging handle that incorporates part of their original ethnic heritage allows these adult adoptees to choose identities that reflect their TRA/TN status; it becomes a means of negotiating their racial ambiguity—to rename themselves as recognition of their hybridized Asian and American selves and as a refutation to their honorary whiteness.

Although all of the bloggers in this chapter happen to be female bloggers, neither gender nor sexuality was the primary consideration for why I chose these blogs for analysis, though it bears repeating that given the gender ratios among adoptees from Asian nations, girls are placed for adoption at much higher rates than boys, particularly from countries that still adhere to Confucian belief systems. Memoirist and freelance journalist Mei-Ling Hopgood writes about the reasons her Taiwanese father placed her for adoption by invoking the gender preference for boys that her first father was culturally raised with: "[Ba] once told me that he decided to give me to Rollie and Chris Hopgood because he felt I'd have a better life, but Ba was also the first man to reject me. He would not have given me away had I been a boy."[78]

In addition to the gender of their bloggers, the blogs that I focus on in this chapter all share the commonality of being written by adult adoptees of Asian descent who write specifically and deliberately about their adoptee experience and who were raised in white families in North America.[79] Most are in their early forties and currently live in the United States (Mei-Ling is in her mid-to late twenties, and Jane lives in South Korea). Three of the bloggers (JaeRan, Paula, and Sume) have children, and in the case of Paula, her youngest child (a son) is an adoptee from Korea, so in her blog she talks about the experience of being an adoptee as well as an adoptive parent. JaeRan also comes from a dual perspective as both an adoptee and as a social worker who is completing a PhD dissertation on adoption, so she writes from a personal point of view (her own experiences, thoughts, and feelings about being adopted) as well as through a professional and academic lens (she has expertise in the area of domestic adoption placement and the foster care system). Sume's blog has the earliest blog start date (November 2004), and Mei-Ling has the most recent start date (April 2007). Though most of these writers are currently blogging, *Harlow's Monkey* and *The Original Heping* are not actively being updated (although they are still up on the Web), and *Heart, Mind and Seoul*'s last entry was November 2011.[80]

These bloggers have different reasons for writing about their adoption experiences. Some, like Mei-Ling and Paula, never state clearly what the purpose of their blog is, nor whether there was an impetus (an event or need or desire) to propel them into the blogosphere; instead, they begin their blogs seemingly in media res, chronicling their daily lives and their thoughts, memories, and experiences with being TRA/TN Asian adoptees. Jane's blog seems to be an extension of her two memoirs, *The Language of Blood* and *Fugitive Visions*, recording her struggles with Korean language acquisition and her relationships with other adoptees and her Korean family. Both Sume and JaeRan specifically state their blogs' purpose. For Sume, it is a place to process her contradictory thoughts and feelings about her adoption: "I float between feeling saved and feeling kidnapped, between gratitude and resentment but in the end, there is always love. We are a close family but I chose not to share these thoughts with them, at least for now. This space serves as a repository for those thoughts and my experiences as I sort through them."[81] For JaeRan, blogging allows her to join a community of fellow transracial adoptees who share her perspective; thus, *Harlow's Monkey* provides a virtual space for community building as well as a place for JaeRan to document her experiences with adoption and to assert her identity as a TRA/TN Korean adult adoptee: "This blog began in the spring of 2006 when I was finishing up my MSW degree and discovered a group of transracial adoptee bloggers. I wanted to connect with these bloggers who were writing about their experiences that so closely matched my own experiences growing up as a child adopted from Korea to a White, Midwestern family."[82] Although the other bloggers may not have stated their intention to join a community in the way that JaeRan does, to repeat the quote already provided by Barlow, "No blog exists alone."[83] The very decision to start a blog signals a desire to be part of a larger group of like-minded people—to find others who share their concerns and experiences as adult adoptees.

Beyond the fellowship aspect of these blogs, one purpose that they serve (whether by intention or not) is to provide a counternarrative to the sentimental adoption story. The figure of the adult adoptee is rarely found in public discourse or popular culture. The standard images that we have within orphan narratives are of babies and children—subjects in need of protection and victims of tragic circumstances (death of parents, casualties of war, loss of fortune or social standing). Little Orphan Annie is not allowed to grow up in her comic book iteration and thus remains forever young. Harry Potter does have an epilogue in which you flash upon him as an adult, but the main drama, the plot of the seven Potter series books, centers on his life from age eleven to seventeen. And certainly in contemporary narratives that describe TRA/TN adoption, the standard images that we have are of white couples with Asian female daughters. From *Sex and the City* (both I and II) to *Then She Found Me* to *The Red Thread*, the adopted children remain children.[84]

These blogs, on the other hand, are written by adult adoptees. They have grown up and have processed the experiences that shaped them as adult adoptees and are recording their familiarity with adoption (and in the case of Paula, with her son's adoption from Korea) in order to give voice to a narrative that is largely absent in American public discourse. In fact, there are no visible adult adoptees who speak from that position. Although there have been many moving and astute documentaries and memoirs about TRA/TN adoption from Asian countries, by and large the figure of the Asian adoptee in the United States is of a Chinese baby girl, not someone old enough to reflect upon her life or to talk about what her adoption means to her.[85]

The mere fact that these blogs exist, then, is a powerful statement in and of itself to counteract narratives that predominantly come from the perspective of adoptive parents. This is not to suggest that adoptive parents do not have a right to tell their stories and to share their observations with one another. However, in the adoption triad of adoptive parents, first parents, and adoptees, the adoptive parents' stories are the ones that are most prominent, particularly in the case of TRA/TN adoption.[86] Celebrities like Angelina Jolie, Sandra Bullock, and Madonna discuss their adoption stories in national and international media outlets. But the voices of their children are never included.[87] Adult adoptees use their blogs as platforms to tell their own stories and create their own knowledge base, for themselves and for others who share their experiences. JaeRan is especially clear about the purpose of her blog and the fact that she does not want to be a "TRA pez dispenser" for parents looking for guidance and education on issues pertaining to TRA/TN adoption: "This blog was not written for adoptive parents. I write to share my experiences and my thoughts for my TRA friends and **those who are our allies**" [boldface in original].[88] JaeRan's blog creates knowledge by, about, and for other adult adoptees.

Moreover, these adult adoptees who blog take a very unsentimental look at their adoption experience and have strong feelings and strong words for describing how they feel about adoption. In a post titled "Angry Adoptee," JaeRan writes, "It has been my experience lately that anything that is critical is mistaken for angry. I've been called an angry adoptee many times. And what I think is humorous about that label is I'm far from being angry. Critical, yes. Unsentimental? Absolutely."[89] JaeRan sums up a central tenet of many adult adoptees: they offer an essential perspective, one that is often mistaken for ingratitude or anger but is, in fact, an analytical one that flies in the face of the sentimental narratives of adoption that portray orphans as grateful for their adoption and adoptive parents as kindhearted and selfless rescuers. Even in contemporary narratives like Hood's *The Red Thread*, Karin Evans's memoir *The Lost Daughters of China*, Scott Simon's memoir *Baby, We Were Meant for Each Other*, or the documentary *China's Lost Girls*, when parents try to be careful about not rehearsing this theme of salvage, emphasizing that their daughters rescued them (ostensibly from childlessness or, as in Hood's novel, various psychic and emotional ailments), as discussed previously, it is hard to escape a language of salvation. JaeRan and others insist on offering a critical perspective that should be understood as voicing their truth and their stories without being misinterpreted as anger from resentful and ungrateful children. "Adult Korean adoptees' assertive claim to their position as knowledge producers within the adoption industry demonstrates their sense of agency and amplifies the need for change," writes Kristi Brian. "Korean adoptees and other adoptees of color are speaking for themselves and, clearly, do not need outside researchers like me to speak for them."[90]

Perhaps first and foremost, these bloggers want to be seen as having the right to their own narratives that have produced a knowledge different from the sentimental adoption stories. As previously noted, in the adoption triad, adoptive parents control most of the discourse around adoption, especially in transnational adoption because language and geography exacerbate the inability of first parents to tell their stories.[91] However, in the past decade, as the adoptees from Asian nations have come into their adulthood, they have begun to form a collective and voice their stories, using new media to produce knowledge about their lives as adoptees.

These blogs represent a different knowledge than the ones promulgated in sentimental adoption narratives or in the official literature that adoption agencies distribute. JaeRan, a social worker and adoptee, knows intimately the various perspectives in the adoption triad, and her blog is a space for providing alternative narratives and information for adoptive parents, particularly ones that offer only one-dimensional, overly optimistic stories: "What burns me now is this incessant, pathological force-feeding of happiness and sunshine narrative that society at large and prospective adoptive parents in particular receive."[92] In *Harlow's Monkey*, JaeRan tells a different story and thus develops a different form of knowledge about her childhood and adulthood. Combined with her professional expertise as a social worker, the insights that she offers on her blog perform the unique work of being expert in terms of her personal as well as professional experiences with adoption.

Yet even if JaeRan had not been a social worker, her experiences as an adult adoptee should count as knowledge. In the inspirational and influential collection *Making Face, Making Soul Haciendo Caras: Creative and Critical Perspectives by Feminists of Color*, editor Gloria Anzaldúa, in her introduction, talks about the need for women of color to have their experiences count as knowledge, to be seen as experts who can theorize and analyze the conditions in which they live as women of color: "We women of color strip off the *máscaras* others have imposed on us, see through the disguises we hide behind and drop our *personas* so that we may become subjects in our own discourses."[93] Paula reinforces Anzaldúa's assertions about being "subjects in our own discourses" when she finds herself dismissed by others for the wisdom she offers as an adult KAD adoptee:

> What I am saying is that YES—adoptees ARE experts—and not only have every right to be included in the discussion, but we damn well deserve to be there as well. Am I an expert who speaks for other adoptees? No, of course not. But I am an expert in my own life whose story is part of the collective history and narrative of other adoptees and esp. other Korean adoptees like me. I may not have one thing in common with the Korean adoptee across town, but we are both experts in the experience of adoption and I believe that each of us has a valid and equal voice.[94]

All too often adult adoptees are not invited to be part of the conversation. In a most recent iteration of this puzzling phenomenon, a panel convened for a Minnesota Public Radio show on transnational adoption featured adoptive parents, social workers, and scholars (who also happened to be adoptive parents), but the panel did not include any adoptees, an oversight that is truly baffling given the number of Asian American adoptees in the Twin Cities area. After a series of phone calls to the MPR station, a second panel comprised of adoptees, scholars, and social workers, all of whom were also adult adoptees, was convened three days later as a corrective to the myopia of the first panel.

For Paula, as for these bloggers, being able to be seen as an expert and to have her story recognized as legitimate, as authoritative, and as authentic is in large measure why she (and others) blog: to be legible as an authority over one's own life. Consistent blogging ensures that these adoptees get to tell their story in the manner in which they want to tell it. These bloggers assert their truths without diminishing anyone else's story or claiming the mantle of "representative adoptee," as Paula makes clear in one of her posts: "I certainly do not profess to speak for all adoptees or all Korean adoptees. Each one of us is entitled to claim our own journey for ourself [sic]. . . . I feel that I am confident enough in my own truth as to not feel threatened by reading or hearing the stories of others, even if they do not support my own life experiences."[95]

Blogging allows these adoptees to not only narrate their own story but to correct the misimpressions that have shaped the dominant discourse around adoption, especially around Asian transnational adoption. Sume tackles the stereotype of Asian war babies head on when she writes:

> To this day, us first generation transracial adoptees from Korea and Vietnam are generally referred to as "war orphans" in the media and by people we encounter on a daily basis, as if it is a self-applied term of endearment. The main assumption is that we were rescued from a tragic past and handed a hopeful future. The public was reassured that we were not going to look back and puzzle together the facts behind our orphan status. Yet, this is exactly what we are doing. And at every turn, we are admonished for daring to not only question the historical interpretations of the Korean and Vietnam Wars, but also other people's motives and methods for transporting us out of our birth countries.[96]

Echoing JaeRan, who announces, "Critical, yes. Unsentimental? Absolutely" about her opinions and writings on adoption, Sume also espouses a discerning view with respect to her own and others' adoptions in the aftermath of the Korean and Viet Nam wars. Her perspective, like those of her fellow bloggers, employs the perspective of critical race theory and postcolonial analysis, perhaps not couched in terms of formal theory but that nonetheless interrogates the flows of global power that have led to her, and thousands of others, being adopted out of their Asian country of origin and into the United States.[97] Writing about the intersection of the lived realities of women of color to theorize their lives, Anzaldúa writes "*Necesitamos teorías* that will rewrite history using race, class, gender, and ethnicity as categories of analysis, theories that cross borders, that blur boundaries—new kinds of theories with new theorizing methods."[98] Sume's blog becomes a repository for her critical interrogation about US state practices of adoption and governance, one that provides a counternarrative to

seeing adopted children from Asian war-torn nations as fortunate orphans rescued into the bosom of America's largess. Her blog and those of the other adult
adoptee bloggers precisely offers a "new theorizing" that blurs boundaries and
write themselves into history.

Besides challenging the dominant discourse around their transnational
adoptions, many adult adoptees want to be recognized for who they actually
are and the cognitive dissonance of their experiences growing up as ambiguous Asian racial minorities in all-white families and largely all-white communities, as Jane says, "For an adoptee raised in rural Minnesota, pretending you're
white is not really a big stretch."[99] KAD Soon Na explains her struggle with the
disconnect between her identity and her family's in her autobiographical essay:
"I struggle with being a person of color who grew up in a white family whose
members deny their white privilege."[100] Not owning their white privilege on the
part of adoptive parents combined with an insistence on not seeing racial differences between themselves and their adopted sons and daughters leads to
the racial ambiguity experienced by TRA/TN adoptees—they grew up believing
themselves to be white, yet every time they looked in the mirror the reality
of their Asian minority selves stared back at them, which JaeRan affirms: "I've
heard TRA's talk about avoiding mirrors because they remind us of our difference and that we're *not* really White" *[emphasis in original].*[101] Similarly Mei-Ling
asserts that "I was born Chinese and raised as a Caucasian. Asian face Asian
body. But with a white mind and a white body language."[102]

Furthermore, the racial ambiguity of adoptees often leads to feeling vulnerable when subjected to racist attacks from those outside their family, as
Paula O. explains: "I was so conditioned to be treated as the daughter of Mr. and
Mrs. X, that when I was no longer under the tutelage of two white parents, I was
left unprotected, unprepared and uneducated on what to do when I was subjected to racist acts and behaviors."[103] Sume also writes about being sheltered by
her parents' white privilege: "As bad as it got for me, I was afforded some protection by my parents' white privilege. It was a small town so everyone knew me
and my family. It wasn't until I ventured away from that protective umbrella that
I really understood what racism was and how it affected me and those around
me."[104] These bloggers articulate the difficulty of navigating their racially ambiguous identities as Asian racial minorities growing up in white families that did
not prepare them for the racism and white supremacy that exists in mainstream
culture outside their supposedly colorblind nuclear family, particularly when
so many of them identified as white and had to adjust to a world in which,
despite how they felt within their nuclear families, they were regarded and
treated like Asian racial minorities.

They also articulate their experiences of embracing their identities as adult adoptees of Asian descent. Jane, JaeRan, and Paula were adopted from Korea. Mei-Ling was adopted from Taiwan. Sume was adopted from Viet Nam. Although the ethnic particularities of their families of origin vary, they all share the experience of growing up as Asian in white families and having to learn how to identify as Asian American on their own, without the benefit of family to connect them to their ethnic heritage or to help them adjust to their racially ambiguous selves. As Paula states, "I may have been raised by a white family and treated as an honorary white person in their presence, but I had not been taught to anticipate how the world would treat me as an *Asian woman, which is what I am*" [emphasis in original].[105] Similarly, JaeRan believes that "75 percent of my 'adoption issues' stem from being raised as the only non-white member of a family and community that did not prepare me for the harsh reality of being a member of American society marked as 'other.'"[106] Discussing the process of recognizing her racial and ethnic difference from her adoptive family, Mei-ling writes, "I am an international adoptee. Sometimes I love that fact, because it connects me between two cultures. Sometimes I hate it, because it reminds me of how eager I was to fit into a white community, and how far the bridge between me and my natural family is because of all the years that have passed."[107] And Sume also articulates the change in her self-awareness of who she is, one that creates distance between herself and her adoptive father: "Furthermore, as I slowly re-align my perspective to one of a woman of color rather than a white woman, my brain must reject much of my father's view of the world as unacceptable."[108] These adoptees had to adapt to being women of color without family or community support; they had to navigate their racially ambiguous identities during the formative years of their childhood, rejecting the honorary white status of their adoptive families.

Yet one of the important things about these blogs is that they form a community. They do not exist in a vacuum but rather serve as nodes in a larger online network of not just adoptee bloggers but adoptees who are connected to different organizations and global networks. As stated previously, blogs do not exist alone but are linked to other sites, other blogs. Certainly this is the case with these blogs—in fact, I chose these blogs for the ways that these particular adoptees form a community within one another's online space. They comment on each other's blogs; they link to one another on their blog rolls and in individual posts. Sometimes they even copy and comment on a fellow blogger's post. For instance, on October, 31, 2007, JaeRan republished a post on *Harlow's Monkey* that Jane ran on her blog, *Bitter Angry Ajumma*, on October 27, 2007. Both Paula and Sume have linked to *Harlow's Monkey*, and JaeRan has also commented on and linked to their blogs as well. And Mei-Ling has actively participated in various threads, sometimes commenting multiple times in the discussion, often in defense of the blogger and as a means of educating a commenter whose perspective would seem to malign or marginalize those of TRA/TN adoptees.[109] These adoptees are intimately familiar with one another's blogs and share similar experiences. But they also share in the joys and sorrows of one another's lives, as documented on their respective blogs. When Sume announced that she had launched a group blog with two other Vietnamese transnational/transracial adoptees, Paula wrote in congratulating her.[110] When Jane discussed her small triumph in passing a Korean language class and the possibility of continuing on to a PhD program, JaeRan wrote a celebratory and encouraging comment, urging her to pursue her PhD.[111] These adoptees actively take part in one another's blogs, creating a coalition of adult adoptees that allows them a sense of solidarity with one another.

The importance of shared community that the blogs represent cannot be overstated. Too often individual adoptees live in places where there may not be a critical mass of other TRA/TN adoptees and/or the cost of commuting to more urban spaces where such groups exist would be prohibitive. Yet in the online world, adoptees can share their experiences as adoptees and find commonality with others that, according to E. Kim, "permits individuals in geographically distant locations to imagine themselves as connected to each other and existing in the same time-space as others who are having similar and simultaneous experiences."[112] Indeed, adult adoptees can be seen as a nation unto itself because Asian American adoptees raised in transracial families are unable to completely identify with their adoptive families because they often do not resemble them racially, and they cannot identify with an Asian-ethnic identity because they weren't raised culturally as Korean/Chinese/Vietnamese. KAD activist Sunny Jo categorizes such a Korean adoptee identity as constituting a specific ethnic nationalism: "Only when KAD culture is recognized as its own ethnic and cultural group (not only as 'Korean' or '_____') can a new identity and heritage be embraced with pride, freeing us from the stereotypes and expectations of both our Korean and adoptive societies."[113] Asian American adult adoptee bloggers have constituted their own culture and their own community, linking their blogs and hence their lives to one another.

No Red Threads, Just Loose Threads

Award-winning filmmaker and Korean American adult adoptee Deann Borshay Liem has written, directed, and produced two documentaries that examine her adoption from Korea to America. In *First Person Plural*, Borshay Liem discovers that she was switched with another Korean child, exchanging her name, Kang

Ok Jin, for Cha Jung Hee, and thus taking the place of a four-year-old girl who was to be adopted by a white American couple, Alveen and Arnold Borshay of Fremont, California. The first half of the film discusses her suppressed memories of who she really is, a girl with living relatives in Korea, versus who she is told she is, an orphan whose parents died following the Korean War. The second half of the film shows Borshay Liem in Korea with both her American parents and her Korean family, and at the end of the film she talks about needing to let go of a childhood fantasy of reunification with her Korean family and to figure out a way of being with them as an adult who has grown up with a different family and in a different culture.

Although the end of this film offers a type of closure for Borshay Liem, ten years later she returns to the topic of her adoption in her second documentary, *In the Matter of Cha Jung Hee*, traveling back to Korea in search of the original Cha Jung Hee, the one whose place she had taken. She calls 101 Cha Jung Hees listed in the Korean phone book, goes on Korean television to tell her story, visits Korea's oldest adoption agency, and interviews multiple women named Cha Jung Hee. Eventually Borshay Liem finds a woman named Cha Jung Hee who was placed in the same orphanage as the filmmaker and whose biography seems to fit the scant details that Borshay Liem has about the original Cha Jung Hee. Yet even with this discovery, there are still unanswered questions: there are three different photos of three different four-year-old girls named Cha Jung Hee. As Borshay Liem says at one point about the latest Cha Jung Hee, "Many of the facts that I thought were important don't match her history." The answers that Borshay Liem has gone in search of, related to her adoption and her early Korean life, do not come in a neat package. The facts she discovers do not necessarily match up with the story of her life or the lives of the various iterations of Cha Jung Hee that she finds in Korea.

Both *First Person Plural* and *In the Matter of Cha Jung Hee* chart Borshay Liem's journey to resolve identities she experiences as conflicted and unable to coexist comfortably within her as Korean, as American, and as an adoptee. What each film makes clear is that there is no resolution—there is no closure. There are answers and there are facts, but what Borshay Liem uncovers and discovers may only produce more questions and less certainty about what she knows and about what she knows about who she is. In *First Person Plural* Borshay Liem's Korean brother and her American mother tell her that she is American—she is culturally different from her Korean family, and this difference may not be easily breached.[114] Yet Borshay Liem desires a connection to Korea and a close relationship with her Korean family. One of the running themes throughout both films is the sense of uncertainty that Borshay Liem feels about her adoption and about her identity. For Borshay Liem as for other transnational and transracial adoptees, a lack of closure and resolution undergirds much of their identities; they live with their racial ambiguity as being both Asian and American and yet feeling, at times, alienated from both their ethnic national identities and ethnic ancestry as well as their adopted family's nationality and white culture.

Which is one of the reasons that the blogs written by Asian American adoptees become a powerful medium for charting the negotiation of this ambiguity. Blogs do not have closure or resolution; they are ongoing testimonials of their writers. They are interactive forms of communication that create a living community of other adoptees. For Asian American adoptees, there cannot be closure because the mourning and loss that they feel over their transnational adoptions is continuous. Just like for Borshay Liem, for these bloggers there are answers without resolution. And just like with Borshay Liem, there are stories upon stories that can be told about who they are, about how they came to the United States, about what their lives might have been like had they remained in Asia. Yet these stories do not have an ending because the nature of transnational and transracial adoption and the ambiguity of their lives leaves these adoptees with more and more stories, ones that produce knowledge first and foremost for themselves and for other adoptees.

At the end of her memoir, *The Language of Blood*, Jane Jeong Trenka leaves her reader with the image of "millions of butterflies, opening and closing their wings," and she concludes her memoir with evocative lines that mimic the butterflies' wings:

Opening and closing.
Opening.
Closing.
Open.
Close.
Open . . .[115]

Trenka literally leaves her memoir open ended with the last word and the ellipsis, an appropriately ambiguous ending for a life rendered racially ambiguous.

3

Cablinasian Dreams, Amerasian Realities

Transcending Race in the Twenty-First Century and Other Myths Broken by Tiger Woods

On a clear Sunday morning on April 13, 1997, in Augusta, Georgia, professional golfers, throngs of spectators, and viewers around the globe stood ready to anoint its next prince, a golfing prodigy who was already known by just a single moniker: Tiger. By the time Tiger Woods walked off the eighteenth hole at Augusta National, one of the nation's most prestigious and exclusive country clubs that hosts the Masters, one of the world's most prestigious and exclusive golf tournaments, Woods had broken several tournament records: he had the lowest recorded score (eighteen under par), won the Masters at the youngest age (twenty-one), with the highest lead (nine) going into the final day of the championship. But perhaps the biggest barrier of all—the reason that non-golfers were as riveted to their television screens as inveterate golf fans—was that the young man who embraced his African American father and Asian American mother at the end of the tournament was not white. Woods's triumph was especially notable given Augusta National's less than illustrious history of racial segregation, discrimination, and upholding of Jim Crow traditions and attitudes. This was the club where founder Clifford Roberts once infamously said, "As long as I live, there will be nothing at the Masters besides black caddies and white players"; the club admitted its first black member only in 1990, thirteen years after Roberts's passing.[1] The image of the mixed race black–Asian American golfer wearing the coveted and iconic green jacket seemed to signal a transcendent moment for both golf and race relations nationwide.[2]

This moment, and the many others that would follow in the decade and a half that Woods has been playing on the Professional Golf Association (PGA) tour, would seem to signal that Tiger has exceeded typical racial categories to become a global symbol of mixed heritage and multiraciality. According to his father, Earl Woods, Tiger is "qualified through his ethnicity to accomplish miracles. He's the bridge between the East and the West. . . . He is the Chosen One."[3] Tiger's mother, Kultida (Tida) Woods, believes that because "Tiger has Thai, African, Chinese, American Indian, and European blood . . . he can hold everyone together. He is the Universal Child."[4] Yet the events following from his 2009 Thanksgiving Day car crash—the revelations of his sexual exploits and infidelities, his entry into a rehabilitation clinic (ostensibly for sex addiction), his time off from the PGA tour, his televised apology event, the disintegration of his marriage, and the tell-all essays, news pieces, and books that followed from the Woods scandal—all point to the ways in which even a golf phenom like Tiger Woods cannot transcend his racialized body.[5]

Although there has been much written about both the golfer and the man Tiger Woods, this chapter examines not simply the flesh-and-blood person but Tiger Woods as text. To analyze Tiger as text is to go beyond his public statements or his numerous biographies (those authorized and unauthorized by team Tiger) and to read and interpret the various discourses that adhere to the figure known as Tiger Woods. Woods as text is a composite of various stories, some well known and rehearsed like gospel in the mythology of Tiger Woods, others more obscure and nearly invisible to the larger public but that are nonetheless part of the narrative that coheres around Woods, a narrative that is, at heart, racially ambiguous. Woods's racial ambiguity derives from the ways in which he is continually referred to as a monoracial African American even while he has proclaimed a multiethnic identity. Indeed, Woods is often discussed and referred to as a monoracial African American, but never as a monoracial Asian American. He is racially ambiguous precisely because of the ways in which the one-drop rule of hypodescent continues to guide US society in defining racial identities as well as the ways in which Woods's Asian heritage remains occluded and illegible to the general American public. This illegibility of his Asian heritage speaks to the larger ways in which Asians in America are similarly ambiguously figured: as not truly American and as model minorities who have not suffered from discrimination and thus are deemed honorary whites. To think of Woods as racially ambiguous is to reject the notion that his exceptional status allows him to transcend race. To view Woods as racially ambiguous allows us to interpret him through alternate stories that are embedded within his family's (and the US nation's) history: the American war in Viet Nam and the Amerasian children produced through that war.[6] Understanding Tiger Woods as a racially ambiguous subject places mixed race Asian Americans, particularly Amerasians, into a legible space with respect to Asian American communities and US society, creating new narratives and new knowledge about the Cold War legacy of mixed race Amerasians as well as new knowledge about Woods and how we should view and interpret him as a racially ambiguous Asian American.

Hello World, I Am Tiger Woods: Woods's Importance
as the Transcendent Racial Healer of Golf

Tiger Woods was born in Long Beach, California, on December 30, 1975. He is the only child of Earl Woods, a retired Army colonel and former Green Beret, and Kultida "Tida" Punswad Woods, a former Army secretary from Thailand who met Earl in 1966 and married him in 1969 in Brooklyn, New York. Earl and Tida's relationship was simultaneously typical and exceptional. The number of US military and civilian personnel who engaged in romantic relationships is at least as great as the number of Amerasian children (largely black and white, although there are a handful of Latino, Asian, and Native American Amerasian children) fathered across Southeast Asia during the American war in Viet Nam. Certainly depictions of US soldiers mingling with Vietnamese women (usually depicted as bar girls and prostitutes) are staples of Hollywood films that focus on the war in Viet Nam. Earl's attraction to an Asian woman would not be atypical. Yet the seriousness of their relationship and Tida's willingness to leave Thailand and move to the United States with this US officer (and to marry him) makes their relationship an exception to the standard narratives of US soldiers who love and then leave the Southeast Asian women that they meet while stationed in Viet Nam, Cambodia, and Thailand.

Tiger's childhood in Cypress, California, by all accounts was a relatively idyllic one. Although various biographies of Woods repeat the stories that Earl has shared about the racism he and Tida encountered when they moved into their largely white neighborhood (stones and limes were thrown at their home, knocking out window panes) and though both Earl and Tiger recount minor incidents of racism, particularly something that Tiger has described as "the look" that he and Earl would receive during the many junior golf tournaments Tiger entered, by and large Woods's childhood is described as the stuff of suburban idyll.[7] Tiger had two supportive parents who claim never to have hired a babysitter and who devoted themselves to their son and his passion for golf. Tiger considered his father his best friend, dutifully did his homework, and went yearly to the Buddhist temple with his mother. Although there are more recent accounts that point to cracks in the Woods's marriage and though critics have often speculated on whether Earl was an overbearing sports father, by and large Tiger's childhood and adolescent years seem to have been relatively drama free, with all three members of the Woods family staunchly maintaining that Tiger's drive for golf excellence was self-motivated.

By the time Tiger entered Stanford University he was a seemingly self-assured young man who was already known as a golfing wunderkind, having appeared on national television (*The Mike Douglas Show, That's Incredible*) and having won countless tournaments, including an unprecedented three junior amateur titles and the first of what would be three unprecedented adult amateur titles. Tiger's exceptionalism remained a constant throughout his life: he was undoubtedly one of the few if not only mixed race African American–Asian American kids in his neighborhood and certainly one of the few if not only golfers of color in the various junior tournaments he participated in. He was routinely noted and mentioned in golf magazines like *Golf Digest* and *Golf Weekly*, and then, as he grew older and continued to dominate tournaments, in mainstream publications like *Sports Illustrated* and *Newsweek* magazine. When Tiger turned professional, leaving Stanford University before the start of what would have been his junior year of college, no one was surprised at his decision, particularly since it led to the most lucrative endorsement deals that any golfer had ever received.[8] Winning two of the seven tournaments he played during the half-year of his professional debut and winning his first major championship the first time he entered as a pro, Tiger would forever be seen as exceptional, particularly because of his racial difference as a non-white, specifically blackbodied, golfer in an overwhelmingly lily-white sport.

Although Tiger certainly profited from the lucrative endorsement deals and the purses that he earned from the golf tournaments he participated in, the institution of golf gained even higher dividends from Tiger, particularly since what he brought was a value beyond mere dollars: his mixed race body was seen as redemption and healing for the racist practices perpetuated for the greater part of the twentieth century by US golf. According to historian Henry Yu, who has written extensively about sports and about Tiger Woods in particular, "Perhaps more than any other sport, golf stands for white male privilege and racial exclusion."[9] Yet the value that Woods brought to golf when he debuted as a professional was not as an Asian American golfer; his Asianness then, as now, was largely ignored, in much the same way as his Thai mother was passed over in favor of the many photo ops and stories of Tiger with his African American father, Earl Woods. Tiger's African American heritage and his visibly black body were seen as redemption for the racial sins of golf's (and the US nation's) past.

In the United States the golf fairway and the country club have been exclusive and elite arenas of power, where selection and segregation based on race, religion, gender, and sexuality are overt and covert means of discrimination—both in the sense of discerning a higher class of people as well as excluding those deemed to be less than desirable. What the golf course and the game of golf have done is perpetuate a cycle of white male privilege.[10] Those who have access to the game continue to meet and do business with others who enjoy the sport. Although this is seemingly not a deliberate way of discriminating or enacting racist policies, in effect golf in America becomes an important institution where deals are brokered, business is transacted, and power circulates among the same groups of people who have access to the sport and to one another, and generally speaking these people have been white men. As Marcia Chambers observes, "The world of golf engages so many influential people, people who are the leaders in their nation, their cities, their towns, their companies. These are people who are among the best-educated in the country—legislators who make state and national laws, executives who manage large and small corporations, judges who sit on state and federal courts."[11]

This is all the more reason to understand golf's attitude toward race and how it has perpetuated institutional discrimination and racism, specifically against African Americans, for nearly a century. Courses were first developed in the United States during the 1880s as private country clubs, with the first municipal course opening in 1895.[12] Despite the rise of public municipal courses, golf's association with country club life and the connotations of exclusivity and privilege that membership in a country club represents became solidified throughout the twentieth century and reflected the typical prejudices of the era. Private golf courses regularly and routinely barred African Americans, Jewish Americans, and women from becoming members.[13] One African American lawyer, noting the lack of advancement among associates of color and women in his firm, realized that the key difference separating white male lawyers from others was access to country clubs: white male associates played golf and associates of color and women didn't.[14] As journalist David Owen attests, "Golf in America is more inclusive than it was thirty years ago, but it remains conceptually inseparable from the country club."[15]

Adding to the exclusivity and elitism of golf was the rise of the PGA of America, formed in 1916 as a regulatory body meant to promote golf among professionals. However, it also promoted discriminatory social values of the time period, most notably ones that excluded golfers on the basis of race, as Howard Sounes writes: "Golf was institutionally racist. Race discrimination was ingrained in the very executive of the game, actually written into the rules of the Professional Golfers' Association (PGA) of America, the organization that represented all golf professionals in the country, including club pros and—at that time—tour players."[16] What Sounes is alluding to is the Caucasian clause that first came into effect in 1934, which stipulated that members of the PGA must be "professional golfers of the Caucasian Race."[17] Noting that golf may not have been any different from other sports, like baseball and football, in preventing non-white athletes from participating, John H. Kennedy rhetorically asks, "But what major sport spelled out those segregationist attitudes in black and white, as the PGA did? The clause officially institutionalized the discrimination that had reigned over the PGA for decades."[18] During this era, the PGA granted membership solely to white men, which meant that only white men could effectively earn their livings from golf as instructors or as professionals playing in PGA tournaments (which were the most lucrative and highly publicized tournaments in the United States at the time). From the years that the Caucasian clause was in effect, the only way that a non-white person, specifically African American, could walk on a golf course during a PGA tournament was as a caddy.[19] The Caucasian clause was lifted in November 1961 only after the California attorney general, Stanley Mosk, threatened a ban of PGA events from public courses in California and enlisted the attorneys general of other states to follow suit.[20]

The PGA's Caucasian clause was only one public and official way of discriminating against non-white golfers, because the reality for non-white golfers in the United States was that they faced many obstacles to even playing the sport. For example, non-white and particularly African American golfers were barred from almost all private and most public golf courses. If a country club did not have a specific rule preventing against membership, other factors like the lack of nomination from a current member or exorbitant membership fees (ones made more financially punitive for the non-white member) effectively acted as barriers to desegregating private clubs. And with public golf courses, even in cases where the racial segregation wasn't explicitly noted, threats of intimidation and not-so-veiled violence kept many non-white golfers from pursuing the sport. Black golfers in Atlanta who pushed to desegregate public courses in 1955 were told that white golfers would start packing guns in their bags to prevent them from playing. During a tournament in Phoenix, Arizona, Charlie Sifford and his fellow African American professionals encountered human excrement filling the cup on the first hole green, a clear signal that their presence was unwelcome.[21] The PGA's forty years of institutionalized racial discrimination, along with the lack of opportunities for non-white players to play the game, has resulted in a professional class of golfers in the United States, almost all of whom are white, who often come from privileged, country club backgrounds.

Yet like all institutions, golf is sensitive to the same cultural changes of society, even when it may be slower to catch up, as Tom Callahan affirms about the troubled history of the Masters tournament: "There was a time when the Masters didn't want black players, and there came a time when it did—desperately."[22] Although Callahan doesn't expressly explain the impetus for this change of heart, anthropologist Rachel Joo is clear about the connections among corporate interests, sports, and desegregation in a post-civil rights era: "The integration of minorities into the Whites-only field of media sport has almost always been associated with capitalist business interests."[23] Given its racist past, golf was in need of a player who could redeem the sport and attract new consumers, which is one reason why Woods's Masters win was historic not only for the records that he broke but for the color barrier that he crossed.

As a mixed race golfer, particularly one who is of African American ancestry, Tiger's triumphant win at Augusta was noted by innumerable journalists as righting so many racial wrongs in a setting where the clubhouse resembles a plantation home and where caddies (and most of the domestic staff) were black and the players white. Golf journalist John Feinstein called Tiger's win "a major social and political event in American history."[24] Dave Kindred of *Sporting News* writes that "the golf records themselves were the least of Tiger's accomplishments. More important than any numbers was one color. The color of [Tiger's] skin."[25] Callahan devotes a chapter to Woods's 1997 win at Augusta by recounting the racism of the club, the discrimination faced by black golfers like Charlie Sifford and Lee Elder, and the redemption that Tiger brings to the Masters, Augusta National, and the PGA. Writing for *Sports Illustrated*, Rick Reilly ends his piece by commenting on the African American employees at Augusta, tying their reaction to the redemption that Woods's accomplishment signaled: "Clear in the back, near a service entrance, the black cooks and waiters and busboys ripped off their oven mitts and plastic gloves, put their dishes and trays down for a while, hung their napkins over their arms and clapped the loudest and the hardest and the longest for the kind of winner they never dreamed would come through those doors."[26] And Sounes asserts that Tiger's win "was also the first time a person of African American heritage had won America's whitest golf tournament—a matter of considerable significance in the United States, and in the history of the game."[27]

Yet in none of these accounts is it noted that Tiger Woods also became the first Asian American to wear the green jacket or to win one of golf's four major tournaments. Though some reporters took care to mention that Woods was both black and Asian, most concentrated on Woods's ties to his African American father. Largely ignored, Tida became an exotic footnote—where and when Asia or Asianness was referenced it was largely cast through tropes of Vietnam War narratives vis-à-vis Earl Woods as a Vietnam vet who named his son after a South Vietnamese soldier and friend of Earl's. As far as the many journalists covering Woods's story were concerned, there was no ambiguity about his race: Woods was black.

Indeed, Tiger's win at Augusta was treated as a salve for the racial wounds suffered by black golfers for more than a century, a chance for golf to absolve itself of its racial sins and a clear sign of racial progress in America. Tiger appeared to be the latest in a long tradition of African American athletes (Jack Johnson, Joe Louis, Jesse Owens, Jackie Robinson, Muhammad Ali, Arthur Ashe) to break down racial and social barriers and to become powerful symbols of social change. Finally an African American athlete is dominating a sport that had relegated African Americans to being caddies rather than golf pros, where their presence on a golf course was in the service sector and not as guests of the club. Finally an African American athlete triumphed in a tournament that had prevented African American men, for decades, from joining its clubs and participating in its tournaments. Finally African Americans could enjoy the sport of golf and point to Tiger's success and feel like they, too, belonged on the golf fairways, both to cheer Tiger to victory but also to play the game themselves.[28]

Certainly the two advertisements that heralded Woods's professional debut (pre-Masters win) solidified the way in which Nike and IMG (his management team) wanted to market and introduce Tiger to the world as both a specific racialized and minoritized body who could represent the oppression that people of color face and as a universal symbol of progress that everyone could identify with. In the first ad, "Hello World," images of Tiger from his childhood to his latest triumph at the US Amateurs flit across the screen as a soundtrack of tribal sounding drums (reminiscent of African rhythms) and indistinct Gregorian-like chanting is accompanied by text that detail events from Tiger's life—shooting in the 70s when he was eight, playing in the Nissan Open at the age of sixteen, and winning his first US Amateur at eighteen. These statistics are punctuated by the phrase "Hello World" as the final lines of the commercial announce: "There are still courses in the US I am not allowed to play because of the color of my skin. Hello World. I've heard I'm not ready for you. Are you ready for me?" The assumption, of course, is that it's not the yellowness of his skin that prevents his ability to play on certain courses but rather the blackness that serves as the racial barrier that can't be overcome. Again, for most of the world who saw Tiger's professional debut, he was a professional black golfer and not a professional Asian American golfer.

However, Nike's second ad featuring its new golf star, "I am Tiger Woods," attempts to market Woods's multiracial heritage, gesturing to both his Asian as well as African American lineage, as the commercial exhibits a multicultural cast of children swinging golf clubs and chanting, "I'm Tiger Woods." Literary critic Hiram Perez offers a trenchant analysis of both commercials, noting that "Tiger Woods's racial celebrity personifies the paradox of '90s racial discourse: a simultaneous institutionalization of diversity politics and colorblind universalism."[29] Images of children, most notably black, Latino, and Asian of both genders, flash across the screen, as viewers are invited to see that Tiger Woods is an everyman that everyone can identify with; his universal appeal crosses all races, ethnicities, and genders.[30] As Perez aptly notes, this ad performs "Nike's construction of Woods's transcendent racial celebrity."[31] The celebratory multiculturalism of the second ad has ideological roots in a colorblind meritocracy where Woods as Nike spokesperson par excellence becomes the transcendent race figure that everyone can identify with. Precisely through his ambiguous multiracial identity Woods becomes the healer of golf's racial wounds. Tiger Woods is such a racially transcendent figure that he can put to rest the racism of the past century.

However, this image of Tiger Woods as racial iconoclast ignores both the longer history of golfers of color (both African American and others) who have paved the way for Woods and those who currently play alongside him. Latino players Chi Chi Rodriguez (Puerto Rican) and Lee Trevino (Mexican American) both played professionally in the 1960s and 1970s during the height of the civil rights movement and broke down color as well as class barriers.[32] As noted previously and as Woods has acknowledged, African American golfers Charlie Sifford, Teddy Rhodes, Lee Elder, and Bill Spillers (and I would add Althea Gibbs) made possible Tiger's entry into professional golf. And though Woods may be the only African American professional currently excelling in the PGA, there are many golfers of Asian descent (including Asian American golfers like Anthony Kim) who have given him a run for his money, often challenging him on Sunday and sometimes besting him as Michael Campbell (Maori from New Zealand), Vijay Singh (Indian from Fiji), and YE Yang (South Korean) have all done in major tournaments. Twelve golfers of Asian descent are listed in the top 100 (as of May 2014), and Woods is not even the only mixed race Asian golfer on tour— Jason Day (Filipino and Irish from Australia) and Rickie Fowler (Navajo, Japanese, and white from the United States) are also visible multiracial Asian bodies on the PGA who are winning tournaments and receiving professional recognition. Furthermore, turning to the LPGA, it is clear that professional golf is dominated by Asian players; seven of the top ten best female golfers in the world are from Asian nations: South Korea, China, Taiwan, and Japan, and female players of Korean descent, in particular, excel within the LPGA, where they represent more than half of the LPGA membership.[33]

Although Asian descent golfers, both men and women, play a prominent role in professional golf, their marginality in mainstream and even sports discourse signals the ways in which Asians in America continue to be regarded as racially ambiguous; they are not "real" minorities because "real" minorities are black or brown. Furthermore, the racial ambiguity of Asian American golfers reinforces the ways in which the discourse around Tiger Woods continues to erase his Asian heritage and his multiracial identification through highlighting his associations with African American golfing predecessors but not showcasing his fellowship with other Asian American golfers, as Joo affirms of seemingly "race neutral" athletes Michael Jordan and Tiger Woods, "they continue to be absorbed in racialized narratives of integration and racial uplift that capitalize on their Blackness."[34] For most of mainstream America, Tiger transcends race specifically as an African American rather than a mixed race or Asian American golfer. Woods is not read as a racially ambiguous figure; rather, he is seen and is desired by many to be a monoracial African American sports phenomenon, despite the fact that he identifies as a mixed race man.

Mixed Race Messages: Tiger as a Thai-Buddhist Black Man

In June 1995 on the eve of playing in his first US Open at Shinnecock Hills in New York, the amateur golfer, Tiger Woods, released the following media statement:[35]

> The purpose of this statement is to explain my heritage for the bene-
> fit of members of the media who may be seeing me play for the first
> time. It is the final and only comment I will make regarding the issue.
> My parents have taught me to always be proud of my ethnic background.
> Please rest assured that is, and always will be, the case—past, present, and
> future. The media has portrayed me as African American; sometimes,
> Asian. In fact, I am both. Yes, I am the product of two great cultures,
> one African-American and the other Asian. On my father's side, I am
> African-American. On my mother's side, I am Thai. Truthfully, I feel very
> fortunate, and equally proud, to be both African-American and Asian!
> The critical and fundamental point is that ethnic background and/or
> composition should not make a difference. It does not make a difference
> to me. The bottom line is that I am an American . . . and proud of it! That
> is who I am and what I am. Now, with your cooperation, I hope I can just
> be a golfer and a human being.[36]

Although it is not clear what prompted Woods to make this public declaration, it would seem that this was his attempt to clarify his ambiguous multiracial identity to a public that had increasingly been portraying him as a monoracial African American individual and to deemphasize his racial difference through employing discourses of multiculturalism and colorblind universalism. The rhetoric of universalism that Woods invokes in this statement signals an unwillingness to engage with not just the complexity of his particular racial identity but an attempt to distance himself from the thorny controversies that adhere to any discussions of race. Claiming that he is an "American" who just wants to be seen as "a golfer and a human being," means that Woods allows all of us to identify with him, because even if we aren't Americans or golfers, we share with Woods the condition of being human; racial difference thus disappears in favor of appealing to common humanity. According to legal scholar Robert Chang, "Multiracialism may constitute a new iteration of colorblindness where color will not matter because (most) everyone will be full of color."[37]

Although Woods's multiraciality does fit into the ideology of colorblindness and while sports journalists and others writing about Woods have made a cursory attempt to acknowledge his mixed heritage, with some going so far as to delineate the exact ethnic percentages that accrue to Woods's various ancestries, Woods is predominantly and consistently portrayed as a monoracial African American man. When Woods triumphed at Augusta in 1997, nearly every story mentioned the historic nature of this win because Woods was the first African American golfer to win the Masters or any of golf's four major championships. Yet, as journalist William Wong observes, "Little was made of the fact that he was the first person of Asian descent to break the Masters color barrier,"[38] and Henry Yu points out that "there was also a seemingly positive desire to paint Tiger in a darker shade, a pulling for Tiger to be a heroic black man who would save America from its racist past."[39] Jamie Diaz, David Feherty, John Feinstein, Howard Sounes, Tom Callahan, John Strege, and Steve Helling, among countless other sports writers, biographers, and journalists, may mention, in passing, that Tiger is multiethnic or mixed race, but in general when they talk about Tiger's racial identity, it is to note his blackness. Moreover, most sports journalists writing about Woods often employ a rhetoric of colorblind multiculturalism, at once affirming his blackness through the historic nature of his dominance in the PGA but then switching to universalist terms that showcase his golf prowess, thus sidestepping any mention of his racial identity. Indeed, after his 1997 win at Augusta, stories that referenced his race disappeared in favor of talking about Woods as an American and a golfer, which is exactly in keeping with the desires expressed in his 1995 media statement.

In his tell-all book about his time as Woods's swing coach, Hank Haney is remarkably sensitive to the constraints that Woods faced as a "black kid in a white sport," which was his initial impression of the teenage Woods's wariness upon meeting Haney.[40] Throughout the memoir, Haney writes frankly about "how skin color might have influenced some of his critics."[41] Yet Haney discusses Woods almost entirely as a monoracial African American man; even when he briefly refers to Tida, it is only to mention that he believes Tiger got his killer instinct from his mother, a statement that a number of journalists have previously made.[42] When Callahan writes, "Is it possible for someone to walk around America for twenty-seven years with a black face and not feel black?," he sums up the attitude of most sports journalists and average Americans who believe that Tiger looks black and therefore must be black.[43] The fact that his blackness is reflected in his father further consolidates not only how he is regarded by sports journalists and the general American public but the ways in which the discourse around sports emphasizes the influence of fathers on their athlete-children. Writing about LPGA phenom Se Ri Pak, Joo provides a quote that could be applied to an analysis of Woods's family as much as Pak's: "Whereas the actions of the father are the basis for the daughter's success, the mother's labor is peripheral or entirely erased."[44] Tida's labor and ethnic influence on Tiger is certainly one that is peripheral if not erased in narratives of Woods.

However, Tiger has never identified solely as monoracial African American (or Asian American for that matter). In a 1997 Oprah Winfrey interview, the one in which he infamously coined the moniker "Cablinasian" to describe the multiethnic heritages that he embodies, he very clearly states that he was raised in two households and that he neither wants nor chooses to deny either his mother or father's heritage:[45]

WINFREY: When you're called one or another [African American or Asian American] does it bother you? To be called African American?

WOODS: Yeah it does. . . . To be honest with you, if I would have to label myself as anything ethnic wise . . . you know you always have to check a box on those little forms and stuff, they say pick one, I can't. I usually pick African American and Asian because those are the two households I was raised under.

WINFREY: You don't want to deny your mom's heritage?

WOODS: No, I'm not going to deny my mom's heritage, and I'm not going to deny my father's heritage. Those were the two I was raised under and those are the only two I know.

Many African Americans focused on the circulating sound bite that Woods was "bothered" by being called African American, interpreting his refusal of monoraciality as a rejection of blackness. Scholar Kerry Ann Rockquemore claims that "Tiger Woods's public statement that he was not black but Cablinasian was immediately interpreted by African Americans as rejection at best, and antiblack sentiment at worst."[46] Certainly there are those who not only see Woods as actively dissociating from African Americans through his embrace of a multiracial, "Cablinasian," identity but also believe him to be an Uncle Tom figure, a convenient token for whites, corporate America, and the PGA. For many, Woods is a branded spokesman whose real color is green, the color of money and greed.[47] Others point to his life choices—living in an affluent gated community in Florida (which is predominantly white), marrying a Swedish model, not taking on a social justice agenda—as evidence that Woods's lack of African American affiliation derives as much from his actions as his phenotype. Indeed, given Woods's apolitical stances on issues such as gender desegregation of private country clubs and the flying of the Confederate flag,[48] many believe that his assertion of multiraciality is meant to reassure his corporate sponsors and consumers that he is not a radical black activist.[49] His mixed race identity, in other words, becomes a new form of racial passing, similar to the form of passing discussed in the previous chapter with respect to the honorary whiteness of transracial and transnational adoptees; except for Woods, it is a passing enacted through the excess of race that literary critic David Eng believes "installs the law of colorblindness under the sign of an antiracism."[50] As a multiracial figure Woods can be a racial everyman precisely because his embrace of all races means he cannot affiliate with a single racial identity—most especially an abject African American one. "A greater onus is placed on those who cannot pass entirely into whiteness to claim multiraciality as an escape from blackness," asserts critic Meredith McCaroll, echoing the sentiments of many African Americans who believe Woods's multiracial identity signals a desire for "white access."[51]

Furthermore, the belief in Woods's abnegation of his African American heritage and his desire for whiteness gained particular force in the revelations of his many extramarital trysts when over more than dozen women came forward post-Thanksgiving 2009 and admitted their sexual liaisons with Woods because, as anthropologist Orin Starn observes, "Tigergate resurrected older doubts about Woods's racial allegiances, and generated new accusations that he was an outright race traitor."[52] Writing about the online comments that he followed on sites such as *Golf Channel*, *ESPN*, *Hollywood Gossip*, and *Bossip* (a website for black celebrity gossip), Starn traces the rhetoric of race betrayal that adhered to Woods in the wake of Tigergate, with comments like "Guess no 'chocolate' ladies need apply'" and "'WHITE WOMEN ONLY. Tiger Woods is a RACIST!'"[53] Others saw his latest preference for white women as confirmation of his rejection of black life: "'I was done with his sorry behind the minute he said he was 'Casublisian' [sic]'" and "since you don't claim to be one of us, you've got to face this on your own" were among the comments left about Woods during Tigergate.[54] Notably, Starn does not mention any commenters discussing Woods's betrayal of Asian American women, community, or lifestyle. Tiger's race betrayal was fixed in the public imagination as one of blackness rather than Asianness or multiraciality.

Although Starn notes that Woods's marriage to the blonde-haired and Nordic Elin Nordegren garnered scant negative attention or racial commentary, the numerous pictures of the white-appearing women affiliated with Woods created a cacophony in online forums that decried Woods as the ultimate race traitor. For many African Americans, Tiger's preference for white women was confirmation of two twinned and potentially contradictory notions: it confirmed his distance and dissociation with blackness and affirmed that he would be perceived as black in the larger public sphere. Writing for *The Root*, Jimi Izrael notes of Tigergate: "It would be hard to look at this story and not see how race makes it even more titillating. The media wolves have been waiting for this day for over a

decade, and his blackness has never been so apparent."[55] Despite Woods's declaration of his multiracial identity on *Oprah* in April 1997, more than a decade later
the mixed race golfer would be both overtly and covertly reduced, in popular
culture, to a cheating black man. Any idea of Tiger transcending race disappeared after Thanksgiving 2009 when the sub rosa discourse of his interracial
sexual desire fueled both mainstream media and tabloids. When Tiger fell from
grace he did so not simply as an American and as a golfer but as a black man
engaged in sexual congress with multiple white women. However, what is most
suggestive in reading through the jokes and parodies of Woods in the weeks and
months following Tigergate are the ways in which stereotypes of both lascivious
black men and passive Asian men cohered to Woods. He was simultaneously
labeled sexually voracious and insecure because of the quantity of his sexual
partners. References to his earlier days as a nerd when he was in high school
were given as reasons for his need to bed as many women as he could. Thus,
whether the media and general public were aware, or not, Woods's multiracial
identity played out through the scandal, a confirmation that Woods as racially
ambiguous figure both cannot transcend racial categories and that he, like
other racially ambiguous multiracial people, resists monoracial classifications.

Although clearly the general public has conferred monoraciality on Woods,
Woods himself has rejected the monoracial hail that would interpellate him as
only African American.[56] Indeed, Woods's insistence on claiming multiraciality
is noteworthy, particularly in a celebrity who has been notoriously tight-lipped
and apolitical in the stances he takes. Woods may be regarded and discussed as
an African American, but he has time and again asserted himself as a multiracial person, resisting the definitions that others place upon him. And though it
may be compelling to interpret Woods's statements as designed to depoliticize
him and thus make him more palatable to consumers and corporate America,
as Thea Lim writing for the blog Racialicious asserts:

> The insistence on designating Woods as solely black—and getting mad
> when he tries to articulate his ethnic heritage in a way that feels true to
> him—is about more than media bias towards black crime. It's about our
> need to simplify all complex racial phenomenons into the binary of black
> and white, effectively erasing anyone who doesn't fit inside. Tiger Woods
> seems like a jackass. He cheated on his wife in a particularly flagrant way.
> But that's no reason to deny him the right to self-identify.[57]

We may not like Tiger Woods, but liking him or approving of him (or his actions
and political stances on or off the golf course) is beside the point when it comes
to his racial identity. Woods, like every other person, has the right to define
himself, regardless of the ways in which others choose or want him to identify.

Critical mixed race scholar Maria Root created a Bill of Rights for People of Mixed Heritage in the early 1990s. In it, she reinforces the idea that people may choose how they affiliate and what racial group they belong to; self-identification for mixed heritage people is framed as an inalienable right.[58]

Although McCarroll and others have likened multiraciality to a form of passing and a desire for whiteness, Woods's public statements about why he eschews monoracial African American affiliation has continually and consistently been linked to his Asian mother—the love and loyalty that he feels toward her and hence toward the heritage she raised him with: "I don't shun away from my black heritage at all. I certainly welcome it. But I don't appreciate when someone doesn't respect that I have an Asian mother. Because she's my mom and I love her to death. . . . By saying I'm only black disrespects my mother and I would never disrespect my mother."[59] Tiger has often referred, in public statements and interviews, to the influence of his Thai ancestry and Asian culture in his life. In a letter he wrote to the king of Thailand, Woods proclaims that he is "Thai in his heart."[60] All members of the Woods nuclear family have acknowledged that Tiger was raised as an Asian child, with Woods stating his preference for Asian over American culture: "'I like Asian culture better than ours. . . . Asians are much more disciplined than we are. Look how well-behaved their children are. It's how my mother raised me.'"[61] And Tiger has also consistently referred to his Buddhist upbringing, a spiritual and cultural practice he inherited from his Thai Buddhist mother. In early interviews and biographies, the Woods family noted that Tiger was raised as Buddhist and that mother and son would visit a Buddhist temple in Los Angeles every year around his birthday. Tiger's Buddhism was most notably on public display when he invoked straying from Buddhist values and principles during his February 2010 apology for his multiple sexual indiscretions:

> I have a lot of work to do. And I intend to dedicate myself to doing it. Part of following this path for me is Buddhism, which my mother taught me at a young age. People probably don't realize it, but I was raised a Buddhist, and I actively practiced my faith from childhood until I drifted away from it in recent years. Buddhism teaches that a craving for things outside ourselves causes an unhappy and pointless search for security. It teaches me to stop following every impulse and to learn restraint. Obviously, I lost track of what I was taught.[62]

At the end of his televised apology, Woods tearfully hugged his mother in a pose reminiscent of a 2006 American Express print advertisement featuring mother and son in a warm embrace.[63] These images of Woods entwined with his mother are rare moments in his very public life that feature Tida—that actually

highlight her—making visible a woman who has always been a marginal figure
in stories and pictures focused on her famous son. Tiger's embrace of Tida, in
both the print ad and at the end of his apology, reinforces Woods as the inheritor of his mother's Asian values. Although we might interpret Woods's invocation of Buddhism to be part of a twelve-step program of making amends and
giving himself to a higher power, the fact that he didn't succumb to the calls
of conservative Fox News commentator Brit Hume to renounce Buddhism and
accept Christianity speaks to the ways in which Woods refuses to be interpreted
and interpellated according to the desires of others. In emphasizing his Buddhist upbringing and the role of his mother in his early moral education, Woods
reminds his audience that he is, in fact, a person of Asian descent: racially,
culturally, and spiritually. The Buddhist references and the embrace with his
mother signal Woods's annunciation of himself as a mixed race Asian–African
American Buddhist. It also serves as a reminder of Woods's racial ambiguity and
the ways in which Asians in America are also considered an ambiguous racial
category in American racial discourse. Asians in America, like Woods's Thai
mother, are hidden in plain sight, generally ignored by mainstream media and
often erased from social consciousness.

Although Tiger would undoubtedly reject being referred to as a monoracial Asian American on the same principle he has rejected monoracial
African Americanness, the absence of any discourse about Tiger as a monoracial
Asian American signals both the ways in which the one-drop rule of hypodescent
remains prevalent in how we regard people with known African American heritage and the ways in which Asian Americans—knowledge about this community and who constitutes this racial group in the United States and what their
particular history has been—remain largely absent and invisible. The category
"Asian" continues to be viewed on a spectrum closer to white acceptance than
black abjection; in a society predicated on white supremacy, the racial hierarchy
dictates that Tiger, as a man of African heritage, be identified first and foremost
as black. Asians, as honorary whites, can have their phenotype and ethnicity
subsumed in this racial matrix, rendering them racially ambiguous.

What does our lack of acceptance and designation of Tiger as Asian American say about how we, in the United States, view Asian Americans? Certainly it
signals the lack of awareness that Asian Americans are part of American society, especially in arenas like sports. It also signals that our ideas of Asianness
are still predicated on an East Asian phenotypic designation—where real Asians
are people of Chinese, Japanese, and Korean descent. South Asians and Southeast Asians are often treated as if they constitute a separate category of Asianness. Those mixed race Asian Americans, especially those without access to
Asian language skills or a discernible Asian surname or phenotype, often feel

excluded from any connection to a monoracial Asian American designation. When these individuals are mixed race black and Asian American, they may also suffer from multiple stigmatizations: from their Asian ethnic homeland, from an African American community, and from mainstream America's disregard of multiplicity and multiraciality. Tiger's refusal of monoracial African American-ness and assertion of his Asian heritage, particularly as a means of making visible the influence of his Thai mother, speaks to the ways in which he becomes a racially ambiguous figure precisely through his Asianness. If he were to choose (as other mixed race public figures have) to identify solely as African American, few would fault him, including other Asian Americans. Tiger is racially ambiguous precisely through his assertion of his Asian heritage; it is his Asian identification that forces people to see him as mixed race and to acknowledge the role of his mother in his life. The refusal to see his Asianness is a refusal to see Tida. It is also consistent with the way that Asian women remain an absent presence in American history. As the next section makes clear, understanding the role of Asian women in the domestic fallout from the American war in Viet Nam and Southeast Asia is crucial to understanding the invisibility of Amerasian children in our public consciousness.

Amerasian Alternatives and the Legacy of the American War in Viet Nam

The specific absence of Asian American discourse surrounding Woods is linked to the many ways that his Asian mother, Tida, is largely ignored: she is a marginal footnote in the multiple narratives of Tiger Woods, overshadowed by her ex–Green Beret husband and by her golf prodigy son.[64] Yet embedded in Tida's story of how she came to the United States and came to raise Tiger lies the story of Cold War politics, US military intervention, interracial romance, and mixed race children straddling two races and two nations. Within Kultida Punsawad Woods's story and her invisibility lie the story of Amerasian children and the twist of fate that could have left Tiger not as a global golfing phenomenon but one among a number of children in Southeast Asia whom Thomas Bass calls "the last casualties of the [Vietnam] war."[65]

Although most everyone knows the basic circumstances around the American war in Viet Nam—how it came about because of the Cold War–era politics and anticommunist ideology of the United States and its allies—what is less well known is what happened to the thousands of children who were the product of unions between US men (mostly military personnel) and Asian women (predominantly Vietnamese, although certainly as in Tida Punsawad Woods's case, there were Thai as well as Cambodian women who had romantic and sexual liaisons with US men during this time period).[66] Approximately 100,000 Amerasians were born during the conflict in Southeast Asia.[67] And though some did leave with their parents for the United States before the fall of Sai Gon on April 30, 1975, those who did not leave after the communist reunification of Viet Nam were often ostracized and harassed because of their racial ambiguity but even more for their mothers' ties to enemy American forces.[68] Robert McKelvey notes that "Vietnamese Amerasians are a living legacy of America's longest and least popular war"; they are also a living reminder for Vietnamese people of a nation that invaded their homeland to fight a war in which millions died, family units disintegrated, and the natural environment was decimated by toxic weapons.[69] Treated as second-class citizens, Amerasians were taunted in Viet Nam as *my lai* (Amerasian), *my den* (black American), and/or *con lai* (half-breed), or in Thailand as *farang* (foreigner).[70] Subject to extraordinary discrimination and prejudice, Amerasians have been denied job opportunities and marital prospects.[71] Indeed, the prejudice against Amerasians in Thailand was institutionalized; quoting a US State Department official, Bass notes that Amerasians are prevented from attending school or claiming Thai citizenship if they list an American father on their birth certificate.[72] In 1987, the US Congress passed the Amerasian Homecoming Act, in part to alleviate the stigmatized treatment that Amerasians were suffering from in Southeast Asia and as belated recognition and responsibility for the American paternity that brought about their existence in the first place. It is estimated that between 30,000 and 69,000 adult Amerasians have settled in the United States as a result of the Amerasian Homecoming Act.[73]

Amerasians in Southeast Asia are living reminders of US colonialism, the product of unions between US men and Asian women that had been occurring for nearly a century of conflict and contact between the United States and Asia. Quoting from John Shade's report on Amerasians for the Pearl Buck Foundation, Bass writes that "two million Amerasians had been born since US troops first landed in Asia during the Spanish-American War, and that 250,000 Amerasians in nine nations were currently alive."[74] The Amerasian children born from 1962 to 1976 were only the latest in a long line of unintended byproducts born out of US imperial conquest and containment of communist forces in Asia. Noting the increase in military installations throughout Asia and various Pacific island nations in the post-1945 era, Christina Klein asserts that "as this expansion unfolded, US policymakers and journalists resurrected the nineteenth-century imperial idea of the Pacific as an 'American lake.'"[75] And where there are US military men, there are war brides and mixed race and intercultural children. Writing about war brides in the twentieth century, from World War I to the war in Viet Nam, Susan Zeiger observes, "In each of these wars, US soldiers returned home with thousands of foreign-born wives and children."[76] Viewing Tiger Woods as Amerasian is a reminder of the long history of US imperialism in Asia and the Pacific, one in which bodies of land, water, and women were the terrain of violence on which the US military enacted their conquest. The multiracial children born in the Philippines, Okinawa, Korea, Viet Nam, Cambodia, and Thailand are the living legacies of US hegemony in the Asia-Pacific region.[77]

Although Tiger Woods may not quite fit the standard definition of an Amerasian because his birth occurred in the United States and after the fall of Sai Gon, he is the child of a union that began during the war in Viet Nam, a direct inheritor of the Cold War logic of expansion and containment that sent Earl Woods on two tours of duty and that enabled Tida to work for a US Army office in Bangkok.[78] Their courtship was repeated countless times throughout the war in less well-known fashion, one in which US servicemen and civilian contractors developed romantic relationships, sometimes for one night or sometimes for the duration of their tour of duty and, in a few cases, sometimes extending beyond the war and resulting in the migration of Asian woman to the United States. Woods's particular story of being a transcendent and mythical figure who exceeds the bounds of race within the game of golf is widely circulated, yet the stories of other Amerasians whose origins mirror that of the famous golfer are less widely known, most likely since the one key difference in their stories from Woods's is that they were not claimed by their US fathers and were left behind (sometimes by both parents) during the war.[79] To call Tiger Woods Amerasian is to consider his racially ambiguous status in light of other stories of less famous Amerasians, to make visible his largely invisible Asian immigrant mother, and to consider the status of mixed race Amerasian adults as part of the undertold history of the war in Viet Nam and of American history in general.

Although Woods has been widely embraced as Thai when he has visited his mother's motherland, he is accepted in Asia not because of his mixed race status but in spite of it.[80] Clark Neher, director of the Southeast Asian Studies Center at Northern Illinois University, is quoted in a *Chicago Tribune* article as stating that "people who are mixed-race-commonly called *luk khuryng*, or 'child half'—are not as accepted as people who can claim to have pure Thai blood lines" particularly if they are "the offspring of the black American GIs who were stationed in the country during the Vietnam War."[81] Jan Weisman, in her essay "The Tiger and His Stripes: Thai and American Reactions to Tiger Woods's (Multi) 'Racial Self,'" affirms the suspicion that Thai people hold about Amerasians and their mothers, noting that though Woods is embraced in Thailand, it is entirely to do with his fame (and fortune) rather than his Amerasian origins: "Many Thais with whom I spoke questioned the media's reports that his mother had been employed as a secretary at a US military installation, insinuating that she had instead met Woods's father in the course of a less legitimate line of work."[82] The biases and prejudices evident in these two quotations speak to the twin oppressions of racism and sexism that shadow the interracial unions that formed to produce Amerasians, particularly those between African American men and Thai women. The common perception of Asian women who became romantically involved with US soldiers is that they were prostitutes. Researchers, like Steven DeBonis and Robert McKelvey, dispute this stereotype; in their interviews with Vietnamese mothers of Amerasians, these women state that they had entered into long-term relationships with their partners and that, whether the unions were legalized or not, they considered the American men to be their husbands. However, despite their findings, the depiction of Asian women as prostitutes endures in popular culture through films that center on the war in Viet Nam and even in certain scholarship on Amerasians.[83] Zeiger confirms that the American public has a tradition of "stigmatizing foreign wives as prostitutes, economic parasites, and breeders of crime and disease."[84] Both in Asia as well as in the United States, Asian mothers of Amerasian children are assumed to be of suspect morality, a drain on resources, and immoral in a host of ways, perhaps most especially for breaking the taboo of racial purity. According to Weisman, "As thousands of Amerasian children were born to non-elite Thai women and American military men, *luk kreung* [half-child] came to be seen as a marker of unbridled, illegitimate, female sexuality and lower-class origins."[85]

Weisman's thorough analysis of the complexity of multiraciality (or its equivalency in Thailand) and her descriptions of the prejudice and racial preference for purity in Thailand is echoed in the narratives of Amerasians, particularly those of African American heritage. In all the accounts of journalists and researchers who have interviewed and written about Amerasians, whether in Viet Nam, the Philippine Refugee Processing Center (PRPC), or after their resettlement in the United States, they have all commented on the extra difficulties that black Amerasians have experienced in Asia and in America.[86] Jan Weisman, Trin Yarborough, Thomas Bass, and Robert McKelvey confirm the color biases that Vietnamese and Thai people have toward mixed race black Amerasians, noting that in Vietnamese and Thai cultures, black Amerasians are believed, by dint of phenotype, to be considered morally inferior, as Weisman writes: "Fair skin is a marker . . . of moral achievement."[87] McKelvey, observes that "while many Amerasians experienced prejudice and discrimination in Vietnam, black Amerasians appear to have experienced more than others" in large part because of "a general Vietnamese prejudice against those with darker skin."[88] Quoting one of her interview subjects, Miss Dao, a Buddhist nun who ran an orphanage during and after the war, Yarborough states that "Amerasian kids, especially the black ones, were so often abandoned by their parents."[89] And Ahn Dung/Clarence Taylor III, an Amerasian resettled in Utica, New York, articulates the difficulty of his mixed race identity: "When I'm with Vietnamese, I'm Vietnamese. When I'm with Americans, I'm American. I am more Vietnamese than black, but the longer I live in America, the less Vietnamese I become. Amerasians don't really fit in anywhere. . . . We don't know who our people are. We don't belong"[90] He appears to be black, yet he identifies as Vietnamese; he is called "chink" by African Americans who cannot figure out what to do with him, a "triple minority . . . black, Amerasian, and foreign-born."[91] Ahn Dung/Clarence cannot blend easily into the world of Vietnamese immigrants, black Americans, or mainstream white America—the only people who seem closest to understanding his particularly fraught racial ambiguity are fellow Amerasians.[92]

One Amerasian, Alan "Tiger" Hoa, is an interesting contrast to the famed golfer. Yarborough followed Hoa through his arrival in the United States to his incarceration in the California penitentiary system. Although she does not speculate on how Hoa received his nickname, she does provide a description of him that could as easily apply to the more famous Tiger: "Many women have been drawn to Tiger . . . powerfully built and muscular, Tiger has curly dark hair, dark skin, and dark long-lashed eyes."[93] However, the similarities between the two Tigers are superficial—both were born in the early 1970s to Asian women who met their African American fathers as a result of the war in Viet Nam, but whereas Woods was born in the United States and had the love and attention of both parents through his childhood and early adulthood, Hoa never knew his father and was raised by his mother's extended family after she died when he was four. Hoa's life, in contrast to Woods, has been marked by extreme deprivation: poverty, loss of family members, serious illnesses, emotional and mental difficulties, drug abuse, prostitution, self-mutilation, and incarceration because of petty thefts after his resettlement in Southern California. Although their stories and life trajectories are vastly different, it is interesting to contemplate what Woods's life would have been like had he been born in Bangkok, Thailand, instead of Long Beach, California; if his father had not married Tida and taken her back to the United States; and if Tiger had to grow up as one of thousands of Amerasians abandoned by their US fathers in Thailand, denied citizenship and education. His story may not look so different from Hoa's; their narratives are intertwined as Amerasians, their lives a consequence of Cold War conflict that resulted in their respective births.

To understand Woods as Amerasian and hence a racially ambiguous figure is to reorient the way in which his story—his exceptionalism and his transcendence—is mitigated by the thousands of others stories of fellow Amerasians, like Tiger Hoa and Ahn Dung/Clarence. If we read and interpret Tiger as racially ambiguous, it forces us to acknowledge his Asian heritage and his Asian mother. It also brings to the fore the ways in which his story as a mixed race Amerasian is part of a larger discourse and story about Amerasians that is largely left out of public consciousness and general awareness. In charting the rise of various foreign war brides throughout the twentieth century, Zeiger notes that "Vietnamese women have not yet created a platform, in print or on the Internet, for their stories or concerns—a significant contrast with the war brides of the World War II generation."[94] For Zeiger, "the war bride disappeared as a signifier of US foreign policy"; in her place rose the figure of the Amerasian, most notably and (in)famously in the guise of the orphaned (or semi-orphaned) Amerasian child as depicted in the mega-musical hit from the 1990s *Miss Saigon*.[95]

Miss Saigon, a retelling of the Madame Butterfly story, recycles the plot of tragic interracial love stories between US military men and Asian women.[96] In this iteration, the mixed race union results in an Amerasian child who will return with his father to the bounty of America, the price of his immigration bought by the Asian mother who is denied entry and who subsequently kills herself as part of a maternal sacrifice to achieve US citizenship for her son. Echoing this plot, the initial policy of the Amerasian Homecoming Act forced Amerasians to choose between their mothers and their spouses: they could bring only one family member with them to the United States. Yet even when they chose their "mother," these women were often paper family members, fake mothers who bought their family ties to Amerasians in order to receive an airline ticket to the United States. Indeed, one could say that unlike the mixed race child left behind at the end of *Madame Butterfly* and *Miss Saigon*, the Amerasian adults who came to the United States did so alone and without knowledge, oftentimes, of their fathers' identities. In the sentimental story of *Miss Saigon* the American father eventually claims his Amerasian child (and with the death of his former Asian lover is allowed to take him home and rebirth him in the bosom of white America); however, the reality for Amerasians in the United States is that only 2 percent ever locate their American fathers, and of those who do find them, often there is no happy reunion, only repudiation and rejection.[97]

It is no wonder that we do not think of Tida Woods; we do not think of Asian women in general and less so Asian women engaged in romantic relationships with US men during times of war. These women are absent from our public discourse, and when they are rendered in popular culture they are represented as silently suffering ciphers. Tida Punsawad Woods's own story, particularly in light of revelations that Earl Woods had committed a number of infidelities during their marriage, would seem to mirror that of her fictional counterparts— Asian women who withstand the disloyalty of their American husbands without complaint.[98] Tida simply does not register within the narratives that America is largely familiar with, a point exacerbated by the fact that she is Thai rather than Vietnamese, rendering Tida and other Thai women like her as doubly erased because in the public imagination Asian women in the era of the war in Viet Nam are all Vietnamese. Furthermore, popular understandings of the war in Viet Nam can incorporate Vietnamese women into these narratives, but the specific details of Tida's Thai experiences as a secretary and not a victimized Vietnamese villager leaves her story outside of the standard narratives that circulate about Asian women in war.

Moreover, the standard narratives we have of Asian women who have been involved, romantically, with US military men during a war with an Asian nation is that they have either remained in Asia or they have died tragically (*Madame Butterfly*, *Sayonara*, *Miss Saigon*) and thus do not have to be dealt with at all. And outside the realm of fiction, many Asian mothers of Amerasian children have sacrificed themselves for the sake of their Amerasian children, remaining behind in Asia to care for elderly family members, or they simply have disappeared into the United States, isolated because of their stigmatized difference from other Southeast Asian immigrants who arrived in the early 1970s. Whether because they are left behind in Asia or secluded in the United States, Asian women who bear Amerasian children are absent from the discourse of the war in Southeast Asia, from the popular stories we have (other than the tragic ones that end in their death or desertion), and from general public knowledge and American history. Like her Amerasian son, Tida is a racially ambiguous figure for the ways in which she is ignored; her story, along with thousands of Amerasians and their Asian mothers, remains undertold within the larger narrative of US history and American culture, particularly in the ways that it rebukes the *Miss Saigon* story by demonstrating that both mother and son can live their lives, if not happily ever after in the United States then certainly not tragically suffering in Asia.

Let Tiger Be Tiger

The man the world now knows as Tiger was born Elderick Tont Woods. Various biographers have noted that Tida (or Kultida) invented the name "Elderick" by making sure that the first letter of both father and mother would begin and end their son's name. Many journalists have recounted that Earl Woods gave his son the nickname "Tiger" in honor of Vuong Dang Phong, a South Vietnamese colonel he befriended on one of his tours of duty who is credited with saving Earl's life twice during the war. Earl gave Phong the nickname "Tiger" because of his ferocious and tenacious personality, qualities he wished upon his son by bestowing the same nickname on baby Elderick. What is never remarked upon is Tiger's middle name "Tont," a traditional Thai moniker that means "royal" or "king." Like the significance of his middle name, the influences of his Thai heritage, ones embedded in his name, his upbringing, and his relationship with his Thai immigrant mother, are similarly ignored. The invisibility of "Tont" is like the invisibility of Tida and Tiger's Amerasian connection: hidden in plain sight.

Woods's many names reflect the many Asian influences in his life and his parents' lives, which is not to say that this signals that he is more Asian than African American, but it does suggest the ways in which some of the most obvious markers of his identity have been glossed over in favor of either concentrating on his African American heritage or the ways in which his subjectivity exceeds and transcends race. Yet it would certainly be erroneous to traffic in the idea of blood quantum—to try to reclaim Tiger as Asian American over and against his African American or multiracial selves.[99] As Henry Yu so trenchantly observes in two different essays about the famous mixed race golfer, those who would break up Woods's ethnicity into specific categories to allege that he is more Asian than African American forget that there is no idea of pure races— the idea of racial purity is a fiction, one that has had world-shattering consequences for all of us, but that still remains a social construction that the modern world has agreed to believe in:

> The fractional nature of the racial and cultural categories in Tiger Woods was as arbitrary as the classification of him as African American. The key factor that undermines Tiger Woods's racial formula is the fiction that somehow his ancestors were racially or culturally whole. When he was broken up into ¼ Chinese, ¼ Thai, ¼ African American, 1/8 American Indian, and 1/8 Caucasian, the lowest common denominator of 1/8 leads to a three generation history. . . . Further and further back in time, these genealogies would reveal that there has never been a set of racially whole individuals from which we have all descended. Whether in purportedly mixed or pure fashion, biological descent that invokes racially whole individuals in the past is delusional.[100]

Yu's point is an important one to consider when thinking about Woods as racially ambiguous and the manner in which the rhetoric of transcendence adheres to him. As so many critical race theorists have asserted, race is a social construction—a fabrication designed to uphold a race hierarchy in which people who get coded and marked as "white" are deemed superior to people coded and marked as "black." The idea that we can break up Woods's ancestry into percentages that will somehow accurately and authentically reflect his ethnic heritage and racial identity is an absurd fantasy; his Asian "blood" does not overrule his African American "blood" just because it might seem to be a greater percentage. After all, the history of race relations and white supremacy in the United States has shown that as far as blood quantum goes, majority does not always rule. Although "Cablinasian" may be a term that only applies to Tiger Woods, that there are other people who share similar mixtures of ethnic groups that include European, Asian, Indigenous American, and African influences is not uncommon to the polyglot of multiracial people living in the world, especially in the United States. In that sense, Cablinasian is just as odd a term to use as Asian American—both compress a plethora of ethnic groups into a single term of limited utility outside of a specific context (Woods on the one hand, people of Asian descent living in the United States on the other).

Yoshiko deLeon (the subject of chapter 1) is deemed racially ambiguous by the state, whereas Asian American adult adoptees (the subjects of chapter 2) internalize their racial ambiguity through the negotiations of their first and adoptive families. Tiger Woods's racial ambiguity, as a mixed race African American–Asian American celebrity, derives from a different source, specifically the dominance of hypodescent—the belief that his "blackness" trumps his "Asianness." The consequences for this type of racial ambiguity—for Woods and for others who share his ethnic ancestries, is that his Asianness is erased, which for Woods means that his Asian mother, Tida, and the history of what she experienced as an Asian female immigrant, as a Thai woman working for the US military during the war in Viet Nam, is also erased. Asian Americans are already ambiguously figured within the US social polity because their racial identity is not legible to the mainstream public. To understand Woods as monoracial rather than multiracial and specifically as African American instead of biracially African and Asian American is to erase the history of state oppression that Asians in America have been subjected to from the time they first came to the United States.

Tiger Woods's continual assertion of his multiraciality and refusal to be interpellated as monoracial, ignoring the hail that calls him into blackness, is a refutation to the erasure of his Asian ancestry. The public's understanding of his multiraciality also forces us to acknowledge both the intimate links to his Asian ancestry, in the form of his mother, as well as the larger history of US imperialism and racialization. Furthermore, Tiger Woods is free to choose his multiracial affiliations because they reflect the reality that Woods and other multiracial people would like to see for themselves (a future forward attitude) rather than the racial climate that has traditionally guided our attitudes on race (a historic awareness of the past). In this way, Woods and other multiracial people remain ambiguous figures precisely for the ways in which they continue to push beyond standard narratives for how one should regard, talk about, and treat people of mixed racial backgrounds.

4

Ambiguous Movements and Mobile Subjectivity

Passing in between Autobiography and Fiction with Paisley Rekdal and Ruth Ozeki

Contemporary Asian American literature was born out of an ambiguous text: Maxine Hong Kingston's *Woman Warrior*. First published in 1976 by Knopf when Kingston was an unpublished and unknown writer living in Hawaii, *The Woman Warrior: Memoir of a Girlhood among Ghosts* heralded the wave of both Asian American literature and Asian American literary criticism in the post-civil rights era. Its multidisciplinary appeal quickly made *Woman Warrior* canonical within the fields of women's studies, Asian American studies, American literature, and autobiography studies.[1] Originally branded as "nonfiction," critics have grappled with its generic ambiguity.[2] Is it truly autobiographical or entirely fictional? Are its imaginative departures a signal of cultural corruption or creativity?[3] Did Kingston willfully mislead readers, pandering to white Orientalist desires for an exotic China, or did she pen a truly postmodern work that blends fact with fantasy in an effort to recount her fragmented childhood growing up Chinese American?[4] In other words, how does one read *Woman Warrior*? The debate about both authenticity and genre that circulates around Kingston's narrative is a debate about passing—about whether the work is trying to be something that it is not. Is *Woman Warrior* passing as autobiography when it is, in fact, fiction? Is Kingston's work passing as an authentic representation of Chinese culture? Do its inconsistencies and inaccuracies about Chinese life and legends render it neither a reliable Chinese cultural document nor an accurate representation of Chinese American life?[5]

Similar indeterminacies mark the narratives penned by two turn-of-the-twenty-first-century Asian American mixed race writers: poet and memoirist Paisley Rekdal's collection of autobiographical essays *The Night My Mother Met Bruce Lee: Observations on Not Fitting In* (2000) and documentary filmmaker and novelist Ruth Ozeki's debut novel *My Year of Meats* (1998). Both Rekdal and

Ozeki's works, like Kingston's canonical text, pass back and forth from autobiography to fiction, weaving elements of both genres into their respective narratives. But beyond generic considerations, Rekdal and Ozeki, as mixed race writers, also grapple with the theme of passing in terms of content as well as form; their respective works fit within a genre of passing narratives because of the self-conscious way both writers address racial issues and at various times ignore one part of their racial identity (or those of their narrators) in favor of emphasizing another aspect of mixed race subjectivity. Furthermore, both use the trope of passing as movement to expound on their respective preoccupations with the ambiguity of their racial identities. Both tell stories about their negotiations of their textual mixed race bodies by utilizing the trope of passing as movement in order to replace a language of visuality with a language of mobility. Rekdal and Ozeki create mobile subjectivities for their narrators as each work moves back and forth—through genre, through identities, through countries—crossing multiple borders of form and content to create a passing story.

In this chapter, I locate the theme of passing as a continually evolving strategy for dislocating one's racial and ethnic identity—to think about passing for what you are instead of passing for what you are not, because to be mixed race and hence racially ambiguous means that passing is a strategy of identification as much as disidentification. According to literary scholar Tina Chen, "Both passing and impersonation wrestle not only with the tactic of how to perform as well as undermine racial constructions but also with the implications and contexts of such performances as they are affected by specific cultural, historical, and political circumstances."[6] Passing should be understood not merely as upholding a racist system and reifying its power dynamics but, as Chen alludes to, passing has the potential to "undermine racial constructions" while simultaneously commenting on the social values of our contemporary times. For instance, mixed race subjects no longer need to choose one race over the other, or, as Teresa Kay Williams queries, "Can a multiracial individual pass for what he or she is? Does passing for what you are count as really passing?"[7] By virtue of blood, descent, heritage, or all of the above, mixed race individuals can choose multiple ethnic and/or racial identities.

By reimagining passing, I consider how mixed race Asian American writers like Rekdal and Ozeki use the theme of passing to contest the very category of racial identification—passing negotiates the racial ambiguity of the category "Asian American" as well as the multiracial condition of these two mixed race writers. When critic Pamela Caughie asserts that "all subjectivity is passing," she makes an astute observation that our sense of self and identity is always a constant performance.[8] It is never static or fixed; rather, subjectivity is passing both in the sense of the inherent instability it connotes as well as in the sense of shifting performances that it conveys. We are all constructions shaped from the social, historic, and cultural forces that surround us. And because, generally speaking, there is not a space or a language for mixed race people to claim a multiple, hybrid, or heterogeneous subjectivity, passing in a post-civil rights era could be seen as challenging a categorical system of thought.[9]

Passing is movement; it is literally active because the grammatical present participle denotes the present time in action, in process. Rekdal and Ozeki create narratives that highlight the mobile subjectivities of their mixed race passing subjects. In *The Night My Mother Met Bruce Lee*, Rekdal writes about her many different selves growing up mixed race in Seattle. Animated by self-reflection, her essays move from place to place and through various periods in Rekdal's life, charting her earliest childhood memories of her racial and ethnic difference to her adult self searching for traces of her Aunt Opal in the South. Turning to *My Year of Meats*, Ozeki's fictional alter-ego, Jane Takagi-Little, literally embodies mobile subjectivity; Jane is continually on the move and cannot stay still. Jane travels from hotel to hotel and from state to state, coming back to New York City to recharge but then leaving, again, in search of new narratives about her place in America as a biracial woman. Additionally, both authors play with generic conventions, passing in and through fact and fiction, because their narratives weave elements of both throughout their respective works.

As passing stories, neither entirely fictional nor entirely factual, neither fully Asian nor not Asian, Rekdal's and Ozeki's works draw attention to passing as a way to tell unique stories of being mixed race mobile subjects and to reveal the ambiguity of race itself. Passing is ambiguous movement: the mobile subject, in transit, is elusory. She or he cannot be fixed because the subject is moving and therefore unsettled and untethered. "The mixed race writer understands herself existing not simply in one single moment," declares literary scholar Raquel Scherr Salgado, "but also in the flux and multiplicity that these contingent moments may generate in her transit."[10] Salgado's allusions to movement as characterizing the writing of multiracial authors replaces an ocular language with one of motion, a useful transposition when considering passing as mobile subjectivity. Too often people are defined, racially, through a language that emphasizes visual cues,[11] which then requires them to be a reflection of someone else's gaze.[12] Asian Americans have long been oppressed through their visually overdetermined and ambiguous bodies, as Chen affirms: "US anxieties about how Asian Americans can or cannot be 'seen' have regularly manifested themselves in a cultural history of considering Asian Americans both 'excessively visible' and 'inscrutable.'"[13] Asian American phenotypic features are most marked through facial characteristics; being defined occurs through others' awareness of one's Asianness as well as one's own visual imprint in the mirror.

In other words, one cannot know whether one is Asian without seeing oneself reflected through the mirror or through others. Asianness, as defined through the visual, is thus always a reflection. Passing as a form of identity predicated on animation allows mixed race Asian Americans to define themselves without relying on the reflective surface of others' definitions or the solipsism of the mirror. Enacting a passing identity allows more choice and more freedom of expression, one rooted in a language of mobile subjectivity and hence not framed as static within either gaze or mirror.

Returning now to a discussion of *The Woman Warrior* as the archetype of ambiguous contemporary Asian American texts, Maxine Hong Kingston articulates the dilemma of ethnic American writing when she observes, "Chinese-Americans, when you try to understand what things in you are Chinese, how do you separate what is peculiar to childhood, to poverty, insanities, one family, your mother who marked your growing with stories, from what is Chinese? What is Chinese tradition and what is the movies?"[14] Here she enunciates the tension between individual and collective representations of an ethnic group as well as the tension over what is real and what is fake—what is part of one's actual family experience versus one's hazy recollections, colored by fantastic stories told by Hollywood and other media representations of "the real." This blurring, though distinctively part of an Asian American literary tradition, is certainly not limited to this ethnic genre. Indeed, the melding of fiction and autobiography has been and continues to be the subject of several studies within narrative theory and autobiography studies.[15] Autobiography has always been plagued by charges of veracity and the imperfections of memory: no one can recall factually accurate activities from minute to minute, hour to hour, and day to day. And even were someone to record, as precisely and minutely as possible, all one's activities, it would hardly make for a compelling or interesting story. Instead, the challenge that critics of autobiography have is not in verifying facts but in finding truth. Similarly, the first-person narration of fiction conceals clear boundaries between the real and the fake, as narrative critic Susan Lanser notes of the inherent unreliability and fallibility of homodiegetic (first-person-narrated) texts: "Homodiegetic texts provide no such formal index of their status as fiction or fact. Indeed, writers and publishers have exploited this ontological ambiguity for centuries, passing off fictions for histories and hiding autobiographies beneath claims of fictiousness; the 'rise' of the novel is indebted to just such practices."[16] Eighteenth-century novels like Daniel Defoe's *Moll Flanders* created a stir with its titillating content and its homodiegetic narration; no longer could readers ascertain the truth of narrators once Defoe created a lively and believable fictional version of a woman's colorful life. Through the speciousness of homodiegetic narration the modern novel was born, ventriloquized through the voice of a man to tell the story of a bold and bawdy woman who crossed borders of propriety and geography.

While first-person-narrated novels have appeared as fictive forms of autobiographies, the genre of the autobiography often contains fictive elements. As countless critics of *The Woman Warrior* have noted, Kingston weaves fabulist elements within her autobiography, projecting stories and imagining scenarios that may or may not have occurred and that may or may not have been told by her mother. Truth is both elusive and illusive, and the truth of Kingston's life cannot be found among the mere facts of her childhood growing up in Stockton, California, during the post–World War II era. Rather, the truth of her reflections lie in her experiences growing up Chinese American at a time when there were no public narratives that mirrored her particular reality of being the first-generation American-born daughter of immigrant Chinese parents.[17] The embellished stories of her No Name Aunt and Fa Mu Lan serve as narrative role models for her coming of age. Giving textual shape and life to these characters allows Kingston to develop her authorial voice and to write herself into being within the pages of *The Woman Warrior*. Truth is no longer about what really happened; instead, as life-writing scholars Sidonie Smith and Julia Watson explain, "Autobiographical truth is a different matter; it is an intersubjective exchange between narrator and reader aimed at producing a shared understanding of the meaning of a life."[18]

Although Smith and Watson carefully distinguish between autobiography and other forms of writing (such as fiction), they recognize the ways in which elements of each genre, fiction and life writing, permeate one another. Similarly, truth can be found within the imperfection of memory, and not simply in spite of it, for how we remember and recount our memories reveals truths that shape our lives and give meaning to our experiences. Maureen Murdock, in her own memoir *Unreliable Truth: On Memoir and Memory*, believes that details, though important, are not the sole facts that shape our understanding of our memories and ourselves: "The meaning of the event is not attached to the details, but details help disclose the meanings of the event. What is important about memoir is the meaning we make of our lives, and of course that meaning is subjective."[19] Meaning is subjective because it shifts and changes, and it shifts and changes because it is attached to a person's point of view and thus subject to the inaccuracies and inconsistencies of one's memories. Yet this shifting, this passing, only further reinforces the complexities of people's lives. People are not static; rather, their lives are marked by growth, development, and the inherent ambiguity of being changeable, complex human beings.

However, understanding the meaning of a life is not limited to the realm of autobiography. Fiction has an epistemological purpose, allowing for a different path to knowledge through the "truth" of someone's story. It also does not preclude facticity, for there can be accuracy within fiction. The historical novel often uses the facts of history—the dates, places, and even real figures themselves—to tell a fictional story, one that contains elements of "truth" and "the real" among its many fabulist conventions. Kazuo Ishiguro's haunting novel *The Remains of the Day* relies on historic details (the aftermath of World War I, the rise of the Nazi regime, Britain's entry into World War II, English country life during and immediately following World War II) in order to tell the story of an English gentleman's butler in the waning period of the British Empire. Set in 1956, the novel follows Stevens, the head butler to Lord Darlington, and it is less an historic look at Britain during World War II than an example of the frailties, failures, and small dignities of one man's life. Whether Stevens or Lord Darlington are based on any actual figures is inconsequential to the epistemological value of reading Ishiguro's narrative and learning about how one man comes to realize and face the missed opportunities and misreadings he has made during his lifetime.[20] The blurring between fact and fiction, between the homodiegetic narration of autobiography and first-person-narrated novels, makes an examination of passing important to see such differences and similarities. Using passing to analyze narratives, whether fiction or nonfiction, allows one to see the borrowings and blendings that occur between these two genres.

Paisley Rekdal's *The Night My Mother Met Bruce Lee: Observations on Not Fitting In*

Narratives become imperative guides, particularly for mixed race people whose racial identity is clouded in ambiguity. Rekdal's collection of autobiographical essays, *The Night My Mother Met Bruce Lee: Observations on Not Fitting In*, abounds with stories about her painfully self-conscious awareness of her multiracial subjectivity. Divided into three parts, six of the twelve essays recount her visits to various Asian countries. But the collection cannot accurately be described as a series of travel essays, because her observations are not focused outward on her foreign surroundings but rather inward. Providing details about the sights and experiences of her myriad travels, her essays explore interior musings and childhood memories—most notably her reflections on being biracial. Born to a Norwegian American father and a Chinese American mother, Rekdal is a third-generation American on her maternal side: both her mother and grandmother were born in Seattle, whereas her father's family is of immigrant origins. Yet as a biracial woman, Rekdal continually questions her national, racial, ethnic, and cultural affiliations, passing in and out of identities as she travels through Japan, Taiwan, South Korea, China, the Philippines, the American South, and even the Seattle neighborhood of her childhood memories.

Although some reviewers have commented on the lack of focus and the haphazard placement of essays within this collection, a closer examination at the three-part division reveals a loose teleology.[21] The work begins and ends with the subject of mythology, specifically the intersection of Asian American mythology with Rekdal's family stories—the ways in which stories take on a life outside their truth-value. The eponymous essay that begins the collection narrates her mother's recollection of meeting Bruce Lee while working at a Chinese restaurant in Seattle. Rekdal's mother is unimpressed with this buffoon, who has yet to become a martial arts superstar and is, instead, an arrogant young immigrant from Hong Kong who breaks dishes and brags about his physical prowess. The concluding essay, "Traveling to Opal," depicts Rekdal in her oldest (and perhaps wisest) incarnation within the collection: she has sojourned from Seattle to various Asian countries and has, temporarily, moved to Atlanta for the sake of her partner. "Traveling to Opal" recalls a trip she takes to Natchez, Mississippi, in search of traces of her Aunt Opal, a Chinese American woman who improbably lived in this small southern town during a period when the idea of Chinese in the South would seem to be sheer myth. The essays sandwiched between these two also show a trajectory of Rekdal's understanding of the power of stories, personal as well as universal, to become myth—larger than the lives they originally recorded. Though each essay can be read out of order as an independent piece, to read the collection in sequence is to recognize the entirety that Rekdal creates, one greater than the sum of its parts. Chinese American and Norwegian American alike, these family anecdotes comprise her mixed race subjectivity, a reflection of her ambivalent feelings about being biracial. All the essays are framed around the question of Rekdal's sense of herself as a misfit; the ways in which her ambiguous racial identity places her outside any normative categories. Taken as a whole, the collection becomes a kind of racial bildungsroman: Rekdal comes of age and accepts her biracial identity by acknowledging the inherent ambiguity of her subjectivity.

Rekdal's work can be characterized as autobiography, memoir, nonfiction, travel writing, and in some instances even anthropology.[22] However, her work also reflects the lyricism of her poetic training, and the essays, informed by such prosody, bear an aesthetic resemblance closer to fiction than to straightforward ethnography or autobiography.[23] Though critics like Smith, Watson, and Lanser have made claims for the fictive qualities inherent within all autobiography, memory's unstable qualities renders all life writing suspect to a certain degree, because one's memories may or may not accurately represent one's experiences as they happened versus how they were remembered. In an interview with literary blogger Ron Hogan, Rekdal very deliberately describes the process of using both prosody and fiction in her autobiographical work:

Maybe it's because I write poetry, but I tend to think metaphorically and I tend to think in terms of emotional events, lining things up emotionally and chronology falls by the wayside. The trick here was to create essays that mimicked a journalistic sense of what had happened at the time, but to manipulate them so that the emotional content of totally random events somehow flowed together and created its own story. That meant I had to change characters occasionally. I had to put dialogue from other friends in different friends' mouths. I had to totally mess around with the chronology in order to line things up.[24]

Referring to people in her essays as "characters" and announcing that she had "to manipulate" both dialogue and events for the sake of having her narrative "flow together" demonstrates Rekdal's reliance on conventions of narrative more akin to the genre of the novel than the autobiography. Her work can be seen as one that passes from states of fiction to nonfiction. Weaving fictional elements within her autobiographical acts, she employs rhetorical art forms to create a life narrative that tells a convincing story.

Rekdal's fictional interventions, as disclosed in the interview with Hogan, do not reveal her life writing as false or untrue; rather, it confirms the porousness of autobiography and Rekdal's own self-conscious admission to the exact problem that other critics have stated about telling autobiographical stories and yet keeping to the "truth" of one's life. *The Night My Mother Met Bruce Lee* tackles the tension between telling a good story and recounting the accuracy of Rekdal's experiences. In "Bad Vacation with Tasaday Tribe, or How My Grandfather Acquired the Laundromat," Rekdal opens the essay with a family anecdote about her maternal grandfather acquiring a laundromat at the start of World War II from a Japanese American man about to be incarcerated. The Japanese American sells the laundromat to Rekdal's grandfather for a dollar, and when the man returns from the concentration camp, Rekdal's grandfather sells the laundromat back to the Japanese American for a dollar. This is the story Rekdal relates, told to her by her Norwegian American grandmother, who, in turn, heard the story from Rekdal's Chinese American mother. It's a story of pan-Asian American solidarity in the face of white racism and xenophobia, one that makes Rekdal's grandfather appear magnanimous and heroic. Yet, Rekdal confesses that "unfortunately it is untrue. Nothing like this ever happened."[25]

Throughout this essay, Rekdal ruminates on the nature of truth and on her desire for this story to be true. She probes her mother (who swears by its veracity), grandmother (who disavows her mother's story), and her Norwegian American relatives (who describe the powerful impact the story made on them) for their versions of the laundromat story. She then juxtaposes their accounts with her discovery of the Tasaday hoax while on vacation in the Philippines. The Tasadays were a supposedly primitive tribe of people still living in a preindustrial state in the late twentieth century. In reality, however, the Tasadays were supported by the Philippine government and were discovered to be smoking and drinking soda at a local town not far from their tribal village.[26] Both the truth of the Tasaday's existence (not primitive but used for touristic purposes) as well as the questionable truth of the laundromat story (her grandfather did own two laundromats, but they were purchased through his hard labor, and he had no Japanese American friends) lead Rekdal to ponder the nature of truth and her desire for stories which are too good to be true—stories that portray the world as a purer, more innocent, and more benign place than it currently seems to be.

Rekdal's ruminations in this essay also address how truth passes in and out of different stories. Like memoirist Murdoch's description of details tied to events, it's the meaning we derive from memory rather than mere factual accuracy that informs our knowledge of the world. The transmission of the story, passed on from Rekdal's mother to her mother-in-law to Rekdal and, finally, to us, the readers of her essay, signals the way that the theme of passing (as movement as well as the idea of something that is false or only partially true) informs Rekdal's narrative structure and her ability to navigate her subjectivity: "It is my version. My mother's story has evolved into the story of her white husband and mother-in-law and daughter. Like the Tasaday hoax, it's what we—the outsiders—want to believe happened. It's what I want to think about when I think about my Asian family in America. . . . Because being Asian in America is a fact that does and does not exist. It disappears from view when scrutinized directly."[27] The story that Rekdal circulates is one that she now owns and that is part of her, even as its veracity remains in doubt. Yet it is the passing on of the story through different family members that makes this version more powerfully Rekdal's own; the ways in which the force of narrative to convey truths can remain, despite imprecision of details. Details are not always reliable, especially when one depends on an ocular examination for verification of existence. Being Asian American is not a fact that can be solely verified or affirmed through direct visual examination alone, particularly for mixed race ambiguous bodies like Rekdal.

The sense of ambiguity—of the undecided, indecipherable, and indistinct that passing suggests—recurs throughout Rekdal's work. As the subtitle to the collection makes clear, Rekdal focuses on how she is marked by difference, on *not* fitting in, whether in Asia or the United States. Indeed, her Asia essays emblematize the indeterminacies and ambivalences that Rekdal carries with her because traveling becomes a trope for passing, a statement about moving in and out of spaces as Rekdal's identity flows and fluctuates during her many peregrinations. To reaffirm the larger thesis of this chapter, passing is not about taking on an identity that you are not; rather, passing for multiracial Asian

Americans proclaims an identity that may not be apparent at first glance. Passing, or mobile subjectivity, attests to the fluidity and ambiguity of racial identities, mixed race or otherwise. For Rekdal, passing is shaped by her location, her companions, her clothes, and how she occupies space. Passing—her ambiguous movements—destabilize her racial identity, both her own notions of her self as well as others' interpretations of her mixed race body.

In "Americans Abroad," Rekdal aptly illustrates the unreliability and inaccuracies of appearance through her passing identity; her body's movements make noticeable the unapparent and indeterminate aspects of her mixed race self. Narrated in the past tense, "American's Abroad" recalls a summer that Rekdal spent studying in Kobe, Japan. The essay opens with her older, more mature voice commenting on the kinds of assumptions she held about knowledge, aesthetics, and ontology in her younger days: "When I was twenty I thought I knew something about Japanese art. I liked it, which I thought meant I must inherently understand it. So in college I applied for and received a scholarship to stay with two families in the seaport town of Kobe for the summer—my first trip out of the country."[28] The key word in this quotation is *inherently*; Rekdal returns to this theme throughout this essay—the connection between the appreciation and knowledge of a subject with what is "inherent," interior, and inside oneself. Must knowledge be inherent (or inherited) in order for one to truly appreciate and understand culture? Can one embody a culture different from one's own and make it a part of oneself simply by understanding it?

Rekdal's choice of Japan for her first trip outside the United States significantly relays another instance of her ethnic ambivalence: "In my application I wrote that I was interested in Japanese aesthetics, a suggestion inspired by my mother. She thought it would be a good idea for me to see other countries China had influenced; to see, if indirectly, my culture."[29] Although Rekdal mentions neither interest nor apathy toward her Chinese heritage, the oblique connection to China through Japan—of having Rekdal experience, "if indirectly," her Chinese ancestry—conveys ambiguity. Is she traveling to Japan to understand and appreciate Japanese art or is she going to unearth a connection with her Chinese ancestry? Indeed, the trip reflects more her mother's ideas of Rekdal's identity (or what it should be) than Rekdal's own inchoate aptitude for Japanese aesthetics. Rekdal's mother has embraced all things Asian, particularly all things Japanese, in a display of Asian American solidarity; both before and throughout Rekdal's sojourn she reminds her daughter about her shared "Asianness" with her Japanese hosts, telling her that "you've got something in common with them at least. You aren't just like any other American."[30]

Yet it is exactly like "any other American" that Rekdal grapples with her national and racial affiliations. Her mother's comments conflate "American" with "white": to be a "true" or "real" American, one must be a white American. American subjectivity itself seems predicated on a compulsory racial identity, one tacitly understood throughout American society. Much like Judith Butler's conception of a compulsory heterosexuality that governs gender identity, the racial default in the United States is to white. For if, as Butler asserts, à la Simone de Beauvoir, that "only men are 'persons,' and there is no gender but the feminine,"[31] then the corollary for racial identity is that only white Americans are citizens, and there is no race except the non-white because the absence of racial markers suggests a white normativity—race is invoked only as difference.[32] However, Rekdal does not and cannot occupy the privileged position of white normativity. As much as she understands that she benefits from the entitlement of being an American abroad, she also knows that despite her initial assertion to her mother that she is "'exactly like every other American,'" her mixed race status renders her as an outsider in Japan as well as in the United States because she is neither a "real" Asian nor a "real" American.[33]

Rekdal displays her ambivalent feelings about her identity through various attempts to define herself for others when they continue to misconstrue her identity or when they cannot see Rekdal in the myriad ways that she, inherently, understands herself to be. Rekdal's passing identity makes visible that which is not apparent. It is not consistent in the sense that she chooses to pass as white, Chinese, or American but rather the kinds of passing she performs varies with the changing contexts of her sojourn, as demonstrated in a scholarship banquet scene. Confronted by the embarrassing prospect of having to sing at a karaoke machine with other foreign students, Rekdal attempts to make a connection with one of the Japanese businessmen attending the dinner. Answering his query as to her nationality, she adds, "'But I'm half Chinese,'" explaining that "I wanted somehow to ally myself with him, his place in the audience drinking beer and watching others perform. *I'm like you*, I silently begged. *Save me from my culture*" [italics in original].[34] Rekdal's wish to align herself with the banquet guest originates out of a desire to escape performance as well as the very specious sense of fraternity for which she mocks her mother, the sense of "Asianness" that she and the Japanese man both embody. Her silent plea, "*I'm like you. . . . Save me from my culture*," exposes a yearning for a connection that can only be established through race, particularly because the historic animosity between China and Japan renders any real solidarity between the two nations superficial at best. Because the businessman may not recognize her "Chineseness," Rekdal must engage in a verbal performance in order to secure a racial alliance that can, potentially, link them. However, the man concentrates on the answer to his original question about nationality, ignoring Rekdal's Asian-ethnic ties by simply replying: "'American. . . . It's too bad what is happening to your country.'"[35] For this bored businessman, Rekdal is simply another American student studying abroad.

The frustration that Rekdal continually encounters over her identity and the ways in which she is seen as only an "American" erupt most passionately in an exchange with her host family sister Fumiko. When the Tanakas discover that Rekdal "love[s] traditional Japanese dancing," her host family takes her to several festivals, where, dressed in a traditional Japanese robe—the yukata—Rekdal quickly learns the steps and follows along with the other dancers.[36] However, the Tanakas view her dancing as an aberration, and Fumiko insists that because of her nationality Rekdal is unable to dance in an authentic Japanese manner:

> "[My father] says you are unusual because Americans cannot do Japanese dances."
>
> "That's true. Americans don't learn Japanese dances."
>
> "Americans cannot do Japanese dances."
>
> "They don't know Japanese dances," I said. "They could do them if they learned."
>
> Fumiko looked confused. "But Americans cannot do Japanese dances," she insisted. "They are Japanese-style, not American-style."[37]

Fumiko believes that nationality is inextricably linked to behavior—it is an essential, immutable quality that precludes one from crossing over into other cultural forms or practices; only real Japanese people can properly perform Japanese dances. When Rekdal argues that "'it's a dance. . . . You learn it by imitating it,'" Fumiko contradicts her by saying "'You can't imitate.'"[38] No matter how authentic Rekdal's performance, no matter how carefully she chooses to learn the correct movements of Japanese dance, her performance always betrays her "American style" to her Japanese hosts.

Yet Rekdal's performance of Japanese dance, along with her insistence that one can learn and imitate behavior, counters Fumiko's belief that only those with inherited Japanese ethnicity can participate in Japanese culture. Rekdal conveys the ease with which she takes part in these dances: "The dances were simple to pick up. I dipped gently and bowed in time."[39] For Rekdal, culture is learned through imitation, which does not signal inauthenticity but rather a strategy for appreciation, one that she embodies through movement. Dancing "in time," Rekdal moves in step with her fellow dancers, which makes her *like* them. Thus, Rekdal enacts the ambiguity of the simile—she is not dancing Japanese-style, but is, perhaps, dancing like the Japanese dancers. Her imitation of Japanese dance gives her license both to admire this form of Japanese culture as well as to enact it through the accuracy of her dance steps. Moreover, the emphasis on movement as performance also illustrates that Rekdal's identity, in motion, serves as a metaphor for her own fluctuating and indeterminate race.

Indeed, Rekdal's precise Japanese dance movements at an end-of-the-summer banquet propel her to pass as white in order to resist being essentialized as an exotic "Oriental." While attending a Bon Odori festival at the Colony Yacht Club, a British ex-pat haven, Rekdal and her fellow foreign scholarship students wear their yukatas and participate in the Japanese summer celebration. Stepping into the line of Bon Odori dancers, Rekdal wends her way through new dance steps by copying the older Japanese gentleman in front of her. A Japanese photographer, spying Rekdal in the line of dancers, accosts her by literally pulling her out of the dance and manipulating her body for his photo: "He began positioning my arms as if I were a doll, trying to make me dance the way I had danced in line."[40] Escaping from the photographer, Rekdal sits down next to an older white British ex-pat, hoping to calm herself. However, noting that the man "raised his glass and drank, looking me up and down."[41] Rekdal finds no comfort in his lascivious presence but is, instead, antagonized by the ex-pat, as first he tells her that her assault by the photographer was justified based on her appearance, and then he exoticizes her based on her movements: "'You managed to learn the dances. . . . You've really gone native. You know, you even have the round face. The more I look at you, the more you look Japanese.'"[42]

For the British ex-pat, Rekdal's performance of Japanese dance, along with her Japanese costume, marks her as both racialized and sexualized, because it is her Asian appearance that titillates him. Affirming the intersection of racism and sexism, Sumi Cho observes that "Asian Pacific women suffer greater harassment due to racialized ascriptions (exotic, hyper-erotic, masochistic, desirous of sexual domination) that set them up as ideal-typical gratifiers of Western neocolonial libidinal formations."[43] Dancing in the Bon Odori festival, Rekdal unwittingly reinforces an Orientalized vision of herself, thereby allowing these men to interpret her mixed race body through a sexual and racial lens that leaves her vulnerable to physical manipulation and verbal harassment. As both Cho and sociologist Yen Le Espiritu argue, Asian American female subjectivity is predicated on the intersection of racial and sexual politics so that Asian American female subjectivity always conveys hypersexuality: to be an Asian American woman is to be a sexual entity, one historically subject to white male interpretation, desire, and control.[44] For the Japanese male photographer, Rekdal becomes an exotic spectacle and an ambiguous subject—white and yet not white, Asian and yet not Asian—whose performance of Japanese dance registers as an anomaly that he wants to frame through his photographer's lens. For the British ex-pat, Rekdal's physical harassment by the photographer is warranted because she has "gone native." And as a racially ambiguous figure, one who could potentially pass as Japanese, Rekdal is simultaneously racialized and sexualized through her dance movements in the eyes of the British ex-pat, trading her innocent white American identity for an overtly sexual Asian identity, as Espiritu affirms: "As the racialized exotic 'others,' Asian American women do not fit the white-constructed notions of the feminine. Whereas white women have been depicted as chaste and dependable, Asian women have been represented as promiscuous and untrustworthy."[45]

Fleeing from the British ex-pat, Rekdal attempts to find refuge among her fellow American compatriots. However, recounting her experience to her peers elicits doubt instead of sympathy, because the American students ascribe her treatment by the ex-pat to her wearing a yukata. Rekdal's insistence that the man's comments were directed at her physical features, her face, prompts one male student to ask, "'Well, isn't your mother Oriental?'"[46] This question again positions Rekdal as a racial other and reinforces the justification for the racist remark. Only someone of dubious nationality—the mixed race Asian American—would be subject to the kinds of harassment that Rekdal has experienced, because according to Lisa Lowe, "The Asian is always seen as an immigrant, as the 'foreigner-within.'"[47] Moreover, the student's use of the word *Oriental* to signify Rekdal's mother's racial background evinces a literal figuring of Rekdal as an exotic other and foreign object in this space.

Reacting to her treatment by these various males (the photographer, the ex-pat, and the American student), Rekdal responds to their collective harassment through the act of passing:

"No," I said sharply. "No. She's American."

"Of course she's American," the American replied sarcastically, but I interrupted again.

"I mean," I continued, "that she's white. We're white. We're completely American."[48]

Far from being a simple repudiation of her Chinese ethnicity or a reflection of racial shame, Rekdal's passing validates her identity through her "insistence on its strange, misplaced patriotism."[49] Passing as "white" in order to be "American," Rekdal attempts to combat the exoticization and harassment to which she has been subjected by insisting that she is not simply a projection of male Oriental fantasies but is, instead, a person who can claim subjectivity on her own terms. Rekdal passes as a white American in an effort to make visible that which others cannot or choose not to see. In this instance her choice of a passing identity—to highlight her white identity over her Chinese heritage—challenges hypodescent constructs. Although Rekdal has falsely described her mother as white, her own claim to whiteness is a choice she is free to make as a biracial

woman. In this light, Rekdal's passing identity can be construed as challenging both essentialized racial categories as well as stereotyped visions of Asian
American female hypersexuality.

In a post-civil rights era, passing is not about choosing an identity out of
social mobility; rather, passing becomes a self-determining strategy to resist
binary identifications—a choice to move in between, in and out, back and forth,
and through racial categories. But to what degree is passing an effacement of
racial identity? Judith Butler's theorization of gender and sexual identity as
products of systems of power rather than universal absolutes is a useful corollary through which to understand the performativity of identity, passing or
otherwise. Stressing the idea that there is no essential or core identity but only
the modes of signification that occur "*on the surface* of the body," Butler notes
that "such acts, gestures, enactments, generally construed, are *performative* in
the sense that the essence or identity that they otherwise purport to express
are *fabrications* manufactured and sustained through corporeal signs and other
discursive means" [italics in original].[50] For Butler, all identity is performance;
there is no internal essence that does not accrue meaning through external
cultural, historical, and political signs, "because gender intersects with racial,
class, ethnic, sexual, and regional modalities of discursively constituted identities . . . it becomes impossible to separate out 'gender' from the political and
cultural intersections in which it is invariably produced and maintained."[51]

Moreover, we could say that the performance of passing, like that of gender
construction, destabilizes notions of race and ethnicity through the continuous reinforcement that identity entails exhibition rather than essence. Yet, if
passing stresses the performativity inherent in every act of identity, let me be
clear in emphasizing that it is the ineffaceable reality of race that guides the
experience of passing itself. Although race may be said to be a social construct,
an illusion based on a collective will to believe in the concept of race, it remains
one of the primary measures of identification that we use to categorize people,
especially those we are meeting for the first time because, to quote Michael
Omi and Howard Winant, "We utilize race to provide clues about *who* a person
is. . . . Without a racial identity, one is in danger of having no identity" [ital-
ics in original].[52] The ambiguous bodies of mixed race people position them
at the crossroads of racial interpretation; their embodiment of myriad racial
identity markers undermines any notions of racial unity or purity. Multiracial
subjects resist normative categorizations of race by using ambiguity as a mode
of identity that revels in the multiple rather than the singular, affirming the
reality of fluidity rather than the falsity of the fixed. Beyond being a strategy of
identity, passing upends a compulsory racial identity of white normativity as
well as subverts hypodescent constructs. Mixed race people, like Rekdal, enact

a passing subjectivity that troubles our belief in any stable or static notion of racial identification.

Ruth Ozeki's *My Year of Meats*

Jane Takagi-Little, the protagonist of Ruth Ozeki's postmodern novel *My Year of Meats*, extols the virtues of racial hybridity and globalization when musing about race: "Being half, I am evidence that race, too, will become relic. Eventually we're all going to be brown, sort of. Some days, when I'm feeling grand, I feel brand-new—like a prototype. Back in the olden days, my dad's ancestors got stuck behind the Alps and my mom's on the east side of the Urals. Now, oddly, I straddle this blessed, ever-shrinking world."[53] Yet despite these auspicious pronouncements at the beginning of the novel, Ozeki crafts a narrative that remains skeptical of such easy transnational and transracial celebrations. Instead, the themes that permeate Ozeki's first novel recall her earlier work as a documentary filmmaker: a sense of ambiguity, fragmentation, skepticism, and self-reflexivity on the topics of race, gender, capitalism, and sex, particularly as these forces mix and intersect in a global arena. The plot of *My Year of Meats* focuses on Jane, a half-Japanese, half-white American woman, whose first-person point of view forms the bulk of the book, as she recounts, retrospectively, the year she spent working on a Japanese television show, *My American Wife!* Jane is first hired as a coordinator and then promoted to be director of the show, which is broadcast Saturday mornings in Japan and is sponsored by an American lobby group called BEEF-EX. The novel alternates between various locales in the United States and Tokyo, just as it alternates between Jane's first-person narration and the third-person perspective of the various wives who cross her path. As Jane creates these television episodes, designed to showcase an American wife making an American meal featuring a main protein (preferably beef), she learns about the dangers of mass cattle manufacturing and the links among the consumption of meat, women, and media.

My Year of Meats follows several traditional narratological conventions: it has a protagonist, an antagonist (in the form of a Japanese ad executive, Junichi "John" Ueno), a clear chronology (although it does rely on flashback), a definite setting (the United States and Japan) and time frame (the central plot of the novel begins in January 1991 and ends one year later), and even employs the literary device of a *deux ex machina*, which takes the shape of Jane's answering machine. Yet, many elements in the novel defy and trouble singular generic classification, because *My Year of Meats* is a postmodern work, one that incorporates memos, faxes, song lyrics, script treatments, newspaper clippings, and extended quotations from Sei Shonagon's *Pillow Book* into the plot. These elements, coupled with the use of footnotes, a bibliography, and a polemical message that warns against the dangers of eating mass-produced beef in the United States (due to the hormones injected in beef, most infamously DES), marries various genres: memoir, protest novel, picaresque, dissertation, and *kunstleroman*.[54]

But beyond its postmodern tag and its didacticism, the novel also passes as autobiography in many respects.[55] Similar to the ambiguity of genres within Rekdal's work, *My Year of Meats* blurs the actual biography of author Ruth Ozeki with the fictional biography of the novel's protagonist Jane Takagi-Little. Lanser, writing about narrative voice, structure, and the issue of attachment that we, the reader, place on texts, notes how the "I" of a fictional narrator can often be confused for the "I" of the author, a state she refers to as "*equivocal*—literally *equi-vocal*—for they not only manifest but, I submit, *rely for their meaning on* complex and ambiguous relationships between the 'I' of the author and any textual voice. The 'I' that characterizes literary discourse, in other words, is always potentially severed from *and* potentially tethered to the author's 'I'" [italics in original].[56] In the case of *My Year of Meats*, the autobiographical elements gleaned from within the text enhance its status as an equivocal text, because the resemblance between author and narrator makes distinguishing between the "I" voice of author and protagonist problematic. Both Ozeki and Jane are biracial women whose Japanese mothers married white American men from small midwestern farming towns. Both author and protagonist lived in Japan for a period of time, where they became fluent in Japanese. Both have worked as independent filmmakers and for transnational corporations in ways they felt were ultimately at odds with their own belief systems.[57] There are moments when the first-person voice of Jane can be confused with the voice of the novel's author, Ozeki, a situation exacerbated both by the homodiegetic narration as well as a tendency to read Asian American literature as veiled autobiography or ethnography.[58]

The slippage between author and protagonist is made more pronounced by the novel's conclusion, which ends with Jane talking about having written the book we, the readers, hold in our hands. The "author's note" that follows the last page of the novel proper and that introduces readers to the novel's "bibliography" states that "although this book is a novel, and therefore purely a work of my imagination, as a lapsed documentarian I feel compelled to include a bibliography of the sources I have relied on to provoke these fictions.—J.T.L."[59] Is this author's note purportedly penned by Jane Takagi-Little and hence still part of the fiction of *My Year of Meats*? Is Ozeki making a tongue-in-cheek reference, playing with genres of fiction and nonfiction as well as playing with conventions of narrative? Is this a work that is passing back and forth between novel and autobiography, between fiction and documentary, between entertainment and education? Much like her main protagonist, or even the author herself, *My Year of Meats* is a hybrid work, one that contains different moments of passing, whose heterogeneous form reflects both an ambiguity of genre and hermeneutics as well as the passing identity enacted by its main protagonist, Jane.

For Ozeki, like Rekdal, passing reflects both the mobile subjectivity of her narrator, Jane, as well as the reality of globalization in a rapidly expanding world: nothing stays still. Rapid technological advances have increased our ability to communicate, to conduct commerce, and to consume products and media images. We allow so many things to pass through our lives, and we, in turn, pass through various worlds via our television screens, our personal computers, our smart phones, and the multiple regions (local as well as global) that we fly to and from. Passing becomes a state of being for the narrator Jane, one that reflects her postmodern global framework as well as her biracial status. Jane is a character on the move—continually passing from one state to another, in terms geographic as well as emotional and mental. When readers are first introduced to her, she is lying rigid in an apartment without any heat. But the minute the phone rings, Jane propels herself out of bed and begins her search for the perfect American wives and the most tantalizing American meat dishes. Ozeki portrays Jane as an active character—she hustles, she runs, she swears, she films—in the words of literary critic Cheryl Fish, "Jane epitomizes a mobile feminist American activist of mixed-race parentage."[60]

Jane is also self-consciously aware of her multiraciality, and she interjects reflections about her biraciality or, Ozeki's term, "hybridity" throughout the novel. Like Rekdal, Jane animates her mobile subjectivity through acts of passing—of ambiguous movements but also of the enigmatic ways she is read and interpreted by others. Passing, for Jane, becomes a strategy of identity rather than signifying betrayal or loyalty. Her passing reflects her place in a globalized world where the local refers to both the small towns where Jane films her American wives as well as the home space of Japanese housewives watching their American counterparts on Sunday morning television. Through the television set, space occupied by both American and Japanese women collapse—two countries on two continents contained in one television show. Similarly, Jane's identity collapses American and Japanese cultural and ethnic signs within her multiracial body. Her circumnavigations of the globe and her circulations throughout the United States are facilitated by her chameleon-like abilities to transform according to circumstances; her racial ambiguity allows her to pass through different states of being.

Although Rekdal continually catalogs the ways she is mis-read as white and not recognized for her Chinese ethnic features, Jane's Japanese ethnicity is consistently commented on by other characters in the text as well as by literary critics.[61] In Jane's case, the context in which she is placed for much of the novel, namely in the company of her Japanese film crew, positions her as Japanese or Japanese American; she is coded through both language and the bodies of others. Aside from Jane's self-description over the phone to her future lover Sloan, "'I'm tall. Very tall, pole thin. . . . Green eyes, shaped like my Japanese mother's with her epicanthic fold. . . . Brown hair. . . . Short but respectable.'" Jane's physical details are limited to being described, by others (and sometimes by herself), as Japanese, even though she periodically refers to herself as hybrid, as mutant, as mixed, or as half.[62]

Literary critic Monica Chiu observes that "[Jane] is a physical, intensely public reminder of the ways in which hybrid bodies represent bifurcated, multiply constituted, and thus visibly notable disruptions to homogenous systems whose smooth operations rely on the suppression of such difference."[63] As Chiu notes, racially ambiguous people disrupt institutions and systems by being very physical reminders of difference. Hence, Jane's passing demonstrates the restlessness of mixed heritage people who reject the status quo while agitating for alternative spaces and places. Multiracial people remind society of their indistinct nature; they are neither the promise of a new world nor its condemnation. Cultural critic Elena Tajima Creef cautions against simplistic celebrations of the mixed race person as a salvational figure. Through her attentive close readings of several multiracial bodies (both textual and visual), Creef warns against those "who find pleasure in the deliberate confusing and mixing of boundaries in their often complex, mixed-race genealogies," because, in Creef's analysis, a language of exile, loss, domination, and racism predominates in the works of multiracial authors.[64]

Indeed, *My Year of Meats* does lapse into a type of Disneyfied celebration of multiculturalism, at least upon a surface reading, through its characterization of the multiethnic and interracial couples and families Jane encounters during her travels. Yet the novel makes clear that a social justice agenda undergirds Jane's documentarian motivations. From the first chapter, Jane believes that her work for *My American Wife!* will serve a higher purpose: "I wanted to think that some girl would watch my shows in Japan, now or maybe even a thousand years from now and be inspired to and learn something real about America."[65] Jane's own hybridity spurs her to show something "real" about America, because Jane wants to depict the United States as racially diverse rather than phenotypically homogenous. The wives Jane selects reflect a wide swath of American life: a Mexican immigrant woman in Texas, a Cajun white woman in Mississippi, a Polish American woman in Indiana, a white–black lesbian couple in Massachusetts, and a white Texas former stripper turned housewife in Colorado. Jane's vision of diversity, and the range of women and families who constitute her racially mixed picture of America, comes directly from her experiences as a multiracial person. Jane cannot contain her idea of America to a single perspective; as someone who is biracial she is continually using it as a metaphor to discuss the ways in which she is split, halved, bifurcated. By challenging normative categories of race, Jane's assertion of her multiple racial subjectivities allows her to escape being fixed by any one person's preconceived notions of who she should be. More important, for the purposes of this chapter, Jane's multiracial- ity allows her to pass through many different states, paradigms, and perspec- tives; it allows her to change her identity in order to operate in the world.

Indeed, Jane credits her biracial identity as the key to her media success: "Being racially 'half'—neither here nor there—I was uniquely suited to the niche I was to occupy in the television industry."[66] Jane's passing identity facilitates her work on *My American Wife!* because she describes herself in the opening chapter not as a filmmaker or a documentarian but as someone who can pass back and forth for commercial purposes, declaring herself to be "a useful go-between, a cultural pimp, selling off the vast illusion of America to a cramped population on that small string of Pacific islands."[67] Yet Jane is not entirely ironic or cynical toward her work on *My American Wife!*; instead, optimism underpins her reasons for taking on the role of cultural go-between: "I had spent so many years, in both Japan and America, floundering in a miasma of misinformation about culture and race, I was determined to use this window into mainstream network television to *educate.* Perhaps it was naïve, but I believed, honestly, that I could use wives to sell meat in the service of a Larger Truth" [italics and capitalization in original].[68]

Despite Jane's professed idealism, she is still caught between the goals of the BEEF-EX sponsor, namely to generate sales of US imported beef in Japan, and her own social activist agenda of promoting a more diverse and hence "authen- tic" vision of American life.[69] As much as Jane's passing identity facilitates her work as a producer, she cannot escape the ways that her body becomes defined by others. Lowe, in discussing interpellation and its ideological functions, claims that "a subject may be multiply hailed by several ideologies whose con- ditions of production are heterogeneous and incommensurable."[70] Jane wants to act as a conduit for social justice, yet she also acknowledges herself to be a "cultural pimp"; she is interpellated as both crusading documentarian and sell- out producer. Thus, when Jane encounters the African American Dawes family, the tension between these two images collide, and she is forced to see herself through the eyes of others and confront the fact that her motives may not be as noble as she believes them to be.

Mrs. Helen Dawes, or "Miss Helen" as Jane consistently refers to her as in the text, lives in the small town of Harmony, Mississippi. When Jane initially con- tacts Miss Helen by phone to convince her to allow the crew to film inside her church, Miss Helen responds by saying, "'I don't think we ever had no white per- son inside of our church before,'" to which Jane replies, "'Well, we're not techni- cally white, Miss Helen. We're Japanese, so really we're mostly yellow.'"[71] Because their exchange is mediated by the telephone, without benefit of visual signifiers,

Miss Helen's identifies Jane as white, causing Jane unintentionally to pass. Miss Helen bases her definition not on an ocular confirmation of Jane or the crew's racial identity but by assumptions of vocal cues and, perhaps, regional codes, because Jane more than likely would have introduced herself as calling from New York. Jane's assertion that she is Japanese and hence yellow rather than white attempts to allay Miss Helen's concerns and potentially ally herself with Miss Helen as a fellow woman of color, especially because Jane and her crew are not white and hence not part of an American hegemonic power structure that has institutionally oppressed African Americans within the United States for centuries. But they cannot fully identify with the historic place and existential space of embodying a black body in the United States, and they may benefit from their indeterminate place on a racial spectrum that continues to affirm black abjection and white supremacy. According to literary critic Leslie Bow, "Attempts to fix ambiguous status along a black-white continuum reveal both the subtle and less-than-subtle work of white supremacy."[72] The exchange between Jane and Miss Helen most tellingly reveals the inability to define the place of Asians in America along a fixed color line. Asian Americans exist in a state of racial ambiguity because of their inability to be coherently interpreted by others.[73] Again to quote Bow: "Asian social status becomes adjudicated within the space between 'not black' and 'not white.' It is simultaneously a signifier of objective distance and non belonging."[74] Because Jane cannot escape the fact that she is not black, she chooses yellow as a metaphor to designate the ambiguous status of being Japanese–Japanese American within a US black–white racial hierarchy.

Yet this racial proclamation is not completely accurate in Jane's case, because she *is* half-white. Growing up in a small midwestern town as the only multiracial Asian American person, Jane may not have completely fit in, but she did manage to grow up relatively free of racial hostility and thereby accrued a measure of white privilege, enhanced by being the daughter of a local white man.[75] Like the transnational and transracial Asian American adoptees of chapter 2, Jane is protected by the umbrella of her father's white privilege. Claiming a Japanese and hence yellow designation for the sake of convincing Miss Helen to take part in *My American Wife!* is part of a confidence game that Jane plays, one she continues when she visits Harmony and introduces herself and John Ueno to the members of Miss Helen's black church:

> "We have come all the way from Japan to make a television program to teach the Japanese people about America. Miss Helen Dawes and her family have generously agreed to help us, and she asked us here today to meet you, because you are part of her family. We believe that people all over the world should try to learn about each other and understand each

other, and that is what our television program is about, so I am here to ask you to share your faith with the people of Japan."[76]

In this moment and in this space, Jane uses her racial ambiguity to pass as Japanese. Embodying the role of Japanese ambassador, Jane's "It's-a-small-world" diplomacy and misleading statement—that she has traveled a far distance in order to reach out to the people of Harmony, Mississippi—relies on a language of movement to elicit an emotional connection with her audience.

Jane passes as Japanese over the phone with Miss Helen and in front of the congregation to gain their trust and thus to use their racially marked bodies in service to her vision of a diverse America. Yet Helen Dawes and her family are no more or less an authentic representation of American life than Becky Thayer, the other wife-candidate Jane has to interview because she must vet two wives for each episode. Even before she visits Harmony, Jane has convinced herself that Miss Helen is the only viably authentic choice because she believes white inn-keeper Becky Thayer and her family to be plastic and self-promoting. The Thayers' town, Magnolia Springs, is "a small but well-known town along the plantation tour circuit"; with their bed and breakfast, antique collection, and other business ventures, the Thayers hope to "to increase their exposure," especially for "Japanese tourists, part of the *Gone With the Wind* boom that had mysteriously swept that country."[77] For Jane, the Thayers are fake because they actively and consciously seek increased business to their inn, exploiting different trends for capitalist gains. Furthermore, the dish that Becky Thayer intends to make, "an exotic Chicken-fried Steak Orientale," clearly appropriates an ethnic cuisine for crass commercial purposes rather than out of any legitimate ancestral lineage.[78]

By contrast Miss Helen's nine African American children, her working-class husband, her attendance in her black church, and her famous chitterlings recipe all signal authenticity for Jane. The real differences between the Daweses and the Thayers are socioeconomic as much as racial or cultural, yet one family is not more authentically American because of their class or race. Although the Thayers may be openly opportunistic, they are not inauthentic in their desire for capital accumulation or social mobility. In fact, as Thorstein Veblen's *The Theory of the Leisure Class* confirms, the Thayers' pursuit of self-promotion and conspicuous consumption may, indeed, make them uniquely American. Despite Jane's good intentions, her desire to capture the authenticity of the Dawes family frames them into a potentially stereotyped portrait of a southern working-class black family. Finally, the whole question of authenticity becomes upended by Jane's own passing identity: her mixed race subjectivity as one who is neither "authentically" Japanese nor "authentically" American. According to critic Nina Cornyetz, "In both macrocosmic and microcosmic form, the questions of cultural authenticity and authority are themselves, moreover, put into question, for example, by Jane's own simultaneous belonging and non-belonging to two cultures and races at once—being neither one nor the other, yet repeatedly representing the one to the other as cultural authority/native informant."[79]

Ultimately Jane's movements in Harmony are limited through the manner in which she passes herself off to the Daweses, particularly once she has lost their trust when Ueno overrides her decision and chooses the Thayers. Yet Ozeki makes clear that Jane's constant movements throughout the narrative signal her character's growing education about herself, her impact on others, as well as her awareness of the dangers of beef consumption in the United States. In particular, the links between factory-farmed cattle and hazardous pharmaceuticals lead to Jane's transformation from self-professed "cultural pimp" to global crusader. Jane's passing in and out of different identities—Japanese, American, mixed race, documentarian, corporate flunky, consumer activist—are fueled by her multiraciality. Writing of her inability to remain fixed by either conviction or geographic space, Jane muses, "I've always blamed my tendency to vacillate on my mixed ethnicity. Halved, I am neither here nor there, and my understanding of the relativity inherent in the world is built into my genes."[80] Jane directly attributes her multiraciality as allowing her to pass in and out of various identities: being biracial informs her multiple perspectives. As one who passes, Jane's racial ambiguity and mobile subjectivity becomes reflected, at novel's end, by Ozeki's self-conscious awareness that like the main protagonist and narrator, *My Year of Meats* is also a work that passes: "There's no denying, I thought. In the Year of Meats, truth wasn't stranger than fiction; it *was* fiction. Ma says I'm neither here nor there, and if that's the case, so be it. Half documentarian, half fabulist. . . . Maybe sometimes you have to make things up, to tell truths that alter outcomes" [italics in original].[81]

Ambiguous Movements in "Traveling to Opal"

To pass is to question the fiction of racial categories *and* to recognize the ways that race is embodied, both as a social construction and as a lived reality. "In a racially ordered, racially invested society," observes Teresa Kay Williams, "the social phenomenon of passing has often been one of the few strategies available to, and utilized by, multiracial individuals to escape the detrimental impact of race."[82] However, I am neither valorizing nor celebrating passing in a post-civil rights era as a simple means of challenging racial prescriptions. Passing is movement, and as such it inherently connotes impermanence, transience, fluctuation. Although this may be useful for upending rigid definitions and hierarchies of race, the actual passing subject is constantly moving and thus potentially perpetually restless and rootless. Unlike previous models of passing narratives, the consequences for racially ambiguous Asian American subjects who pass are not betrayal and tragedy but indeterminacy and instability.[83] Indeed, in the case of Rekdal, although her performance of a passing identity in "Americans Abroad" liberates her from restrictions to her identity (gender, racial, national, ethnic) that others attempt to place on her, it also exacerbates her unease and discomfort as an outsider, for she cannot fit herself into others' concepts and definitions of herself. In Jane's case, liminality and instability have consistently marked her life—the choices available to her as well as the choices she makes. Although the novel ends on a relatively positive note, Ozeki carefully tempers that happy ending with a reminder of Jane's status as a DES daughter and with Jane's first-person ruminations on the fact that a happy ending cannot simply be willed by being written; rather, reality dictates a "wait-and-see" policy—a state of suspension.

Yet passing as a strategy of resistance remains a powerful means for mixed race subjects to challenge monoracial designations by making apparent their bi- or multiple-racial identities at all times; by passing one consciously chooses a reality of racial ambiguity over the fiction of racial stability. Like literary critic Gayle Wald, I believe that while "passing is problematic as a paradigm of 'resistance,' it nevertheless renders visible the conditions that produced identities as sites of struggle."[84] A passing identity that continues to move across all boundaries challenges totalizing narratives that restrict and constrict one's ability to self-identify as multiple rather than singular: it is the choice of heterogeneity over homogeneity, a subversion of both the one-drop rule of hypodescent and rigid definitions of ethnic nationalism. Because passing is based on ambiguity, mixed race subjects must embody the racial identity that they choose to pass into, and their bodies must also contain the hint of racial uncertainty. Questions of authenticity or subterfuge no longer adhere to passing subjects because "in the dynamics of passing one cannot worry about being exposed as either the real thing or the fraud, for passing contaminates the distinction between the two."[85]

By way of concluding this chapter, let me end with a discussion of ambiguous movements in the last essay of Rekdal's collection, "Traveling to Opal." The piece begins with Rekdal setting out for Natchez, Mississippi, to look for traces of her Great Aunt Opal, who died in Seattle four years prior to Rekdal's southern sojourn. Newly moved to Atlanta with her partner, Rekdal fills her unoccupied time with daytrips and daydreams. Her restlessness—her movements—propel her toward family history: "I was investigating the history of Po Po's sister, Opal, who had lived in Natchez in the early part of the century with her husband, a Chinese grocer whom she divorced and ran away to Seattle to avoid."[86] Although this is the ostensible reason that Rekdal gives for her journey, the larger point of her trip seems less an investigation about Opal and more a way to give movement and hence meaning to Rekdal's own internal struggles over being a mixed race Asian American in the South, a place that historically has understood race along a black–white axis. An outsider by region as well as race, Rekdal's preoccupation with finding hints of Opal speak more to her own nebulous understanding of herself than to her pursuit of material evidence of Opal's brief existence in Natchez.

For example, when Rekal queries a Visitor's Center employee about whether there is or has ever been a Chinese community in Natchez, the woman's confused and careful reply, "'There's just us. Just Natchez . . . Everyone—blacks, whites, Chinese, we're all in here together,'"[87] leads Rekdal to parse the cloudiness of this woman's statement as she walks away from the center: "It is difficult for me to interpret her remark: does she mean that Natchez was simply too small to have distinct communities, or that Natchez is not—has not ever been—segregated by the virtue of being free-thinking, liberal Natchez?"[88] Rekdal cannot decipher the precise meaning of this woman's remark, so she keeps moving. And it is her movements—driving in the car, walking down the sidewalk, flipping through photographs at the Historic Natchez Foundation, and literally passing through various civic offices (city hall, the library, and the visitor's center)—that inspire her thoughts on race and identity. Her every movement incites more speculation about herself: "Every time I turn around here I am confronted with another way I might perceive myself—a kaleidoscope view with a million glittering edges."[89] As the visual language and analogies that Rekdal uses makes clear, a reliance on the ocular is a fragmenting proposition, particularly for a biracial woman searching for traces of a Chinese American relative in the US South.

Travel gives meaning to Rekdal's movements and to her very identity. By literally propelling herself into space while searching for Opal, Rekdal enacts her mobile subjectivity, because who she is changes as she passes through the town of Natchez and encounters herself being encountered by others. Calling a local Natchez figure on the phone, Rekdal is confronted with his speculation about whether she, herself, is Chinese.[90] She describes being stared at by men in a diner and cannot decide if it's due to her racial features or her gender.[91] She notices a couple, tourists of Chinese background, who receive hard stares from fellow gambling patrons aboard a casino riverboat, and Rekdal recognizes the looks they receive as the same type of gaze she has been subjected to during her trip.[92] Unlike in previous essays, where Rekdal has commented on the lack of recognition people have of her mixed status, through her many different movements in Natchez she continually narrates others' awareness of her Chineseness—her racial ambiguity. Her passing, in this essay, takes the form of identifying as Chinese and of taking on the role of Chinese American researcher, searching for her aunt but also trying to find her own place as a biracial Chinese American, and perhaps even as an Asian American woman in the South.

When Rekdal does find proof of her aunt's existence in Natchez, it arrives in the form of two photographs of Great-Aunt Opal's ex-husband, T. E. Wang, with their two children. Although Opal's image is absent in these photos, the address and name on the back of the pictures affirm that they did belong to her.[93] Copies of the Natchez phone books further confirm that a T. E. and Opal Wang lived above the grocery store that they owned from 1912 to 1929. Rekdal has at last found physical evidence of her aunt, but it is telling that it is an absent presence that she has found, because the only true remnant of Opal is in the bracketed textual notation next to her husband's name in a set of crumbling phone books.[94]

Though Rekdal may feel that her Chineseness is easily overshadowed by her more dominant Anglo features, like her unrelenting search for signs of Opal, Rekdal is determined to assert her biraciality: "When I think of those hard, irritated stares I get sometimes from white strangers who discover my racial background in conversation or by accident, when I recall a man telling me angrily I shouldn't talk about it because it isn't important, I rebel. I become like Opal: I start to talk and talk about all the embarrassing things. This is the past, yes. But it is the present, too, and the future; wishing race out of existence is not the same as its simply not existing."[95] It is in conversation and in movement that Rekdal identifies herself, even if others do not see her as she *feels* herself to be.

In the very last pages of the essay, Rekdal invokes the simile of movement to discuss the ambiguity of her mixed race position: "I find that race is not really a choice for me, either, like traveling to one town and not to another. . . . For me to choose to become one ethnicity so that I can define myself for strangers is to fall victim to a monolithic, constructed idea of race that nothing in my personal history would support as true. . . . Ethnicity, for me, is not Chinese America versus white America. . . . I cannot choose one identity without losing half of myself."[96] As Rekdal notes in the previous passage, she is not content to sit still with a single racial designation but instead fails to make a choice that would only limit her full subjectivity. Her biracial identity is irreducible to quantitative divisions of half and half; instead, she is a sum that is more than the combined parts of her parental ancestries. For Rekdal, any "monolithic, constructed idea of race" cannot accurately or adequately reflect what is true about her experiences as a mixed race woman.

Furthermore the "truth" about race, like the truth-value in texts, lies not in their adherence to a monolithic or absolute facticity or singular generic definitions. Just as it is impossible to parse out the parts of Rekdal's identity into Chinese and white, so too is it impossible to parse out the moments in her essays that are factual and hence authentic to her experiences and lived reality versus the moments that she embellishes and fabricates as part of her craft as a creative writer. Similarly, in *My Year of Meats*, there are slippages between the "I" of the first-person narrator Jane Takagi-Little and the "I" of the flesh-and-blood author Ruth Ozeki. As an equivocal text, one that embeds facts about DES and factory farming into an invented story about a mixed race woman, the fiction of *My Year of Meats* like the fiction of race is not easy to dismiss as being not truthful because it is a creative construction. Understanding the "truth" of race like the "truth" of fiction is less a function of pure facts than about the power of fiction to tell truthful stories, and the ability to move in and out of fact and fiction, like the generic porousness of Rekdal's and Ozeki's texts, demonstrates that both creative works and racial identities can be ambiguously constructed.

Movement, travel, passing—these themes permeate both Rekdal's essays and Ozeki's novel, because they gesture to the ambiguity of the narrators' mixed race subject positions. Therefore, as a strategy for resistance, it is important to read Rekdal and Ozeki's works not simply as examples for how multiracial people should identify but as a type of theorizing about racial identity formation that promotes a richer understanding of multiracial subjectivity. Indeed, for critic Kandice Chuh, it is crucial to read Asian American literature in this manner because "this move of defining Asian American literature as theory potentially effects both the disruption of the multiculturalist sedimentation of Asian American and other minoritized literatures as seemingly transparent vehicles of authentic otherness, and the unbounding of 'theory.'"[97] Rekdal's essays and Ozeki's novel, viewed as theoretical interventions in mixed heritage discourse, provide a useful analysis for understanding mixed race identity through passing, one in which movement replaces the ocular as the central analytic for understanding passing. And the need for such analysis is critical because issues of multiraciality will only increase as the year 2043 approaches, the projected date when white Anglo-Saxon Americans will cease to constitute the majority race in the United States, and issues of ontology will cease to be merely academic exercises but instead will have political, legal, social, and cultural ramifications for everyone in US society. Whether passing is ultimately libratory, subversive, or a means of gaining and maintaining privilege, the concept of passing will change and shift as we continue to move and progress into the twenty-first century.

5

Transgressive Texts and Ambiguous Authors

Racial Ambiguity in Asian American Literature

At the 2008 Association of Asian American Studies (AAAS) conference awards banquet, the prize for best work of Asian American fiction was given to James Janko's *Buffalo Boy and Geronimo* (2006).[1] When Janko, a white American man in his mid-fifties, strode up to the podium, I heard murmurs of confusion and consternation from surrounding tables. A friend turned to me and asked, "Is that a white guy who just won the award for Asian American fiction?" I nodded my head slowly and in the days following the banquet polled people for their reactions to Janko's winning this award. The Asian American literary scholars I spoke with, in person and by e-mail, were baffled and uncomfortable with the Asian American fiction award going to a white American author—to someone who did not appear to identify as Asian American. And I must confess that I shared the initial sentiments of my tablemates, friends, and colleagues in academia. No one I knew had read his novel, so we were not questioning the literary merits of his work; rather, our reaction was due to the fact that a white American writer had just won an Asian American fiction award.

In the months following the banquet, I have mused on what this award signals for the field of Asian American literature; officially the AAAS, a professional organization of scholars, students, and activists working in Asian American studies, has now recognized a non–Asian American author as producing a valid work of Asian American creative writing. Although I do believe, from an intellectual point of view, that Asian American epistemology should be inherently anti-essentialist, emotionally I felt uncomfortable when Janko won the fiction prize. I believe my visceral reaction stemmed from my awareness of the myriad ways in which Asian American voices have been silenced and marginalized by white supremacist forces in US history and society—the ways in which Asians in America have had themselves represented by white Americans often for purposes of vilification (anti-Asian propaganda during World War II, the Korean War, and the war in Viet Nam come to mind). I am all too aware of the double bind that Asian American writers face—that they are often pigeonholed into being "race" writers; damned if they weave an ethnic tale and damned if they step outside their ethnic and racial backgrounds in their creative endeavors.[2]

When sorting out my reaction to the 2008 AAAS fiction award, I recognize that I am also trying to understand how my knowledge of Asian Americans is transmitted through texts that we, the gatekeepers of academia and shapers of literary canons, call Asian American literature. This chapter addresses the racial ambiguity of categories and knowledge production: Can a non–Asian American author pen a work of literature that is defined or described as Asian American, and can this work produce legitimate knowledge about Asian Americans? Specifically, I turn to an investigation of racially ambiguous literature, "transgressive texts," texts in which the identity of the author does not correspond with the identity of the main protagonist or main characters of the work in question. According to literary critic Shelley Fisher Fishkin, transgressive texts are those "in which black writers create serious white protagonists, and white writers black ones."[3] Although Fishkin's study concentrates on African American–white transgressive texts, she acknowledges in a footnote that the theme of transgressive texts is applicable to other ethnic American literatures, like Asian American.[4] Taking Fishkin's central conceit, the disjunction between the body of the author and the body of the text, this chapter questions the racial ambiguity embedded within transgressive texts, particularly in determining their contribution to Asian American epistemology. Furthermore, which bodies matter more when trying to define Asian American literature, the bodies of the writers who create the material or the bodies of the characters who populate the fiction? And what is at stake in defining Asian American literature by either/ both the writer and/or the material? How does knowledge about Asian Americans become produced in and through Asian American literature? Who are the recipients of this knowledge—scholars, students, general readers?—and what is the responsibility of academics in evaluating Asian American creative fiction as forms of knowledge?

The questions raised by transgressive texts are entangled in ambiguity because neither the authors nor the novels can be definitively claimed as Asian American; the disconnection between the identity of the author and the content of the work presents multiple interpretations, manifold meanings, and a plurality of responses. Nothing is lucid or clear when trying to determine the value of transgressive texts to Asian American epistemology, yet I want to investigate what scholars and teachers of Asian American literature may find productive about imagining these works as Asian American literature. In his analysis of Nam Le's short story collection *The Boat*, literary critic Christopher Lee asks, "What does it mean to read a text whose identity is ambiguous by referencing the intellectual and political traditions of Asian American Studies?"[5] In similar fashion, this chapter asks how transgressive texts reflect racial ambiguity and how this ambiguity forces scholars to redefine their understanding of what constitutes the canon of Asian American literature as based on content versus authorial subjectivity. Moreover, how does understanding transgressive texts as a type of racial ambiguity help us to theorize about Asian American literature and the knowledge produced in and through these texts?

Canonical Questions in Asian American Literature: Which Bodies Matter More?

Asian American literature—what constitutes it, who writes it, how to define it—has been debated, discussed, and contested from the publication of the first collections of Asian American writing in the early 1970s to the present-day conference proceedings of the annual meeting of AAAS. The term "Asian American" stakes a claim in the United States through its invocation of nationality, which Sau-ling Cynthia Wong believes is important because "by 'claiming America,' I refer to establishing the Asian Americanist presence in the context of the United States' national cultural legacy and contemporary cultural production."[6] Anchoring Asian American studies in the United States becomes an important element in fighting the stereotype of Asian Americans (many of whom are second-generation Americans and beyond) as perpetual foreigners and aliens. Yet even this rooting of Asian American literature in US soil does not stabilize its meaning; according to Susan Koshy, because "Asian American literature inhabits the highly unstable temporality of the 'about-to-be,' its meanings continuously reinvented after the arrival of new groups of immigrants," the sense of a cohesive Asian American polity or literary canon is not tethered to an unchanging past but is, instead, connected to an ever-fluctuating present.[7] Thus, Asian American literature is as much subject to issues of time as well as space.

Another dimension to consider when trying to define Asian American literature is how the field of Asian American studies developed, because Asian American literature and literary studies is tied to the formation of the category "Asian American." As already noted in this book's introduction, the coinage of "Asian American" was a means of claiming identity grounded in a language of the nation-state in order to discard the colonizing and racist phrase "Oriental," but beyond just claiming a new name, "Asian American" was a social justice call to arms, one intimately linked with the Third World strikes, anti–Vietnam

War protests, and pan-racial civil rights agitation during the 1960s and early 1970s.[8] Scholars who study and teach Asian American literature first emerged through this crucible of protest and human rights, so the attention to social justice as far as the interrogation and analysis of texts marked and labeled as Asian American literature (which generally speaking were understood as texts written by people of Asian descent in the United States about Asian descent people living in the United States) has always been with an understanding that scholars were pushing at the boundaries of the Western, Eurocentric, white male canon of literature. To offer a course in a university setting on Asian American literature meant questioning the very nature of canonicity and what counts as authorized knowledge in an institution of higher learning.

Given the political, activist beginnings of Asian American literary studies, it is no surprise that Asian American literature has also typically taken on political dimensions within the larger publishing world as well as in institutions of higher learning. The editors of *Aiiieeeee! An Anthology of Asian-American Writers*, one of the first collections of Asian American creative writing, made bold claims for defining Asian American literature by including only authors who, as the editors assert in the introduction, exhibit a sensibility favoring American culture blended with an understanding of racial discrimination faced by those of Asian ancestry living in the United States. Frank Chin, Jeffrey Paul Chan, Lawson Inada, and Shawn Wong, the editors of the 1974 *Aiiieeeee!*, were pioneers in the field of Asian American literature not only for discovering and collecting Asian American writing under a single rubric but also in creating the first theory toward an Asian American aesthetics. Most notably, in their 1991 follow-up anthology *The Big Aiiieeeee!: An Anthology of Chinese American and Japanese American Literature*, Asian American provocateur Frank Chin boldly laid out prescriptions for Asian American literature in his controversial introduction, "Come All Ye Asians of the Real and the Fake."[9] In this essay, Chin definitively claims that Asian American literature should promote a masculine, positive, and virile vision of Asian Americanness and that this literature should be defined as writings by Asian Americans about Asian American experiences set in the United States and written in English.

Chin's essay garnered severe criticism for its sexism but also for its intractable definition of what constitutes "real" Asian American writings. Yet his literary prescriptions can perhaps be seen as a reaction to an exponential growth in Asian American literary production, literature classes, and literary criticism. Both the publication of Asian American literature and the field of Asian American literary studies emerged simultaneously in the mid-1970s and 1980s. Creative works written by authors of Asian ancestry, like John Okada and Hisaye Yamamoto, were being rediscovered and republished, while newer writers, such as Maxine Hong Kingston and Amy Tan, were published and consumed by both general readers and college students who had these texts assigned in various courses.[10] Indeed, the success of student activists in the 1970s led to the growth of Asian American literary studies offered in college campuses across the nation, which in turn led to scholars publishing Asian American literary criticism based on the emergence and recovery of Asian American literary voices.

Today the field of Asian American literary production, both from a creative and critical point of view, has exponentially increased. Where once upon a time in the not-so-distant past it was possible to read both the entire canon of Asian American literature and Asian American literary criticism, today both the genre of Asian American literature and the analysis of this creative writing has grown beyond the ability of a scholar to read the entirety of either field. Additionally the content of both Asian American literature and literary studies has shifted from the purely representational to engage with matters more aesthetic and theoretical. Whereas early Asian American works—those that had been redis-covered and republished or recovered and published for the first time—typically depict immigrant scenarios of linguistic difficulties, employment discrimina-tion, racist state practices, cultural confusion, and generational conflict, today's Asian American fiction may encompass those themes or may simply describe life as a con man in New York City,[11] mourning the death of one's mother,[12] or the experiences of various suburbanites living in a coastal California town.[13] Asian American literature is no longer ghettoized into describing racial or eth-nic conflicts; today's Asian American writer creates fiction that depicts Asian Americans as more than the sum of their ethnic and racial parts. Similarly, crit-ics of Asian American literature are producing work that speaks to the diversity and multiplicity of this literature. In the current field of Asian American literary discourse, the term "Asian American" is not simply an ontological category; it is a type of hermeneutics as well as an epistemology—a way of interpreting and a way of making knowledge.[14]

Although as a profession Asian American studies is anti-essentialist (there are many fine scholars producing Asian American literary criticism who do not identify as Asian American), Asian American literature, especially what gets taught in the classroom, is still centered on the body of the creative writer. Which is not unusual. Most literary categories tend to form around the body of writers rather than the content of literature. For instance, Zadie Smith is gener-ally regarded as a black British writer, even though some of her protagonists have not been black (*The Autograph Man*) and her settings have been located outside the United Kingdom (*On Beauty*). Definitions of American literature have also emphasized the identities of writers, with the implicit assumption being that the bodies that matter most are those of white male authors, as evidenced by the overwhelming majority of white male authors that populate anthologies and works of literary criticism under the rubric "American literature." Indeed, according to literary critic and American studies scholar Paul Lauter, "What gets included in significant American studies texts, which works and authors, events, issues, understandings get valorized" have to do with the predominance of a Eurocentric vision that has been preoccupied with European Americans of Anglophone literature, a preoccupation that emerges in canonical American studies texts such that "from them one would hardly know that Indians had culture, that Latinos produced intellectuals, or that Asian Americans exist in American history."[15] What Lauter astutely points out is the ways in which non-white voices are marginalized within the scholarship of American studies—they are either ignored or relegated to the sidelines of American history, society, and culture. Asian American literature is American literature, but it is first and foremost highlighted for its foreignness—its deviance from the mainstream and canon of American literary studies.

Writing is not an apolitical endeavor, and most scholars of Asian American literature believe that teaching is not an apolitical practice either. As a colleague once told me, the imperative to teach works written by Asian American writers derives, in part, from a desire to promote Asian American voices. Many of us teach from an antiracist perspective; we are not interested in further Orientalizing Asian American culture or talking about Asian essences. Although questions of authenticity and representation are vexed subjects, the history of racism and white privilege in the United States, as well as in US institutions of higher education, compel me, and I dare say many of my colleagues, to populate our syllabi with both writers of Asian American descent and works of Asian American content that reflect a diversity of Asian American experiences and an attention to issues of social justice, whether along a racial, class, sexual, or gender axis. In this fashion, we participate in a type of literary affirmative action—ensuring that the works of Asian American writers and the experiences of Asian Americans will be consumed and, we hope, understood.

Indeed, most literature scholars, myself included, tend to define Asian American literature as works created by writers who identify as Asian American. An informal survey of Asian American literature courses I collected through an appeal to the AAAS List Serv in January 2008 confirms the previous statement. Out of the twenty-seven syllabi I amassed from fifteen different English professors, none listed a non–Asian American work of creative fiction on their syllabus, and nearly half of the introductory courses listed Maxine Hong Kingston's *The Woman Warrior*. Indeed, one can imagine that *The Woman Warrior* qualifies as Asian American literature because Kingston claims a Chinese American subjectivity and writes about Asian American experiences. *The Woman Warrior*, written in English and set mostly in the United States, contains themes standard within Asian American literature: generational conflict, immigration woes, acculturation difficulties, and the assertion of an Asian American social if not political identity; this description fits nearly all of the creative fiction listed on the twenty-seven syllabi that I collected.[16] Moreover, most Asian American literary scholarship focuses on literature authored by Asian American creative writers about Asian American experiences.[17] Yet a clear and stable definition of Asian American literature has never been uniformly or consistently applied to the field because Asian American literature has always been contested for what it should include (or exclude) and who is qualified to write Asian American literature. For example, according to conventional wisdom, although Filipino American Jessica Hagedorn's novel *Dogeaters* is generally accepted as Asian American literature, even though its setting is Manila and its characters are primarily Filipino, not Filipino American, white American Robert Olen Butler's collection of short fiction *A Good Scent from a Strange Mountain* is not, even though his work mainly features Vietnamese American characters living in Louisiana and concentrates on a pivotal event in Asian American history, the influx of Vietnamese exiles following the end of the war in Viet Nam. Likewise, Sri Lankan Canadian Michael Ondaatje's *The English Patient*, a work set in Italy with no Asian American characters and just one Asian (Sikh) character, has been featured on the program of the annual conference of AAAS. Whereas Asian authors of non-English works, like Haruki Murakami or Gao Xingjian, generally do not have their fiction labeled as "Asian American," because the category has traditionally privileged English as its main language, the United States as its primary setting, and American (whether US or Canadian) citizenship or identification as a key factor in defining the author and his or her work.

However, this centering of English and the United States in terms of Asian American literature has been challenged by texts and authors that defy easy categorization. For example, Ha Jin is an exiled Chinese national who was forced to remain in the United States post–Tiannamen Square and has only acquired naturalization as an American citizen in the past decade. Jin's subject matter, with two exceptions, has centered on Chinese people living in post–Communist China, and he writes all his works in English, not Chinese.[18] Yet, his novel *A Free Life*, written after he had become a US citizen, is set in the United States and engages in tropes common to Asian American literature: exile, difficulties of assimilation and linguistic acquisition, and the search for the American dream of private ownership. In terms of region, post-9/11 the AAAS witnessed a growth of comparative studies of Arab American and Asian American literature and experiences, with a growing awareness of communities and people with origins in the Middle East considered part of an expanding notion of Asians in

America, such that Afghani American writer Khaled Hosseini's *The Kite Runner* is now considered West Asian American literature.

As demonstrated earlier, the unspoken rule in defining Asian American (or any ethnic/national) literature has rested on the body of the writer. In the examples of Hagedorn, Ondaatje, Jin, and Hosseini, all these writers reside in the United States or Canada and, more important, all could be included under the larger rubric "American"—whether by birth, naturalization, or simple identification. Thus, Chang-rae Lee's novel *Aloft* can be considered a work of Asian American literature, despite its Italian American protagonist, because the writer Chang-rae Lee identifies as Asian American.[19] Even in the case of Ondaatje, by broadening the contours of America to include Canada Ondaatje can be seen as an Asian North American writer, reminding us that America has a geographic frontier much greater than the shape of the continental United States.

Yet this capacity for expansiveness when considering Asian American authorship has not generally extended to non–Asian American writers. The motivation to close the boundaries of the field around the body of the Asian American writer shares an impulse with an activist agenda of creating a space for underrepresented voices as well as safeguarding against Orientalist and racist depictions of Asians in America—ones that white writers have been generating about Asian Americans for well over a century. Canonical white American literary figures like Jack London, Frank Norris, and Mark Twain have often depicted Asians in America, particularly Chinese Americans, in less than flattering and humane terms.[20] Even in cases where the writer in question, Pearl Buck, is deemed a friend to the Chinese,[21] her depictions of Chinese peasants, most notably in the Pulitzer Prize–winning *The Good Earth*, stood as the canonical representation of not only Chinese in China but Chinese in America, resulting in an astounding revelation that most Americans derived their knowledge about Chinese people from this single source well over two decades after the publication of *The Good Earth*.[22]

If the field of Asian American literature expands beyond the borders of the United States, and if literary criticism of Asian American works are increasingly focusing on nonracial issues that affect Asian American lives, like sexuality and class,[23] and if we agree that authenticity becomes a suspect category when evaluating the degree of Asian Americanness a work or writer exhibits,[24] what would the field look like if it included non–Asian American authors writing about Asian American topics and Asian American writers penning non–Asian American–themed fiction?[25] In other words, what knowledge do transgressive texts offer to Asian American literary criticism? Furthermore, what is the pedagogical purpose of teaching Asian American literature and the epistemological efficacy of what constitutes the current canon of Asian American literature: is it to introduce students to Asian American writers or Asian American subjects in writing, in which case, would a transgressive text written by a non–Asian American author about an Asian American topic satisfy both the pedagogical and epistemological goals of Asian American studies?

For example, what do we do with Korean American writer Ed Park's acclaimed novel, *Personal Days*, a narrative describing the working lives of a group of Manhattan twenty-somethings who are not clearly marked, racially or ethnically, and whose focus seems more regional (life in Manhattan) and work related (tech industry) rather than based in any particular Asian American experience? Or what about white American author David Guterson's *Snow Falling on Cedars*, a novel that chronicles, in part, the removal and subsequent incarceration of Japanese Americans during World War II and that features several central characters who are Asian American? Does Park's work qualify as Asian American literature simply by virtue of his Korean ethnicity? Does Guterson's work become disqualified because he is a white American? How would students feel if the books they read in an Asian American literature class were written by Asian American writers but featured virtually no significant Asian American characters and did not focus on themes of immigration or assimilation, like Vikram Seth's *The Golden Gate*?[26] How do literary critics and Asian American studies scholars reconcile the racial ambiguity of these works, and how do we square the potential epistemological value of works either written by Asian American authors on non–Asian American subjects or non–Asian American writers authoring novels with Asian content? What do we do, for example, with Chinese-Panamanian-German American writer Sigrid Nunez, whose body of fiction, save her first autobiographical novel, features no legible Asian American characters and no discernible Asian or Asian American content?

The Ambiguous Authorship of Chinese-Panamanian-German American Writer Sigrid Nunez

Sigrid Nunez, born in the early 1950s to a Chinese-Panamanian immigrant father and a German immigrant mother, is the youngest of three girls, all of whom grew up in various working-class neighborhoods of New York City. Nunez's first novel, *A Feather on the Breath of God*, weaves autobiographical elements into its narrative, yet Nunez has been careful to say that the work is not a memoir: "It's a very self-revealing and personal, even intimate book, but it isn't strictly autobiographical. Were I to write a memoir, it would be a very different book, even though many of the episodes and the characters would be the same."[27] Divided into four parts, each section focuses on a different character, with only the titular chapter devoted exclusively to the unnamed narrator's experiences and her love of dance. All other chapters manage to reveal elements of the narrator's life through her relationship to the main characters of each chapter: her Chinese-Panamanian immigrant father, her German immigrant mother, and a Russian immigrant lover. Throughout her work, Nunez ruminates on various aspects of her identity—on who she is, how she was influenced by those closest to her, and why she is the way she is. In particular, her identity as a mixed race woman raised in a mixed heritage family is a running theme throughout her first novel.

A Feather on the Breath of God not only launched Sigrid Nunez's successful literary career, it established her as an Asian American writer. Nunez was nominated for and won several awards for her first book, most notably the same AAAS fiction prize that James Janko's book would be recognized for thirteen years later. Excerpts from *Feather* have been featured in four different Asian American anthologies; Nunez has an entry in the reference work *Dictionary of Literary Biography: Asian American Writers*, and *Feather* is regularly taught as Asian American literature in college classrooms. So it would seem that Sigrid Nunez is an Asian American writer; because this first novel firmly establishes her literary credentials as one who writes about themes typical to an Asian American experience, ones that seemingly come from her own life history.

Yet when interviewed about whether she will return to the themes of her first book, Nunez claims that she has "said everything I have to say about growing up the child of a German mother and a Chinese-Panamanian father, both of whom happened also to be American immigrants, in that first book," and her subsequent works do not engage with themes of mixed heritage or questions of Asian American identity and interracial immigrant family dynamics.[28] Instead, in her second novel, *Naked Sleeper*, Nunez writes about a woman of indistinct ethnicity who engages in an affair and discovers that her own father has also lived a double life; her third novel, *Mitz: The Marmoset of Bloomsbury*, whimsically imagines life with Leonard and Virginia Woolf through the eyes of Leonard's pet marmoset; her fourth, *For Rouenna*, tells the story of a white female nurse's tour of duty in Viet Nam; her fifth, *The Last of Her Kind*, recounts the turbulent period of the late 1960s and early 1970s of a young radical rebelling against her privileged white upper-class upbringing; and her latest novel, *Salvation City*, describes the life of a teenage protagonist who has survived an outbreak of a plague-like virus that has decimated swaths of the United States and the world, including his immediate family. None of the works that follow *A Feather on the Breath of God* return to the subject of her multiraciality or family background.[29]

However, the narrator's voice from *Feather* seems to reappear in her fourth novel. *For Rouenna* is told by an ethnically indistinct and unnamed narrator, who could be white, yet she so closely resembles the narrator in *Feather* that one could make the argument that the narrators of *Feather* and *Rouenna* are one and the same.[30] Unlike *Feather*, the narrator in *For Rouenna* does not talk about her own racial identity or mixed race family; in fact, the story that *For Rouenna* tells is not that of the unnamed narrator but her friend, Rouenna Zycinski, a Polish American woman who grew up in the same Staten Island housing project as the narrator's family and who completed a tour of duty during the American war in Viet Nam as a US Army nurse. Approached by Rouenna to help write about her wartime experiences in Viet Nam, the narrator initially refuses, but after Rouenna's suicide the narrator devotes the middle portion of her three-part narrative to Rouenna's life—her early years growing up in an abusive working-class family, her escape from poverty through her nurse's training and subsequent tour of duty in Viet Nam, and her mundane and routine life following her stint in Viet Nam, a life of quiet desperation, one might say, because Rouenna, who never married or had children and who kept no close friends and had no career ambitions, ends up feeling as if "'Vietnam was the biggest thing that ever happened to me.'"[31] The narrator's recounting of Rouenna's life helps readers to understand just how and why Rouenna would come to utter those words.

Although Nunez's novel focuses on a pivotal event in Asian American history, the American war in Viet Nam, and although Nunez identifies as someone with Asian-ethnic ancestry, does it automatically mean that *For Rouenna* should be considered a work of Asian American literature? The American war in Viet Nam is described through the unnamed narrator's recollection of the stories that Rouenna told her and supplemented by research that the narrator conducts while teaching as a visiting writer at a small New England liberal arts college. There are no voices or experiences rendered in the first-person or even the restricted third-person perspective of Vietnamese or Vietnamese Americans. Indeed, actual Vietnamese people (along with Asian Americans) are largely absent or silent in this novel. Vietnamese men, when they are described by Rouenna via the narrator, are portrayed stereotypically as short, dark, incomprehensible, and incoherent objects. Rouenna recounts being spit upon by a Viet Cong soldier she was attempting to treat in the ward, and the language she uses to describe her patient encapsulates the sentiments she routinely expresses about Vietnamese men during and even following her time in Viet Nam: "The goddamn motherfucking gook bastard had spat at her."[32] The narrator, while not employing similar racist and troubling language, also does not flesh out the lives of Vietnamese or Vietnamese Americans beyond a passing one-page description of her uncle's wife, a war bride whose English, the narrator relates, "was not yet good enough for us to get to know her well," although the narrator continues by admitting "I would never know her well."[33] The main description of this unnamed aunt has her eating chili peppers out of a jar with her chopsticks while watching television. Additionally, the narrator's aunt is the only Vietnamese person to have her speech directly quoted by the narrator, and the two phrases she utters, "For you like eat napalm, right?" a response to the narrator's inability to eat hot chili peppers,[34] and "You number-one son!" directed at her first-born child, hardly depicts her aunt in a three-dimensional or fully fleshed-out fashion.[35]

The only other portrait of Vietnamese women comes from Rouenna's observation that US soldiers fetishized them but that "everyone knew most guys would have chosen a plain blond round-eye over the most beautiful girl in Vietnam" and that "you got the feeling that what some guys liked about having Vietnamese girls was that you could do whatever you wanted to them. It was like having an Oriental slave."[36] Rouenna's observation seems to be confirmed in the next paragraph when the narrator recalls overhearing a husband verbally abuse and berate his wife, telling her, "I'll break every bone in your body and ship the pieces back to the hold where I found you, *chop-chop*" [emphasis in original].[37] Although Nunez omits the ethnicity and race of the couple, the reference and emphasis on the racist phrase "chop-chop" as well as the placement of this anecdote immediately following Rouenna's observations on the oppressive nature of interracial desire between US soldiers and Vietnamese women suggests that this dynamic, begun in Viet Nam, has continued in a US setting.[38]

Viet Nam exists as a memory for a former US Army nurse, complicated by her wartime experiences, which were filled with horror, trauma, and tragedy as well as laughter, camaraderie, and small moments of heroism and dignity. The perspective of the war in Viet Nam is consistently filtered and narrated by non-Vietnamese participants: Rouenna, the unnamed narrator, her British lover, and Graham Greene's novel *The Quiet American*.[39] Reading *For Rouenna* does not provide any sense of a Vietnamese subjectivity or perspective, nor does it shed any light on Vietnamese American lives or those of any other Asian Americans. The novel does not give voice or agency to any Asian American people, Vietnamese or otherwise. The subject and content of the novel is announced by its title: it is a novel told as a tribute for Rouenna, to commemorate her time in Viet Nam as a combat nurse, and not for the unnamed, silent, and largely invisible and ignored Vietnamese population.

Is Sigrid Nunez an Asian American writer? To the extent that she identifies as someone with Asian-ethnic ancestry, one would have to say yes. Yet even as an Asian American writer, Nunez is racially ambiguous because of her mixed race heritage as well as the ambiguous nature of her writing. Even in the novel for which she is most associated as an Asian American writer, *A Feather on the Breath of God*, Nunez does not so much identify as Asian American as recognize her father's Chinese-Panamanian background, but she does so in a way that signals her own distance from both her father's culture and her identification as

Asian American. Nunez's Spanish surname and her mother's German ethnicity preclude her instant identification as Asian American.

In returning to Nunez's body of fiction, is *For Rouenna* or any of her other works following her autobiographical first novel Asian American fiction? I would have to say no. The content of *For Rouenna* rests squarely on the experiences of the Polish American former army nurse Rouenna Zycinski. Although the novel does tackle issues of race, class disparities, and sexism—issues of social justice often found within Asian American literature—it does so without an attention to any legible or discernible Asian American community.[40] Of all Nunez's post-*Feather* narratives, *Rouenna* comes closest to delving into subject matter found within Asian American fiction: the American war in Viet Nam and the traumatic and complicated emotions that this war evokes in its survivors. Yet, ultimately, we learn nothing about a Vietnamese perspective from this novel, and it's difficult to discern what this novel contributes to Asian American epistemology because it does not seem to engage with Asian American people, experiences, culture, or history. Nunez may, indeed, have "done her homework" as one reviewer complimentarily writes of *For Rouenna*'s verisimilitude in detailing the wartime experiences of one US Army nurse, but it does not illuminate the exile of over a million Southeast Asians who fled the war-torn region during and after US involvement in Viet Nam.[41]

Sigrid Nunez is considered an Asian American writer by virtue of her first novel and her ethnic ancestry. Yet her subsequent novels, her transgressive texts, demonstrate a racial ambiguity that announces a disjunction between a writer's identity and the material that speaks to her and gets transmitted through her, particularly in the form of her creative output.[42] This dissonance produced by a writer of Asian ancestry creating narratives that have no discernible Asian American content or characters opens up questions of categorization and canonization. If Sigrid Nunez is an Asian American writer who authors non–Asian American narratives, then what would we make of the converse: a non–Asian American novelist who writes a work with Asian American characters and content? In other words, how do we reconcile the racial ambiguity of a writer like Cuban American Cristina Garcia and her novel *Monkey Hunting*, a work in which the Chinese and mixed Chinese–Cuban American characters appear to solidify its Asian American literary credentials?

Traveling through the Flesh in Cristina Garcia's *Monkey Hunting*

In an interview with *The Atlantic*, Cristina Garcia, an author whose previous works had centered on the experiences of Cuban and Cuban American women, describes the process she undertook to create the Chinese male character Chen

Pan, the patriarch of *Monkey Hunting*, admitting that she "was fighting self-charges of fraud all along the way."[43] Garcia's creative act of breathing life into this character was one that took a great deal of research, time, and energy, so why should she express any doubt over the authenticity of a fictional character? Her self-reflexive questioning reveals the anxieties of authoring creative works that cross gender and racial boundaries, where assumptions of autobiographical experience and expertise particularly plague ethnic American writers. We expect Garcia to write about what she knows: what it is like to be a Cuban American woman. However, as Sigrid Nunez pointedly observes, often writers are more interested in where their fiction will take them rather than simply rehearsing events from their own biography: "I think it has everything to do with the desire to be engaged in inventing a story, rather than reporting a story—in other words, with what makes me want to write fiction in the first place. . . . There's something that pulls you away from yourself and your own experiences. That delicious pull toward the unknown and the need to give full play to the imagination."[44]

In a similar vein, Garcia describes the ways in which she came to linguistically embody her Chinese-Cuban male protagonists: "I kind of epidermally moved into the muscle tissue until I finally got into the bloodstream."[45] Far from being parody or appropriation, Garcia describes her writing process in terms of cross-racial mimesis, which speaks to her dedication in authenticating the life of her character, one born in a different century of a different culture and gender than her own. Yet Garcia, in doing research for any of her fictitious creations, must delve into a skin not her own, must travel through the flesh, as it were, to create believable, true-to-life characters. Is the demand for verisimilitude stronger when a writer like Garcia dons a racial mask in order to pen a transgressive text? Can that verisimilitude be so authentic that a writer like Garcia who identifies as Latina can author an Asian American novel? Does the ambiguity of categorizing *Monkey Hunting* lie in the body of the literature or the body of the author?

I turn to a close reading of *Monkey Hunting* to show that the novel's concerns with globalization and a Chinese American diaspora are themes typically found in the canon of Asian American literature, which makes Garcia and her third novel ripe for exploring the racial ambiguity inherent within transgressive texts, for *Monkey Hunting* is a novel that defies simple categorization or singular interpretation. Garcia, a writer born in Havana and raised in New York City who currently lives in California with a daughter of mixed Cuban, Russian Jewish, and Japanese ancestry, had written two novels previous to *Monkey Hunting* that concentrated on the lives of Cuban and Cuban American women both in Cuba and in the United States: *Dreaming in Cuban* and *The Aguerro Sisters*. Although her third novel may seem like a departure from these earlier works, *Monkey Hunting* continues the themes of her two previous novels by intimately portraying the landscape and culture of Cuba and by depicting more than a century of Chinese-Cuban affiliations and communities against a backdrop of Cuba's history with colonialism, independence, and eventually communism. Garcia weaves a postmodern tale that moves through time and space from nineteenth-century Hong Kong, to Cuba of the 1920s, to China under Mao's dictatorship, as well as to the United States and Viet Nam of the late 1960s. Told from three different perspectives—the patriarch Chen Pan, his Chinese granddaughter Chen Fang, and his great-grandson, Domingo Chen—each protagonist follows different plot trajectories and experiences, yet all three are tied to the history and culture of Cuba and China, and all three can be seen as transnational characters who cannot be constrained into a specific ethnicity. As Ann Marie Alfonso-Forero observes, by "privileging cultural and religious hybridities over fixed racial identifications, García celebrates her characters' ability to create fluid and dynamic identities."[46]

One character whose identity is fluid and dynamic is Chen Fang, who appears to be the most traditionally Chinese in terms of her upbringing yet is the most cosmopolitan in her outlook. Chen Fang, born and raised in China, finds employment at an international school in Shanghai. While teaching at the school she has an affair with Dauphine, the French mother of one of her students. Chen Fang lives through the Japanese occupation of Shanghai only to be jailed, later in life, as a counter-revolutionary during Mao's regime because of her foreign connections: her Cuban father, her relationship with Dauphine, and her facility with languages and literatures outside of China. Indeed, one may interpret Chen Fang as a victim of racial ambiguity, because her multiple ethnic, cultural, and racial border crossings (in addition to her gender and sexual border crossings) render her subjectivity open to speculation on the part of the Chinese Communist government.[47] Because of her various ethnic associations, Chen Fang, as racially ambiguous, is also a potentially subversive figure for those agitating for a unified Communist Chinese identity.

In the last segment of Chen Fang's narrative Garcia portrays her nostalgically remembering a scene from her time with Dauphine, the two of them dancing a Cuban bolero while Chen Fang sings to her lover in Spanish.[48] Although Chen Fang's fate is left uncertain (yet certainly dire and desperate—she is eighty and jailed in a Chinese communist prison), Garcia's portrait of her as a woman influenced by forces outside of China, in terms both global (Mao's communist revolution) as well as intimate (her foreign lover) suggests that even a Chinese woman in China has an identity impacted beyond the borders of her nation-state. The last image of Chen Fang that Garcia leaves us with has her imagining a trip she will make to Cuba to find her father and to smoke a cigar on a balcony of Havana's Chinatown.[49] This portrait of Chen Fang is one of would be sojourner whose life has been intimately tethered to a larger Chinese American diaspora.[50]

In contrast to Chen Fang, Domingo Chen is the most hybrid of the characters: his hair, grown out, is described as puffing into an afro; after fleeing Cuba with his father, he finds a job at a Chinese-Cuban restaurant, the Havana Dragon; and while stationed in Viet Nam during the war, he "rescues"[51] and impregnates a Vietnamese prostitute, Tham Thanh Lan, thus continuing the mixed race lineage begun with his own grandfather, Chen Pan.[52] Domingo muses on this genealogy, as Garcia infuses a language of migration as well as exile into a description of this diasporic family: "Domingo wondered about these migrations, these cross-cultural lusts. Were people meant to travel such distances? Mix with others so different from themselves? His great-grandfather had left China more than a hundred years ago, penniless and alone. Then he'd fallen in love with a slave girl and created a whole new race—brown children with Chinese eyes who spoke Spanish and a smattering of Abakua. His first family never saw him again."[53] Domingo's ambivalence about his upcoming paternity is linked with both his immaturity as well as his ambiguous feelings about hybridity, particularly the sense of exile that appears bound up with such cross-cultural desires. His union with Tham Thanh Lan will result in a fifth-generation mixed race, multi-linguistic Chen: a child of Vietnamese, Chinese, African, and Spanish ancestry. The nature of these multiple migrations makes Garcia's work a uniquely Asian-American text [hyphen added for emphasis], one that challenges previous understandings of hybridity and interraciality, as literary critic Marta Caminero-Santangelo affirms: "The figure of hybridity—in its nineteenth-century sense of racial miscegenation as well as, though perhaps more prominently than, in its more recent meaning of cultural hybridity—is of primary importance in García's novel."[54] Garcia's representation of mestizo cultures embodied through this one particular lineage of the Chen family, emphasizes that "purity" is a myth—how one identifies as Cuban or Chinese or African or Spanish or Vietnamese is never constant and is certainly not based on phenotype or genetics.

The clearest evidence in favor of understanding *Monkey Hunting* as an Asian American narrative that bridges and connects multiple cultures is the Chinese Cuban patriarch Chen Pan. At the age of eighty, Chen Pan sentimentally immerses himself in Chinese culture—choosing the foods of his youth and memories of Chinese poems and his family as succor in his old age. Yet he recognizes that he is not purely Chinese, for he speaks a mish-mash of Chinese, Spanish, and a host of other languages and dialects picked up over the years living in the port city of Havana: "After so many years in Cuba, Chen Pan had forgotten much of his Chinese. He mixed his talk with words from here and words from there until he spoke no true language at all. There were only a few people left in Havana with whom he could comfortably communicate. Long ago he'd lived in China, known all its customs and manners. How useless these had been outside their own geography! Still, it was easier for him to be Cuban than to try to become Chinese again."[55] Chen Pan is neither wholly Cuban nor wholly Chinese. Yet simply hyphenating the two—Chinese-Cuban—doesn't adequately account for the decisions he made and the identity he created for himself as one who chose to fight for Cuban independence during the Ten Years' War, as one who chose to love, until his dying day, a woman not of his race, and as one who chose a country to die in, far from the bones of his ancestors. As Sean Moiles attests, "Garcia's characterization of Chen Pan presents identity as fluid, multiple, compounded, and, to a significant extent, chosen."[56] Indeed, Chen Pan's acknowledgement of the various cultural influences, Chinese and Cuban, on his subjectivity reveals an inherent ambiguity of his character, one that perhaps coheres around all immigrants, but particularly those whose physical appearance may not coincide with that of the dominant society in which they live. Or in the case of Cheng Fang, a Chinese woman whose multiple ethnic affinities rendered her a perpetual outsider, it is an ambiguity of affiliation, revealing an inherent multiplicity and plurality within the act of identification itself. Chen Pan is, by the end of his life, part of the Chinese diaspora, and his descendants, particularly Domingo, will also become part of the Chinese as well as Cuban diaspora—making Chen Pan's legacy not only one of racial ambiguity and globalization but a truly Asian and American lineage, one originating in China but whose lines crisscross around the globe, linking to various Asian as well as American locales.

In many ways it does not take a great leap of imagination to consider Garcia's third novel a work of Asian American literature; it both expands the definition of the Chinese diaspora and the contributions of Chinese immigrants to Cuba, as well as explodes the boundaries of the Americas that Asian American literature has traditionally adhered to by refocusing attention south of the United States to the Caribbean. With its breadth of both region (the three primary storylines take place over four countries) and languages (there are at least five different linguistic references—Spanish, English, Chinese, Vietnamese, and the African languages of Abakua and Lucumi) *Monkey Hunting*'s global scope forces readers to recognize Asian American literature, and by extension Cuban American literature, as uncontained by traditional borders of the nation-state, thereby de-privileging the United States as the site for (and English as the primary language of) Asian American literature.

Going beyond Biology: Pushing the
Limits of Asian American Epistemology

From the point-of-view of knowledge creation, *Monkey Hunting* does contribute to Asian American epistemology, and as such, I think we need to consider how expanding the canon of Asian American literature to include transgressive texts can deepen the body of knowledge about Asian Americans available to us in American letters. Taking Colleen Lye's *America's Asia: Racial Form and American Literature, 1893–1945* as one example, Lye's analyses of white American canonical literary texts, like those written by Jack London, Pearl Buck, and John Steinbeck, contribute to Asian American epistemology by illustrating how Asian American subjects were formed by white American writers' portraits of Asians—and how those portraits influenced popular perceptions of Asians in America.[57] As Lye asserts in her introduction, *America's Asia* "attempts a critical intervention through an attentive observation of racism's object, generating a contextualized description that incorporates a strong interpretation of race's social meaning."[58] Similarly, the epistemological value of Garcia's *Monkey Hunting* offers scholars a broader understanding of the Chinese diaspora, an expanded notion of the signifier "America," and a historic re-visioning of the place of Chinese in the transatlantic slave trade and the sugar plantation economy of Cuba, as well as the United States. Indeed, scholars like Lisa Yun and Moon-Ho Jung have investigated the role of Chinese in plantation labor during the late nineteenth century, in the Caribbean and the American South. Like *Monkey Hunting*, Yun and Jung's works open up the field of Asian American studies by placing Asian American scholarship in conversation with other disciplines like Southern studies, Caribbean studies, and African American studies.

So to return to the question that propels this chapter: is there a value in expanding the canon of Asian American literature to include transgressive texts? My simple answer is yes. I believe that expanding the canon of Asian American literature to include transgressive texts can enrich and enliven Asian American epistemology. The strength and frustration of Asian American studies as a discipline has always been the diversity, breadth, and expansiveness of the field. The category "Asian American" has never had singular coherence; it has been able to traverse multiple disciplinary as well as geographic boundaries in its engagement with producing knowledge about Asian Americans. As noted in the Introduction to *Racial Ambiguity*, "Asian American" is and has always been a racially ambiguous classification. Acknowledging the racial ambiguity of transgressive texts and allowing these works to be considered as Asian American literature recognizes the multiplicity and fluidity of racial identities and ideologies. Moreover, including transgressive texts into an Asian American canon need not be mutually exclusive, since currently the genre of Asian

American literature is not a mutually exclusive category. Just as *The Woman Warrior* is regarded as an example of postmodern fiction, memoir, American, contemporary, Women's, California, and Chinese American literatures, so should *Monkey Hunting* be read as a work of Cuban American, Chinese diasporic, Asian American, Caribbean, and American literature.

Although there are those who will be uncomfortable with opening up the category of Asian American literature to non–Asian American writers, fearing appropriation and inauthenticity, what I must remind myself and others who feel disquiet over including transgressive texts in this canon is that the careers of writers of Asian ancestry will not end nor does it necessarily mean that non–Asian American writers are stealing a literature that does not belong to them. When it comes to literature, there are no borders, and the study of Asian American literature should be virulently anti-essentialist in this regard. I, and others, must learn to take our discomfort with transgressive texts and apply our intellectual rigor to understanding the forces that cause this discomfort as well as to think productively about what these works can offer in terms of pushing the boundaries of Asian American epistemology.

Yet beyond opening up the canon of Asian American literature, understanding transgressive texts as racially ambiguous is imperative to understanding how we arrive at knowledge by and about Asians in America. I believe that what is at stake is a more honest reckoning about how we (those of us who do research in and teach Asian American literature and literary criticism) are crafting knowledge about Asian American literary studies. Currently Asian American studies and the knowledge produced about Asian Americans is largely driven by identity politics, which becomes problematic because it implicitly casts racial identity as the barometer for authenticity and hence valued knowledge and inclusion on a course syllabus and validation in the field of Asian American studies. The underpinning of identity politics that functions as disciplinary knowledge in the realm of Asian American literary critique and epistemology means that those who are mixed race, adoptees, or figured as racially ambiguous—the topics of the various chapters in this book—can be rendered as illegitimate or seen as illegible as far as Asian American knowledge is concerned. Opening up Asian American literature and literary study to racially ambiguous works, to transgressive texts, helps to decouple the body of the author from the body of knowledge found in the literary work and to legitimate and make legible the Asian American subject matter that pushes beyond questions of authenticity or identity politics. Categorizing people, literature, or knowledge as Asian American need not rest on notions of an absolute authenticity reducible to issues of blood quantum, since the language of blood and percentages—the terrain of the racially ambiguous body—has its own history of eugenics and white supremacy, one that the field of Asian American studies works to combat through a commitment to social justice. Furthermore, as an academic discipline, Asian American literary studies has a tradition of breaking tradition—of pushing boundaries and barriers and of questioning categories, which makes accepting transgressive texts as Asian American literature a not unusual move for this cutting edge field.

However, let me be clear in saying that admittance into an Asian American canon is not done by committee. There will surely not be consensus on deciding that Cristina Garcia's *Monkey Hunting* should now be taught in Asian American literature classes or sanctioned through journal articles or scholarly monographs. I, myself, while admitting Garcia's novel as Asian American literature would hesitate to give either Robert Olen Butler's *A Good Scent from a Strange Mountain* or David Guterson's *Snow Falling on Cedars* the same imprimatur, most especially due to what I perceive to be a not-so-subtle sexual exoticization of Asian American women in both texts, which perpetuates rather than upends stereotypes of overly sensual Asian women as the objects of white male desire. Furthermore, as much as I wish to move away from the author's identity in determining the text's categorization, I am aware of the admonition posed by literary scholar Rajini Srikanth, who astutely notes that "when European American writers depict the experiences of and speak in the voices of people of color, their works are seldom received without consideration of questions of power."[59] Both Butler's short story collection and Guterson's novel, in my reading, reflect a kind of white male privilege that I do not find in Garcia's novel, which may or may not be due to the different life experiences of one set of writers (white American men) versus the other (female Latina immigrant). Although I am certainly not saying that only other writers of color can sensitively depict Asian American characters (white American writer Deborah Iida's *Middle Son* readily comes to mind), I do believe that as a writer of color, Garcia may feel a particular social responsibility in her literary creations, because writers of color, like Gish Jen, recognize the impact of their literary endeavors on their reading public: "I support social responsibility in writing. I think I'm a rare writer in saying that. Most writers argue for artistic freedom. But to imagine that your images have no effect on what happens in society and the way people see themselves is completely naïve. I think also that you are a better writer as you start considering questions like *representation*. I don't see how writing stereotypes about blacks or Asians or anybody else could possibly make you a better writer" [italics in original].[60]

If we are to take seriously Kandice Chuh's call for an anti-essentialist "subjectless discourse" in Asian American studies, then we need to consider opening up the canon of Asian American literature to include works by Garcia,

Iida, and others, like Mark Salzman's *The Laughing Sutra*.[61] As Chuh states, "If we accept a priori that Asian American studies is subjectless, then rather than looking to complete the category 'Asian American,' to actualize it by such methods as enumerating various components of differences (gender, class, sexuality, religion, and so on), we are positioned to critique the effects of the various configurations of power and knowledge through which the term comes to have meaning."[62] The key word in the above quotation is "power." Understanding the power we, as scholars of Asian American literature, have in Asian American epistemology is crucial. Which means it is our responsibility in our scholarship as well as our teaching to be attendant to issues of power that arise in Asian American literature, whether or not they are written by authors who identify as Asian American. Including transgressive texts into the category of Asian American literature allows us to truly envision Asian American epistemology as a subjectless discourse that has come into being through various axes of power, in which the players and actors involved in the history of Asian America and the creation of knowledge about Asian Americans are people with multiple ethnic affiliations and national associations.

Furthermore, acknowledging the power dynamics within Asian American literary studies and through an acceptance of transgressive texts hearkens back to the foundations of Asian American studies as a movement invested in human and civil rights that extend beyond the borders of Asia and the boundaries of racial classifications. Unlike other disciplines, Asian American studies, and by extension Asian American literary studies, was formed out of a commitment to social justice and a desire to question the power dynamics of the existing university structure and national society in which questions of race and racialization are concerned, especially for people of Asian ancestry living in the United States. What we choose to count as Asian American literature, what we choose to research and publish in our scholarly pursuits, and what we teach in our college classrooms have ideological components to them.[63] Writers like Amy Chua, who pen memoirs and treatises that uphold the model minority myth or that traffic in a language of eugenics, are roundly denounced by Asian American literary scholars.[64] Although Chua, by virtue of her ethnicity and race, may be deemed to be an Asian American writer, I doubt many if not any teachers of Asian American literature would teach *Battle Hymn of the Tiger Mother* as an accurate and laudable memoir that upholds a commitment to social justice and antiracism. And certainly no scholar of Asian American studies would positively promote Filipina American Michelle Malkin's *In Defense of Internment: The Case for "Racial Profiling" during World War II and the War on Terror* in a scholarly article about the Japanese American incarceration or as a secondary source in an Asian American literature class. We may not always talk about it directly, but the social justice and human rights roots of Asian American studies precludes scholars of Asian American literature to accept, uncritically, works that run directly counter to this foundational ideology of the field.

This means that transgressive texts, whether written by authors of color or white writers, should bear a responsibility and a commitment to the principles of social justice and anti-essentialism that the discipline of Asian American studies has been dedicated to from its founding moment. I understand that defining Asian American literature through a social justice perspective runs the risk of creating yet another barometer for authenticity. Yet acknowledging the ideological underpinnings of Asian American literature is different from demanding an ethnic or racial authenticity that identity politics would dictate. As noted previously, there is already an ideological bent to what scholars of Asian American literature teach in our courses and use in our research. Our approach to the study of Asian American texts is not apolitical; how we shape and frame the meaning of Asian American literary texts for our students in the classroom, and for our colleagues in the journals and conferences we participate in, arises from our investment in creating knowledge about Asian American subjects that derives from an inclusive pedagogy and epistemology. Relying on content in defining Asian American literature, one that attends to issues of social justice commensurate with an Asian American studies ideology, undermines identity politics and notions of authenticity simultaneously.

Writing about the need to understand Asian American literature as theory (which is also the subtitle of his essay "Blurring Boundaries"), literary critic Donald Goellnicht takes an approach that pushes beyond simplistic borders and binaries, asserting that "I offer these alternative categories, not in order to decide on one over the others, but to draw out the arbitrary and ideologically grounded nature of taxonomic classifications, which seek to contain texts through maintaining generic—and genetic—purity."[65] Goellnicht seeks to push beyond borders of generic or genetic purity in his analysis of Asian American literature. Racially ambiguous transgressive texts similarly subvert oversimplified notions of genre and upend ideas of genetic purity. Allowing transgressive texts into the canon of Asian American literature is one of the most antiracist actions that we can take as critics of Asian American literature. Transgressive texts prove that race is a social construction. If we move away from biology, if we, as a discipline, declare that one's biography should not dictate one's creative output, we recognize the fictive state of not just creative writing but racial construction. We affirm that the ability to write with sensitivity, respect, and accuracy about race is not limited to those whose claim to an ethnic culture or racial category is verified by phenotype or surname. The ability to misrepresent an ethnic group or engage in racial self-loathing is not solely the realm of the majority; to quote Srikanth, "Reductive representations are by no means the shortcoming of white writers alone; writers of color frequently fall into the same mode even when narrating the experiences of those within their own racial or ethnic group, let alone characters from other groups of color."[66] Allowing works by non–Asian American writers to be considered as Asian American literature is a progressive, antiracist maneuver, one that envisions Asian American fiction and literary critique as free spaces open to all allies who wish to promote Asian American experiences sensitively and respectfully in their writing.

Returning to this chapter's opening anecdote about the 2008 AAAS fiction award given to James Janko for his novel *Buffalo Boy and Geronimo*, has my opinion of Janko's winning this award changed from my visceral reaction at the banquet? Yes.[67] When I finally read *Buffalo Boy and Geronimo* I was struck by two things: Janko is a good writer, and there is little in the way of traditional Asian American content in his book. The novel, which takes place entirely in Viet Nam along the Cambodian border during the last stage of the American war, is alternately narrated by the two title characters: Antonio Lucio Conchola, a Chicano medic for the US Army nicknamed "Geronimo," and Nguyen Luu Hai, a North Vietnamese teenager who is also called "Buffalo Boy." We learn about Conchola's platoon, Nguyen's village and family, and about the animals and landscape of Viet Nam. As the novel progresses, the narratives of the two protagonists eventually intersect, and we learn about American and Vietnamese attitudes toward one another—the mistrust but also the moments of intimacy, which Janko's novel renders in vivid detail.

There is little discernible Asian American content in Janko's narrative. However, considering the writings of Hagedorn, Jin, Park, and Ondaatje discussed previously, a non-US setting and an absence of Asian American characters does not preclude a work from being defined as "Asian American." Moreover, as noted in my argument for including transgressive texts into an Asian American canon, an attention to and sensitivity toward social justice issues should be a salient quality when evaluating whether a work should be included in the category of Asian American literature. Janko's novel has, at its core, an antiwar ethos and pro-environment message and depicts, with respect and care, the landscape and people of Viet Nam, creating Asian characters who are fully fleshed out and multifaceted rather than two-dimensional stereotypes or caricatures found in mainstream Vietnam War narratives.[68] Indeed Janko, himself a veteran of the American war in Viet Nam, developed the novel out of a workshop he took with Maxine Hong Kingston; he conducted meticulous research for this novel, living in Viet Nam for a year, becoming fluent in Vietnamese, and listening to and learning from the Vietnamese people he met and befriended there.[69]

Like Garcia's *Monkey Hunting*, Janko's *Buffalo Boy and Geronimo* qualifies as Asian American literature through its attention to social justice themes and its thoughtful, multidimensional, and careful depiction of Asian characters and experiences. Moreover, unlike Nunez's *For Rouenna*, Janko's novel gives significant voice and agency to Vietnamese people rather than describing the war from the point of view of US soldiers and Army nurses. Janko renders Luu Hai and his family and fellow villagers as fully developed characters. The racial ambiguity of Janko's identity as a white American man narrating a story in the voice of a North Vietnamese boy opens up the possibility that the novel is not simply an act of inappropriate ventriloquism but a creative effort on the part of a writer who wishes to provide an Asian voice and perspective not typically heard from (that of a North Vietnamese protagonist), in either American or Asian American literature.

The AAAS, the governing institutional body of Asian American studies, sanctioned James Janko's *Buffalo Boy and Geronimo* as Asian American fiction when it awarded the prize to Janko and his novel, thus opening up the field of Asian American fiction to include works written by non–Asian American writers. Therefore, it became incumbent, in the weeks and months following the 2008 banquet, to discern why the prize committee had awarded this novel one of the highest accolades in the field of Asian American scholarship. It is why I began to think about the place of transgressive texts in Asian American literature and to consider, seriously, works authored by non–Asian American writers as part of an Asian American literary canon. The contexts for understanding the racial ambiguity of transgressive texts may differ from the perspective of the publishing house, college curricula, or professional awards. I doubt that either Curbstone Press (the publisher of Janko's novel) or AAAS gave much thought to the larger implications of what it meant for a non–Asian American–identified writer to publish a book that would be nominated for an Asian American fiction award—publishers are generally non-ideological, and AAAS has a history of non-essentialism whose logical culmination can be understood through this award. Which means that it is incumbent on the scholars of Asian American literature to investigate the meaning of this transgressive text to Asian American epistemology because once the AAAS 2008 Asian American fiction prize committee authorized Janko's novel as Asian American fiction, the genie was out of the bottle, so to speak, and it seems only a matter of time before we, as a field, must contend with which works to include or exclude from the category Asian American literature.

Finally, I close this chapter by moving to the realm of pedagogy because I believe that nearly all of us who teach and pursue research in the field of Asian American literary criticism find that theory meets practice in the classroom.

Whether we are teaching an essay by Sau-ling Wong that engages with literary theory through an Asian American perspective or helping students to explicate passages of Jhumpa Lahiri's *Interpreter of Maladies*, we practice Asian American literary theory by validating the very topic of Asian America for students and showing them how Asian Americans fit into a national, cultural, social, and literary landscape. By teaching our students the subject of Asian American fiction, we introduce them to a new way of thinking about American literature and a new understanding of Asian American epistemology. Although I recognize that an Asian American literature syllabus featuring all white American authors is problematic, such a syllabus could also speak directly to issues of racism, white privilege, and the institutional power and persistence of both. Whether through a critique of potential Orientalism and its effects on Asian American communities and people, a syllabus focusing on white American writers (or other non–Asian American authors), writing Asian American fiction would provoke debate and discussion in an Asian American literature classroom, forcing both teacher and students to question issues of authenticity, representation, institutionalization and canonization as well as epistemology.[70] If nothing else, it would foreground issues of power by examining the social, cultural, and political ramifications of cross-racial mimesis; for example, what does white authorship of Asian American characters add to our knowledge of Asian American subjects?

During the end of one semester that I was teaching a course on Asian American literature and theory, I engaged my class in a writing exercise, asking them to describe what their definition of Asian American literature was prior to entering this classroom and whether or not their idea of Asian American literature had changed after completing this course. Here is one student's response: "The question to ask instead of 'What is Asian American Literature' should perhaps be how does a definition of Asian American Literature best meet the needs of this class, this paper, this conference . . . always remembering that there can be no definitive definition."[71] As this student demonstrates, it is the questions and not the answers that matter in the quest for Asian American knowledge; it is the journey rather than the destination that counts. The great strength of Asian American studies as a discipline is its protean quality, its ability continually to reflect back on itself and to interrogate the meaning of what constitutes not only membership within an Asian American political identity but the very nature of Asian American epistemology. This quality of thinking through and about knowledge production inspires us to realize that these aren't simply academic questions, as in ones that don't matter, but academic in the best spirit of intellectual inquiry—ones that keep us reading and writing and asking questions that have no answers. Because at the end of the day, it's really the questions that matter most.

CODA

Ending with Origins

My Own Racial Ambiguity

In Monique Truong's novel *Bitter in the Mouth*, protagonist Linda "Linh-dao" Nguyen Hammerick explains the difference between the optics that govern how one's identity is perceived versus the more complicated ways in which factors other than the visual govern one's racial identity: "I was often asked by complete strangers what it was like to grow up being Asian in the South. You mean what was it like to grow up looking Asian in the South, I would say back to them with the southern accent that had revealed to them the particularities of my biography."[1] Linda may look Asian, but her voice announces a different identification, one that registers her as an anomaly in a region that has traditionally understood race in black and white terms.[2] As I've demonstrated in the chapters that precede this coda, the ways in which racial ambiguity operates as an optic, a lens with which to view Asian American subjects, their negotiation of their racial identities, and the place of Asian American culture in our present society is as varied and variable as the population of Asians in America in their mixed and monoracial forms.

Yet optics are only one measurement in determining a person's racial identification (an often imperfect measurement at that), and how various Asian American subjects identify, even in the face of others' attempts to fix them into specific racial boxes, signals the ways in which Asian American racial subjectivity exceeds singular categorization, which is illuminated by the subjects of this study. The difference between what you look like versus other factors such as to whom you are married (Yoshiko deLeon's interracial marriage), the family you are adopted into (the white families of Asian American adult adoptee bloggers), and the parents who raised you (Tiger Woods's black and Asian parents) are critical determinants to understanding the ambiguity of race. And as the last two chapters illustrate, how we even understand the label "Asian American" varies given the context of one's subject position (multiracial Asian Americans in Asia and the United States) and the content of narratives (Asian American themed writing by non-Asian identified authors).

Because I believe all research projects derive out of the personal, I end this book by explaining the origins of my interest with racial ambiguity: my maternal family. Linda's southern accent tells readers that she is not simply an Asian immigrant in the US South. Similarly, the food at my maternal family gatherings, from childhood to adulthood, reveals a racial ambiguity that belies our distinctly Asian features: oxtail stew, ackee and saltfish, rice and peas, and Jamaican beef patties are standard fare during the meals that I share with my Chinese Jamaican extended family. We may look like any other Asian immigrant family in North America, but our palates tell a different story.

How my maternal family came to Jamaica by way of Hong Kong and how my Kingston-born mother met and married my Chinese immigrant father in New York City's Chinatown is a tale not common among standard immigration narratives found in Asian American history books and Asian American studies courses.[3] My Gung Gung was the fourth son of a poor farming family.[4] When an opportunity arose to join his second brother in Jamaica, he left Hong Kong for Kingston. Deciding that he could make his living there, he came back to the New Territories region of Hong Kong and married and impregnated my grandmother, and then left to return to Kingston. After giving birth to a daughter, my Po Po left her infant firstborn with my Gung Gung's youngest sister, a Buddhist nun, and traveled from the New Territories region to Hong Kong harbor, where she embarked on a boat bound for Vancouver.[5] From there she boarded a transcontinental train to Halifax, where she caught another boat that took her to Kingston.[6] She had left behind her daughter with family because it was unclear whether she would join her husband in Kingston permanently or whether she'd return to the New Territories and be part of the number of Chinese wives whose husbands were dispersed throughout the diaspora. Unfortunately for my grandparents it was the late 1930s. By the time my Po Po had decided that she wanted to stay and could send for her daughter to join them, with the advent of World War II it was not safe to travel international waters, and my eldest aunt would grow into her adulthood in Hong Kong, separated from her nuclear family.[7]

While my grandparents were not part of the earliest wave of Chinese immigrants to settle in Jamaica, they did comprise a distinct economic niche of shopkeepers.[8] My grandfather opened the Caribbean Bakery, and my grandmother birthed and raised eight children, including another daughter, her fourth born, my mother. As one can imagine, life in Kingston with eight children was not

easy, for either my grandmother or my mother. My grandparents retained traditional Chinese attitudes about gender roles and work; as the eldest girl in
Jamaica (and the only girl until my youngest aunt was born thirteen years later)
my mother was expected to perform domestic labor alongside her mother (cook-
ing, washing, laundering, cleaning, caring for the younger children). Though my
grandparents were not poor, they were not wealthy, and all the children had
to find their own ways in the world, which led my mother to pursue a nursing
degree in Guilford, England, after she graduated from her Catholic high school
at the age of seventeen.

After spending three years abroad, she returned, nursing degree in hand,
and worked at a hospital in Kingston. A year later, she learned about a job in
New York City at Beth Israel Hospital, so she relocated to Manhattan. While
living in New York, my mother received a letter from her friend Dorothy, who
wanted my mother to meet her friend, a young man living in New York City's
Chinatown. Dorothy and her friend had met during a Catholic Youth Summit in
Kingston a few years ago and had remained pen pals. Dorothy sent my mother
his contact information, which is how my mother came to meet my father. A
year after their first date, a dance at the Transfiguration Catholic Church in Chinatown, they would be married in that same church, and two years later I was
born in Queens. After another three years my brother was born, and a year after
that our family left New York for the Bay Area of California, which is the place I
most consider my "home" and where I'm from.

Of course, as I discuss in the beginning paragraph of this book's introduction, the questions "Where are you from?" along with "What are you?" become
reminders of the alienation of Asian Americans, the ways in which we cannot
simply be from the United States or only identify as American—these questions
reinforce the ambiguity that Asians in America face due to their racial difference. And for those of us who feel a distinct ambiguity due to our difference
from standard narratives of Asian American racialization, these questions can
prove even more fraught. In my childhood and adolescence I described myself
as Chinese Jamaican because I was the product of my parents: my father was
born in China and my mother was born in Jamaica, which thus seemed to logi-
cally make me Chinese Jamaican. Furthermore, my mother's Jamaican cultural
upbringing was a major influence in our family. Although the architects of the
Mixed-Marriage Policy of 1942 may have believed that the father's ethnicity
would prevail in the family's home, in our house it was my mother's Jamaican
roots that were palpable in the food that we ate, in the music that my parents
listened to (reggae), and in my mother's accented English; she spoke Jamaican patois like her siblings and half of my cousins.[9] When people asked my
younger self, "What are you?," and when I replied, "Chinese Jamaican," I could

see the confusion in their eyes. As a child I thought that the question "What are you?" was the same as "How do you understood yourself belonging in the world?" rather than "What variety of Asian are you?," making my reply all the more enigmatic for my questioners because "Chinese Jamaican" did not square with their sense of what I looked like. They could not integrate the image they saw in front of them, a phenotypically Asian girl, with their idea of who Jamaicans are (black). The standard response I received from my interlocutors, "You don't look Jamaican," confused me since I believed that I looked like the biogenetic material of my mother's family.[10]

It was not until I began taking undergraduate courses in critical race theory and ethnic studies at University of California-Santa Barbara that I began to understand the nuances and ambiguities of identity—of one's national, racial, ethnic, and cultural affiliations and the intersectionality of class, gender, sex, religion and a host of other factors affecting one's subjectivity. It was during this time that I stopped telling people that I was Chinese Jamaican, partly out of a growing activist identification with being Asian American, but also due to my inability to reconcile the ways that I internally identified with my maternal Jamaican cultural roots and the ambiguity of my external Asian phenotype. My nascent attempts to join the Chinese American Association or the Asian American Student Union had me feeling like a fraud because I spoke neither Mandarin nor Cantonese and because I could not completely relate to my Asian American peers, whose childhoods seemed to be more immersed than mine in Asian cultural behaviors and values: attending Asian language schools, visiting family in Asian countries, consuming the products of their Asian-ethnic homeland. I felt then, as I sometimes do now, a distinct lack of affinity with my fellow Asian American peers because my maternal family's Jamaican roots, combined with my lack of Asian linguistic knowledge, made me an outlier, someone whose relationship with ethnicity and race was ambiguous.

I am the child of immigrant Chinese parents, but this statement does not tell the full story of my family's background and the less well-known tale of my maternal family's Chinese diasporic roots in the Caribbean. My identity as an Asian American woman would seem to be absolute, born out of my biogenetic ethnic materiality, my parents' ancestry in an Asian nation, and my scholar-activist interests, which began at UC Santa Barbara during my first Asian American studies class in 1989 and continues through the Asian American literature classes I teach and the research in Asian American topics that I pursue. Yet I will always feel a sense of ambiguity, a distinct racial ambiguity, because I do, at heart, identify as Chinese Jamaican. And though I continue to be selective in when and where I share this part of my identity, mostly because I do not wish to exoticize my maternal family or have to describe either my family's specific immigration history or provide a more general explanation of why there are Chinese people in Jamaica, I do, in fact, feel myself to be Chinese Jamaican. It is part of my cultural DNA, reflected most distinctly in the tastes of home, ones that are unmistakably Jamaican.

I identify as a racially ambiguous Asian American, and I believe, as the chapters of this book demonstrate, that one's genetic makeup and what one looks like is not the barometer for identity—optics do not unconditionally determine racial classification. This study aims to add to the archive of what constitutes Asian American subjects and to provide a different lens to view those of us who do not fit into the standard narratives of Asian American immigration, racialization, and subjectivity. Who Asian Americans are, what they look like, where they reside, and who is qualified to write about Asian Americans is a racially ambiguous endeavor, one that I hope other scholars will continue to investigate because understanding Asian Americans in the fullness and complexity of their racial ambiguity adds to the richness of our Asian American epistemological inquiries. As a scholar who is deeply invested in antiracist teaching and practices, I believe that an acknowledgment of the ways in which race continues to be a subjective and ambiguous quality can only enhance our abilities to dismantle the structures of racist state practices and oppressive institutions. Theories of racial ambiguity are ultimately theories of antiracism, ones that affirm the plurality, syncretism, and hybridity of all Asian American identities.

NOTES

INTRODUCTION: AMBIGUOUS AMERICANS

1   Although one may interpret the veteran's speculation about Jane to be based solely on her mixed race identity, within the context of this scene, Jane is in the company of a Japanese film crew, and it is the spectacle of these Asian figures at a VFW (Veterans of Foreign Wars) hall that Ozeki describes as the impetus for the veteran's verbal harassment of Jane. *My Year of Meats* and Jane's racially ambiguous identity are discussed further in chapter 4.

2   Bow, *Partly Colored*, 18.

3   To be clear, I am not arguing that Asian Americans experience more ambiguity than other racialized groups (including white Americans), simply that the ambiguity that coheres to Asian Americans is unique and different from other racialized peoples. Furthermore, I use the phrase "racial pentagram" to refer to the five categories into which people in the United States are often divided: Caucasian/white, African American/black, Asian American, American Indian/Native American, and Latino/Hispanic. I also recognize that while Latino/Hispanic is more of an ethnic rather than a racial category, in the United States it functions as a social category of race. I also note that increasingly "Middle Eastern"/"Arab"/"Muslim American" are terms used largely interchangeably in order to function as a sixth prong in the US racial taxonomy. I want to make clear that I recognize the vast differences among the terms "Middle Eastern," "Arab," and "Muslim"; however, within the (il)logic of racialization and in response to the xenophobia that followed 9/11, these three terms have been operating together within the US public imaginary to create a, potentially, sixth racial category.

4   Creef, *Imaging Japanese America*, 177.

5   *Hapa* is the Hawaiian word for "half" and has become a term to identify people who are mixed race Asian American, regardless of the actual percentage of their Asian heritage. However, *hapa* is also a contested term, one that many scholars now eschew because of contestations from Hawaiian indigenous people who point out that the phrase has been inappropriately appropriated from their culture. For more on the debates over the use of the word *hapa* see Wei-ming Dariotis's "Hapa: The Word of Power." I use the term "hapa" within the context of its usage by other scholars, but generally speaking, my own preference is to use the phrase "mixed Asian" or simply "mixed race" Asian American.

6   Fulbeck, *Part Asian*, 248.

7 The Red Apple Boycott was initiated in January 1990 after a dispute between a Haitian woman, Ghiselaine Felissaintin, and a Korean storeowner, Bong Ok Jang. For a year and a half, African Americans in the Brooklyn and other New York boroughs boycotted Korean-owned businesses. Latasha Harlins was an African American teenager who was shot in the back by a Korean storeowner, Soon Ja Du, on March 16, 1991. Mrs. Du was acquitted of the murder on the grounds of self-defense and sentenced to five years' probation, a judgment that angered many African American community members in the Los Angeles area and were cited as one rationale for the targeting of Korean businesses for looting and incineration during the Los Angeles uprisings. I use the term "uprising" rather than "riots" in keeping with labor historian Mike Davis's belief that the violence that erupted after the Rodney King trial in Simi Valley was evidence of ethnicized class divisions rather than irrational rioting. For more on the Red Apple boycott see Claire Jean Kim's *Bitter Fruit: The Politics of Black-Korean Conflict in New York City*. For an artistic take on the Latasha Harlins–Korean American conflict see Anna Deveare Smith's *Twilight: Los Angeles 1992*, and for more on Mike Davis see chapter 10, "Uprising and Repression in L.A.," in Davis, *Reading Rodney King/Reading Urban Uprising*.

8 In order to fully appreciate the multiethnic scope of Jin's work, one should listen to the entire album.

9 I say "predominantly by and about Asian Americans" because as will be evident in chapter 5, the question of who is authorized to pen an Asian American work is central to this later chapter.

10 A word about terminology used in this study. In general, I employ the term "Asian American," rather than "Asian Pacific American (APA)" or "Asian Pacific Islander (API)" to designate the racial category of people whose ancestry comes from the continent of Asia (which includes the area commonly understood as the Middle East) as well as the Pacific Island/Pacific Rim nations. My choice of "Asian American" over "APA" or "API" comes from a nuanced understanding of the complicated race relations that exist between Pacific Islander/Pacific Rim communities and Asian immigrant populations (and their descendants). Because the subjects of this study are predominantly not from Pacific Islander nations (indeed, the subjects of this study are predominantly East and Southeast Asian), I have opted to use the term "Asian American" to be precise and to differentiate between those who appear to be descendants of Asian nations versus those from Pacific Island nations. Many who identify as Pacific Islander find it inaccurate and patronizing to be collapsed into the term "Asian Pacific American" because they often see this as a flattening of all Asian-ethnic difference. Finally, like the editors of *War Baby/Love Child: Mixed Race Asian American Art*, I use the term "mixed race" without a hyphen to underscore "this idea [of mixed race] as a social construct and not as a biological reality, which would be implied by the compound term 'mixed-race'" (243).

11 I am indebted to Leslie Bow for the helpful observations about the various concerns of each chapter and how they unfold in this monograph.

12 Christian, *Black Feminist Criticism*, 226.

13 Prince, *Dictionary of Narratology*, 60.

14 Foucault, *Society Must Be Defended*, 7.

15 Ibid.

16 Anzaldúa, *Borderlands*, 101.

17 Ibid., 103.

18 Gilroy, *Postcolonial Melancholia*, 14.

19 I acknowledge Stephen Sohn for letting me borrow the phrase "poststructural invest-
    ments" during a reading of this chapter. Needless to say, shades (and citations) of
    Antonio Gramsci, Louis Althusser, Michel Foucault, and Jacques Derrida appear in my
    work, as well as in the scores of ethnic, gender, and race critics whom I directly quote
    within this study.

20 Chuh, *Imagine Otherwise*, 9.

21 Bow, *Partly Colored*, 4.

22 I mention the myriad perspectives of mixed heritage scholarship to acknowledge that
    as with any discipline there are varying voices and contributions to the field that are
    sometimes at odds with one another and sometimes in concert. I am not, however, sug-
    gesting that mixed heritage scholarship is more contentious than any other academic
    discipline or that I refer to a specific controversial tension within this body of work.

23 Houston and Williams, "No Passing Zone," x.

24 I note here that not all mixed Asian American scholarship or mixed heritage scholar-
    ship is the purview of multiracial people, although clearly scholars like Kip Fulbeck
    do identify as multiracial.

25 The first Critical Mixed Race Studies conference was held at DePaul University in
    November 2010 and has become a biennial event and established an e-journal of the
    same name.

26 Nguyen, *Race and Resistance*, 7.

27 It has almost become conventional wisdom to recite the claim that there is no bio-
    logical basis to race and that race is a social construction because critics like Stuart
    Hall, Paul Gilroy, Lisa Lowe, Randall Kennedy, Etienne Balibar, Immanuel Wallerstein,
    Michael Omi, Howard Winant, and many others have made this assertion in various
    forms in their respective works.

28 Balibar, "Is There a Neo-Racism?," in Balibar and Wallerstein, *Race, Nation, Class*, 21.

29 See Omi and Winant's *Racial Formation in the United States*, particularly chapter 4,
    "Racial Formation."

30 Another excellent source for an overview of how racial identities, particularly white
    racial identities, became consolidated in the United States is Ian Haney Lopez's
    White by Law: The Legal Construction of Race.

31 Zack, "Preface," ix.

32 Kwan and Speirs, *Mixing It Up*, 4.

33 See Elaine Kim's preface to *Asian American Literature: An Introduction to the Writings and
    Their Social Context* (xii–xiii) and Robert Chang's *Disoriented: Asian Americans, Law, and
    the Nation-State* (2).

34 The term "Asian American" emerged in the late 1960s, during the height of the civil
    rights movement and antiwar protests against US military presence in Viet Nam and
    other regions of Southeast Asia. Asian American activists, largely student led, joined
    in pan-ethnic and pan-racial alliances to protest racism in the United States and to
    demand courses taught in US universities that focused on the histories and experiences
    of Asian Americans. Thus both subjects, Asian American people and the study of experi-
    ences about people descended from Asia in the United States, emerged simultaneously
    out of a coalition centered around Third World rights, social justice, and antiracism. For
    more on the history of the Asian American activist and student movements, see William
    Wei's *The Asian American Movement* and Yen Le Espiritu's *Asian American Panethnicity*.

35 I am indebted to Mia Tuan's work *Forever Foreigners or Honorary Whites: The Asian Eth-
    nic Experience Today* for elucidating the tension between Asian American status as

either over- or underdetermined, racially and nationally, within US social and cultural discourse.

36 Okihiro, *Margins*, 33.

37 Ian Haney Lopez's observations about these similarities from a legal perspective are quite astute—for more see *White by Law*.

38 For more on violence in the US West toward Chinese Americans see Kwong and Miscevic's *Chinese America* and Jean Pfaelzer's *Driven Out!: The Forgotten War against Chinese Americans*.

39 The Yellow Peril stereotype developed at the turn-of-the-twentieth century with the rise of American imperialism and a fear of Asian hordes, represented by Japan's and China's taking over Anglo-Saxon territories like the United States and Western Europe. For more on the Yellow Peril stereotype see chapter 4, "Inner Dikes and Barred Zones," in Robert G. Lee's *Orientals*. For a thorough history of anti-miscegenation laws see Randall Kennedy's *Interracial Intimacies: Sex, Marriage, Identity, and Adoption*.

40 The model minority stereotype avers that Asian Americans are higher achieving than all other racial minorities in the United States. The term was first used in a magazine article on Japanese American academic success, and it has since become a shorthand phrase to denote Asian Americans' success in assimilating to American norms, their achievements in academic arenas, and their supposed lack of racial victimization and discrimination—their unfettered access to the American dream. The model minority myth perpetuates divisions between Asian Americans and other ethnic and racial minority groups by confirming, for white Americans, the pathology of black, Latino, and American Indians in their inability to achieve success like the Asian American "model" minority. This myth has been debunked by various critics, such as legal scholar Robert Chang in *Disoriented* and journalist Frank Wu in *Yellow: Race in America beyond Black and White*.

41 This is particularly true for indigenous Hawaiians, who have recently begun working with various First Nations groups to agitate for their land rights in Hawaii.

42 See Sau-ling Cynthia Wong's "Denationalization Reconsidered: Asian American Cultural Criticism at a Theoretical Crossroads."

43 As acknowledged in a previous note, although the field of Asian American Studies or more specifically Asian Pacific American studies does encompass indigenous groups such as Hawaiians, Samoans, Guamanians, and other indigenous Pacific Island communities, for the purposes of this study I am using the term "Asian American" because the cultural productions that I examine are almost all Asian American and not Asian Pacific American; hence, I wish to remain respectful to the different discourse of Pacific Islander studies while simultaneously acknowledging its place within API studies.

44 A perusal of the conference proceedings of the annual Association of Asian American Studies will reveal the diversity and multidisciplinary nature of Asian American scholarship, as presentations that range from contesting the very linguistic efficacy of the phrase "Asian American" versus "Asian Pacific American," to sociological studies on transracial Korean adoptees, to discussions of life for West Asian and Muslim Americans in a post-9/11 world illustrates the range of Asian American scholarship.

45 A small sampling of recent scholarship in Asian American studies reveals its diversity and range in challenging the limits of what the analytic "Asian American" encompasses. Anthologies such as *AfroAsian Encounters: Culture, History, Politics*, edited by Heike Raphael-Hernandez and Shannon Steen and *Alien Encounters: Popular Culture*

in Asian America, edited by Mimi Thi Nguyen and Thuy Linh Nguyen Tu illuminate multiple perspectives on Asian American epistemology. And two monographs, Anne-Marie Lee-Loy's *Searching for Mr. Chin: Constructions of the Nation and Chinese in West Indian Literature* and Cathy Schlund-Vials's *War, Genocide, and Justice: Cambodian American Memory Work* push at the boundaries of where Asian America is located and the objects (and subjects) of Asian American scholarship.

46   Early anthologies of Asian American literature such as the pathbreaking *Aiiieeeee!* and Elaine Kim's *Asian American Literature* explored mostly East Asian American ethnic groups and Filipino Americans. However, recent anthologies are more inclusive and expansive in the range of voices featured; for example, Jean Wu and Min Song's *Asian American Studies: A Reader* (as well as the updated version edited with Jean Wu and Thomas Chen, *Asian American Studies Now*) includes essays describing not only ethnic diversity (South Asian and Southeast Asian communities, mixed race communities) but attend to differences of sexuality, gender, class, and region.

47   Yu's original musing originated in a post he wrote on his blog, tympan, titled "Has Asian American Studies Failed?" which subsequently became a roundtable topic in the *Journal of Asian American Studies*, the topic of a plenary session in the annual meeting of the Association of Asian American Studies, and a panel at the 2013 Modern Language Association convention.

48   As anecdotal evidence, I offer up the recounting by a colleague (who remains unnamed due to the pre-tenured status of this person) who was told by a senior colleague at her institution that Asian Americans were not a group worthy of study because they were not a disenfranchised nor an oppressed minority in the United States. And at a forum on bridging the achievement gap (January 2006, UNC Chapel Hill) that I had been asked to participate in, the place of Asian Americans were seen as analogous to their white American peers and therefore not worthy of inclusion in thinking about their place as students of color in the American education system.

49   I have had well-intentioned colleagues at my institution ask me about the difficulties of finding works in translation for my students, inquiring whether my own linguistic deficiencies in Mandarin and Cantonese prevent me from conducting research in Asian American literary criticism, and others who continually confuse Asian Studies with Asian American Studies.

50   Edwards, *The Practice of Diaspora*, 7.

51   Lovinik, "Talking Race and Cyberspace," 60.

52   Nakamura, *Digitizing Race*, 5.

53   Kim, *Writing Manhood*, 247.

54   Ibid., 247.

55   The one-drop rule refers to the social convention established during the antebellum period in the United States that governed racial identities for mixed race African American–white people—a belief that one-drop of black blood rendered a person's identity black. Legally, if someone could claim 1/32 (a great-great-great grandparent) of their ancestry as African American, they were deemed legally black. For more on the concepts of the one-drop rule and hypodescent see Omi and Winant's Part II in *Racial Formation in the United States*.

56   In keeping with scholars who work in Southeast Asian studies, I will be using the convention of using two words to refer to the country of Viet Nam.

1: FROM ENEMY ALIEN TO ASSIMILATING AMERICAN

1   Outline of Mixed-Marriage Policy, September 24, 1943, file 291.1, Records of the Western Defense Command and 4th Army and Wartime Civil Control Administration General Correspondence, Record Group 499, National Archives II, College Park, MD (hereafter cited as RG 499, NAII) 1. A note about terminology related to the events around World War II that affected Japanese and Japanese Americans living in the United States and its allied territories: the general phrase used to describe this phenomenon is "Japanese American internment." However, many Japanese American groups prefer the term "Japanese American incarceration," believing it to be a more accurate phrase for the experience of being unconstitutionally targeted, detained, removed, and held in concentration camps. The term "concentration camp" rather than internment camp will be used whenever possible out of accuracy for both the time period in question, because this was the language that the Franklin D. Roosevelt administration as well as the War Relocation Authority (abbreviated to WRA) and Wartime Civilian Control Authority (abbreviated to WCCA) used in its internal documents and since this was the condition that the Japanese and Japanese American community found themselves in. Although the phrase "concentration camp" has been irrevocably linked with another type of concentration camp in this time period—the Nazi camps used in the Final Solution for the genocide of Jewish people—I believe most readers will be able to distinguish between the Nazi regime's genocidal program that led to the Jewish Holocaust and the US government's unconstitutional program that led to the abrogation of civil rights for Japanese Americans. For a very lucid rationale for these terms, see the Densho website, www.densho.org/densho.asp, and historian John Howard's excellent work *Concentration Camps on the Home Front: Japanese Americans in the House of Jim Crow.* Additionally *The Final Report*, published in 1943, lists seventy-two women of Japanese ancestry as exempted; Peter Crosby of the WCCA lists ninety-four "full-blood" individuals as being exempted, and historian Paul Spickard cites ninety Japanese women married to non-Japanese men as being exempted. Given Spickard's extensive research in this area, I am quoting his number.

2   According to a memo by Peter J. Crosby of the WCCA, the final number of exemptees living in the restricted area of the West Coast as of September 1, 1943, was actually 568, with 360 mixed-blood minors, 154 mixed-blood adults, and 94 full-blood individuals, and of these 608 exemptions, 36 permits had been cancelled due to families moving outside of the restricted zone and 2 were cancelled due to deaths; a recount of exemptees was done after the June publication of *The Final Report*. Peter J. Crosby, September 1, 1943, file 291.1, RG 499, NAII, 2. "Mixed-blood" was the language used in Crosby's report and is used herein whenever quoting the papers from this era, and the records of the WRA and WCCA refer to the program as the "Mixed-Marriage Policy," with "Mixed-Marriage" both capitalized and hyphenated. Elsewhere in this chapter and in the book as a whole I do not use hyphens when talking about mixed marriages, mixed race, mixed heritage, or mixed as an adjectival descriptor.

3   Gen. John L. DeWitt to John McCloy, Assistant. Secretary of War, June 16, 1943, file 291.1, RG 499, NAII, 1.

4   Paul Spickard's essay stands as the best researched and detailed account of the Mixed-Marriage Program to date. See Spickard's "Injustice Compounded: Amerasians and Non-Japanese Americans in World War II Concentration Camps." Tetsuden Kashima briefly mentions the Mixed-Marriage Program and quotes from DeWitt's report but

does not elaborate beyond a few paragraphs and three footnotes on this phenomenon. See Kashima's *Judgment without Trial: Japanese American Imprisonment during World War II* (135–136, 144). Klancy Clark deNevers profiles a family exempted from incarceration, the Moyer family of Hoquiam, Washington, and briefly states the circumstances of their exemptions. See *The Colonel and the Pacifist: Karl Bendetsen, Perry Saito, and the Incarceration of Japanese Americans during World War II* (177–179).

5 To be fair, most scholars of the Japanese American incarceration are aware that there were exemptions to incarceration; however, I believe that general knowledge of this, even among Asian American scholars, is still underacknowledged.

6 Navy Secretary Frank Knox believed that Pearl Harbor was a result of sabotage by a fifth column of Japanese in the Hawaiian Islands. Although such intelligence was found to be false, rumors of a fifth column in both Hawaii and on the West Coast predominated in the media and among the US military and were a leading reason for Gen. DeWitt's endorsement of incarceration, despite the fact that the Munson report issued in November 1941 unequivocally stated that "there will be no armed uprising of Japanese. . . . For the most part the local Japanese are loyal to the United States or, at worst, hope that by remaining quiet they can avoid concentration camps." For more on the myth of military necessity and the Munson report see Ronald Takaki's "The Myth of 'Military Necessity' for Japanese-American Internment," in *Strangers from a Different Shore* and Wendy Ng's *Japanese American Internment during World War II.*

7 Spickard, "Injustice Compounded," 6. For an excellent work documenting the theme of loyalty in the decision of incarceration and whom to release during the Japanese American incarceration see Eric Muller's *American Inquisition: The Hunt for Japanese American Disloyalty in World War II.*

8 *Nisei* refers to the second generation of Japanese Americans; the first, *issei*, generation is the immigrant generation of Japanese. I follow Evelyn Nakano Glenn in the lack of capitalization when referring to issei, nisei, and sansei.

9 Poston was one of ten concentration camps used to incarcerate Japanese and Japanese Americans under Executive Order 9066. Others include Jerome, Rohwer, Manzanar, Tule Lake, Heart Mountain, Topaz, Minidoka, Amache (Granada), and Gila River.

10 The document in question is part of a list that the WCCA compiled of "Exempted Persons of Japanese Ancestry now Resident in Evacuated Areas" dated September 1, 1943. There are two entries for DeLeon [*sic*]: Yoshiko and Martin, aged twenty-four and four respectively; the date of their exemption is listed as October 6, 1942, and their residence where exempted is listed as San Luis Obispo, California.

11 Excellent sources for the history of the Japanese American incarceration (and the repercussions of incarceration) include Michi Weglyn's *Years of Infamy: the Untold Story of America's Concentration Camps*, Roger Daniels's *Concentration Camps USA: Japanese Americans and World War II*, Greg Robinson's *By Order of the President: FDR and the Incarceration of Japanese Americans*, and Mitchell T. Maki, Harry H. L. Kitano, and S. Megan Berthold's *Achieving the Impossible Dream: How Japanese Americans Obtained Redress.*

12 I am indebted to the Dorr and deLeon families for first alerting me to the existence of Yoshiko deLeon. All information regarding Yoshiko deLeon and members of her family came from a variety of personal interviews, telephone conversations, e-mail correspondence, photocopied articles, and family anecdotes collected throughout my friendship with Trish Dorr, beginning in September 1988. More formal conversations with members of the Dorr and deLeon families about Yoshiko's exemption from incarceration occurred from approximately May 2004 through July 2008. Information on

the deLeon family is incomplete because of the nature of incomplete remembrances and information that family members had about her. Additionally, Yoshiko deLeon did not keep records or share many stories of her life during World War II.

13 It should also be noted that during this time marriage was clearly coded as a heterosexual enterprise between a man and a woman; any queer unions would not have been recognized by either the US government and larger US society or by any Japanese American communities; therefore, the emphasis in this chapter is on mixed marriages between men and women because these were the only ones officially considered for exemption.

14 Executive Order 9066 mentions people of Japanese ancestry both "alien and non-alien"; there is never any mention of Japanese Americans or American citizens, a discursive move meant to reinforce the foreign nature of the Japanese as well as to obscure the fact that the government was incarcerating American citizens.

15 In a section subtitled "Public Opinion and Public Fears" (*Judgment without Trial*, 52–54), Kashima reprints segments of a 1985 interview with Edward Ennis, one of the architects of the incarceration, in which Ennis admits that the incarceration of Japanese in the United States was necessary to "assuage public fears" and that "public relations" rather than the threat of espionage or sabotage was the prime factor behind the incarceration (53). Similarly, a selection of editorials (11–26) reprinted in the collection *Only What We Could Carry: The Japanese American Internment Experience*, illustrate the level of anti-Japanese hostility and support for the incarceration among mainstream publications like the *Sacramento Bee* and the *San Francisco Chronicle*.

16 Executive Order No. 9066 reproduced in Ng, *Japanese American Internment during World War II*, 155.

17 Daniels, *Concentration Camps USA*, 70–71.

18 Qtd. in Weglyn, *Years of Infamy*, 71.

19 Both Roger Daniels (*Concentration Camps USA*) and Greg Robinson (*By Order of the President*) assert that President Roosevelt's anti-Japanese prejudice, as well as popular opinion, fueled his decision to sign Executive Order 9066 and to specifically target only Japanese and Japanese American people.

20 It is well documented that the "military necessity" that DeWitt and others invoked as the rationale for incarcerating Japanese Americans was greatly exaggerated and motivated by racial prejudice and national vengeance. And although there were Italian and German nationals (like the issei) who were rounded up, interrogated, and imprisoned based on their status as an alleged threat to national security, only the Japanese and Japanese Americans were specifically targeted for mass removal. For more see Weglyn's *Years of Infamy* and Maki et al.'s *Achieving the Impossible Dream: How Japanese Americans Obtained Redress*.

21 Although *The Final Report* lists one-sixteenth as the cut-off for inclusion for incarceration, in practice, the WDC allowed mixed race adults to return to the West Coast as long as they had less than 50 percent Japanese ancestry and could prove that they had been raised in a Caucasian home. For more, see Spickard's essay "Injustice Compounded."

22 Austin E. Griffiths, March 27, 1942, file 291.1, RG 499, NAII.

23 Lt. Col. William Boekel, April 3, 1942, file 291.1, RG 499, NAII.

24 Ralph Harrison, March 30, 1942, file 291.1, RG 499, NAII, 4.

25 Thomas A. Clark, March 31, 1942, file 291.1, RG 499, NAII, 2.

26 I put "Eurasian" in quotations both to signal that this terminology was used in the correspondence found in the WCCA files and to refer to the archaic use of the term for

a person of mixed Caucasian and Asian heritage. Thomas A. Clark, March 31, 1942, file 291.1, RG 499, NAII, 2.

27 Ibid.

28 Ibid.

29 Ibid. Keeping families together was one of the policies that marked the US incarceration of Japanese relatively more humane than their Canadian counterparts, who routinely neglected to take this crucial aspect into account during their evacuation and incarceration procedures.

30 In a few cases, non-Japanese spouses elected to be incarcerated along with their Japanese partners, while some non-Japanese spouses were allowed to leave the restricted zone with their mixed race children. For more on instances of non-Japanese partners being interned see Steven Okazaki's documentary *Days of Waiting*, and for an example of a non-Japanese (white) spouse moving out of the restricted zone with her multiracial children see Cynthia Fujikawa's filmed performance piece *Old Man River.*

31 One letter, found within the correspondence of the WCCA from the vice president and provost of the University of California-Berkeley, Monroe Deutsch, inquires, on behalf of Mrs. Ansel Adams, for the removal of Art History Professor Chiura Obata and his wife and son to Mrs. Adams's residence in the Yosemite Valley; the request was denied. Monroe Deutsch to Frank Kittredge, Superintendent of Yosemite National Park, March 19, 1942, file 291.1, RG 499, NAII.

32 Under the "synopsis" of the correspondence index of files found in the military records of the National Archives in College Park, MD, the subject is listed as such: "Mixed-Marriage Policy." Included in this line #; "The stated policy on handling Mixed-Marriage cases with Var. reports & actions on said cases," file 291.1, RG 499, NAII. Unfortunately, this synopsis and the accompanying index in which it is listed is the only record we have of this correspondence since the entire file is not locatable at the College Park, Maryland, National Archives.

33 Maj. Herman P. Goebel Jr. to A. H. Cheney, July 12, 1942, file 291.1, RG 499, NAII, 1.

34 Ibid. As is evident from the wording of this memorandum, as well as subsequent documents related to the Mixed-Marriage Program, there was a clear gender bias for exemption; no Japanese/Japanese American men married to white women (with or without unemancipated children) were included in the program.

35 Ibid.

36 See *Final Report.*

37 List of Exempted Persons of Japanese Ancestry now Resident in Evacuated Areas, September 1, 1943, file 291.1, RG 499, NAII. The files of the Mixed-Marriage Program indicate that the Regasa family was not the only family released from Tanforan on August 31, 1942. In total there were three families released (Bantugan, Pontillas, and Regasa), and all were the earliest recorded exemptions listed in the mixed marriage exemption files.

38 Despite the fact that the terminology of "race" referred to distinct ethnic and national groups, in the application of racist ideology during World War II there are key moments when we can see how individual Asians in America become lumped together as either "Oriental" or "Asian." For instance, while Chinese, Japanese, and Indian people were seen as distinct races, the Asiatic Barred Zone (part of the Immigration Act of 1917) compressed these three groups into a distinct "Asiatic" category to prevent their immigration into the United States. For more see Sucheng Chan's discussion (54–55)

of anti-Asian immigration restrictions and the "barred zone" in *Asian Americans: An Interpretive History.*

39   See Omi and Winant's *Racial Formation in the United States: From the 1960s to the 1990s.*

40   Ibid., 15.

41   Hisaye Yamamoto's short story "Wilshire Bus" includes an instance of a Japanese American woman remembering Chinese Americans wearing such buttons and reacting with feelings of anger.

42   "How to Tell Japs from the Chinese," 81.

43   Spickard, *Japanese Americans*, 57.

44   Qtd. in ibid., 57.

45   Qtd. in ibid., 57–58.

46   Both the 1882 Chinese Exclusion Act and the 1924 Immigration Act deemed Asians (specifically Chinese and Japanese) ineligible for citizenship; at this time, Asians were the only ethnic-racial group excluded from naturalization. The McCarran-Walter Immigration and Naturalization Act of 1952 modified the 1924 Immigration Act, allowing for great numbers of immigrants from Asian countries, as well as allowing for their citizenship.

47   Three months after Ozawa's case, *United States v. Thind* made its way to the Supreme Court, where Bhagat Singh Thind's petition for naturalization was also thrown out because though he was understood as Caucasian (as a Hindu and member of the Indian subcontinent) he was not understood to be white, thus consolidating the emphasis that whiteness was necessary for nationality. Ozawa's and Thind's cases form what legal scholar Ian Haney Lopez calls the "prerequisite cases" which "provide an invaluable study in the construction of the White race and offer important insights into the structuring and content of Whiteness as a legal and social idea" (139). For more see Lopez's *White by Law: The Legal Construction of Race.*

48   Ng, *Japanese American Internment*, 9.

49   Unlike the Supreme Court's decision in *Thind*, "Caucasian" appears as synonymous and interchangeable with "whiteness" within the WDC and WCCA documents.

50   I say "somewhat" because while the rationale for the Mixed-Marriage Policy might have had a desire for mixed race children to be assimilated as closely to white Americans as possible, there is no indication that they were actually regarded or treated as if they were, actually, white.

51   It is worth noting that Franz Boas, the legendary Columbia University anthropologist, was one of the first to claim that race was not a primordial fact; however, Park and his colleagues were among the first to focus on the topic of race and assimilation. For more on the different race theories of the early twentieth century, see Omi and Winant's section on "Ethnicity" in *Racial Formation in the United States*. For a very thorough look at the connection of the Chicago School and Robert Park in promoting a progressive theory of race in the 1930s and 1940s, one that shaped race theory in the coming decades, see Henry Yu's excellent work *Thinking Orientals: Migration, Contact, and Exoticism in Modern America.*

52   DeWitt, *The Final Report*, 145.

53   Outline of Mixed-Marriage Policy, September 23, 1943, file 291.1, RG 499, NAII, 1.

54   Gen. John L. DeWitt to John McCloy, Asst. Sect. of War, February 15, 1943, file 291.1, RG 499, NAII.

55   Ibid.

56 Gen. John L. DeWitt to John McCloy, Asst. Sect. of War, June 16, 1943, file 291.1, RG 499, NAII, 1.

57 Col. Karl Bendetsen to Capt. John Hall, May 24, 1943, file 291.1, RG 499, NAII, 5.

58 Theresa Takeyashi had her case championed by First Lady Eleanor Roosevelt, who wrote a personal letter to Secretary of War Henry Stimson supporting Takeyashi's exemption from incarceration and urging for her resettlement to Seattle. Needless to say, Mrs. Roosevelt's petition was unsuccessful. For more details see Spickard's essay "Injustice Compounded" (9–10) and the following telephone transcript, Col. Karl Bendetsen to Capt. John Hall, May 24, 1943, file 291.1, RG 499, NAII, 1–7.

59 Col. Karl Bendetsen to Capt. John Hall, May 24, 1943, file 291.1, RG 499, NAII, 3.

60 Ibid., 5–6.

61 Ibid., 6.

62 The bias against Asian male–white female miscegenation was prevalent among the military and can be seen in the rationale for the Mixed-Marriage Policy because no Japanese American men married to white women were exempted.

63 Indeed, until the Cable Act was repealed in 1936, white American women who married Japanese or other Asian immigrant men lost their citizenship—a move clearly designed to punish particular types of interracial relationships because white men who married Asian immigrant women were not subject to the same treatment and white women married to aliens eligible for citizenship, like Italian or German immigrants, did not have their citizenship revoked.

64 Col. Karl Bendetsen to Capt. John Hall, May 24, 1943, file 291.1, RG 499, NAII, 3–4.

65 Furthermore, the status of these exempted Japanese women were wholly dependent on their relationship with their husbands. The "Outline of Mixed Marriage [sic] Policy" states that if a Japanese/Japanese American woman's non-Japanese husband dies or if these interracial couples divorce, there will be a review process to determine whether the "status of the exemptee has changed" and appropriate action will follow; a woman and her children were only allowed to remain in the restricted military zone through the auspices of the husband's identity. In other words, these women were exempted only through the umbrella protection of male privilege.

66 Spickard, "Injustice Compounded," 8.

67 Although Spickard, in his essay "Injustice Compounded," confirms that Japanese fathers married to non-Japanese (predominantly white) women with unemancipated mixed race children "could leave camp, but not return to the jurisdiction of the Western Defense Command," he writes that "whether the offending Japanese parent were the mother or the father, the entire family was allowed to leave prison together" (8). Yet, the example of Jerry Fujikawa, his white wife, and their three multiracial children counter this assertion since Fujikawa was incarcerated in Manzanar while his wife and children were allowed to reside in Denver and visited Fujikwawa before he was inducted into the 442nd regiment. For more about Jerry Fujikawa see the filmed performance piece *Old Man River*.

68 Qtd. in Spickard, "Injustice Compounded," 7.

69 I refer to Yoshiko Tanaka Nakamura deLeon by her first name, Yoshiko, throughout this book not out of disrespect but to acknowledge that her first name was her most stable name and identity throughout the myriad changes that occurred in her various families of origin and matrimony.

70 The only recollection that the family had about Yoshiko's biological father was that his surname had originally been Watanabe, but they do not know his first name nor

any other relevant information about him after he departed California for Japan. Although it may seem to be an unusual and progressive practice for a man to take his wife's surname, it was not uncommon in Japan of this era for a husband to take on his wife's surname if her family lacked a male heir. Essentially, he, and his sons, would become the male heirs to his wife's family. I am indebted to Paul Spickard for confirming this fact.

71 Based on historical precedent, it is likely that Eju was a picture bride (a woman who was married, in absentia, to a husband living abroad and who subsequently journeyed to the United States to join her now husband) because the majority of Japanese of the laboring class immigrated to the United States as bachelors or without their families. In 1908 the Gentleman's Agreement between United States and Japan restricted immigration of Japanese laborers to the United States, but a loophole remained that allowed for the continuing immigration of wives and children until the 1924 Immigration Act. However, no one in the Dorr, deLeon, or Nakamura families could confirm whether Eju was, in fact, a picture bride.

72 For more on the conditions of issei women living in rural areas in the early twentieth century see Evelyn Nakano Glenn's *Issei, Nisei, Warbride: Three Generations of Japanese American Women in Domestic Service.*

73 Ibid., 49.

74 Masa is the preferred name of Masako Nakamura Frost, Yoshiko's youngest sister. All references to Yoshiko deLeon's life were gained through personal interviews with Masako Frost and Patricia Dorr, Yoshiko's daughter.

75 Gabriel deLeon was, by all accounts, an extremely personable and charismatic individual who, like his wife, also led an exceptional life. He entered the United States as a ward of the state based on the US occupation of the Philippines, learned English, and succeeded in his farming business to become a civic leader in the postwar era, despite having never graduated from high school. In 1976 he became the first Filipino American mayor of any US city on the mainland, Arroyo Grande, California.

76 Again, let me assert that by the standards of society in the pre–World War II era, a marriage between a Filipino immigrant and a Japanese American woman would have been seen as an interracial union in a way that we no longer regard such marriages in our current political times. Also, although this chapter looks at the deLeon marriage primarily through Yoshiko's perspective, one of the practical and structural reasons for Gabriel deLeon's choosing a bride of a different "race" has to do with scarcity: there were very few Filipina women in the United States to marry pre-1965—the Filipino male-to-female ratio pre–World War II was around 14:1, and more than half of the women who did immigrate to the United States pre-1965 were married women. For more see Juanita Tamayo Lott's *Common Destiny: Filipino American Generations.*

77 Gabriel and Yoshiko temporarily relocated to the Philippines because Gabriel's mother was dying. They always expected to return to California.

78 Patricia Dorr was born in 1944 and was too young to have any memories of World War II, but she does recall life on the family farm during the 1950s and early 1960s.

79 Yoshiko's silence about her wartime experience is in keeping with the silence of other Japanese Americans incarcerated during this time period. The theme of silence pervades Japanese American narratives that recount the era of World War II, particularly related to their incarceration. And many historical, anthropological, and ethnographic accounts make note of the silence that pervades the incarceration experience for Japanese Americans. Examples of both fiction and nonfiction depictions of silence

include Joy Kogawa's *Obasan*, Maki et al.'s *Achieving the Impossible Dream*, and Inada's *Only What We Could Carry*.

80 Ng, *Japanese American Internment*, 98.

81 A Japanese (and to certain extent Japanese American) custom is to eat mochi (a Japanese rice flour dessert) on New Year's Eve; in the deLeon family, the children and grandchildren of Martin and Yoshiko consume pork adobo, a Filipino dish, every Christmas Eve, thereby exchanging a Japanese custom for a uniquely Filipino American family tradition.

82 The deLeons extended Filipino family included actual family members of Gabriel (a brother in particular) but it also included extensive social networks of honorary aunts, uncles, and cousins who were not necessarily related to the deLeons by blood.

83 According to family lore, Yoshiko's exemption came about because of Gabriel deLeon's relationship with the Filipino consulate in San Francisco—because he knew someone in the consul's office he was able to obtain a permit allowing Yoshiko to remain in San Luis Obispo County and thus able to evade incarceration. It is probably true that Gabriel did seek the advice of his friend in the consul's office. However, it is clear from the archives at NARAII that Yoshiko and Martin became part of the Mixed-Marriage Program, and therefore it was not simply based on individual connections that Yoshiko and Martin were kept out of the concentration camps.

84 Gen. John L. DeWitt to John McCloy, Asst. Sect. of War, June 16, 1943, file 291.1, RG 499, NAII, 1.

85 DeWitt, *The Final Report*, 145.

86 Indeed, from the point of view of constitutional civil liberties, *Korematsu v. United States* (1942) has not been challenged in the Supreme Court (*Korematsu*'s original conviction was overturned on November 10, 1983, in San Francisco's Federal District Court, but the issue of the incarceration was not addressed) and therefore could still be invoked to imprison a specific ethnic group during times of military and national crisis, as unlikely as that might be.

87 For instance, she could have changed into Yolanda deLeon in keeping with her husband's Filipino culture or chosen a more Anglicized name, like Kathy.

88 Morrison, *Beloved*, 104.

2: ANTISENTIMENTAL LOSS

1 In both *Then She Found Me* and *Did You Hear about the Morgans?* an adopted girl from China serves as both films' literal denouement and plot resolution in the concluding minutes.

2 The adopted Asian girl is the latest in a series of transracial adopted children featured in popular culture. The 1980s featured two sitcoms with two different African American children adopted into white families. Arnold (played by Gary Coleman) from *Different Strokes* and the eponymous *Webster* (played by Emmanuel Lewis), were used for neoliberal effect to showcase the overcoming of racism through white adoptive families' incorporation of black infantilized bodies (both Coleman's and Lewis's diminutive statures rendered them perpetually childlike in appearance and in performance on their respective shows). The most recent cinematic portrait of the black infantilized male incorporated into a white neoliberal family has been dramatized in the 2009 film *The Blind Side*. Although this chapter does not have the scope or length to analyze the gendered and racial dynamics of Asian female adopted bodies versus black male adopted

bodies, it bears further scrutiny, particularly as I discuss later in this chapter the gendered and raced manner in which Asian female adoptees are seen as more assimilable subjects within the United States. I thank Ariana Vigil for pushing me on this point.

3 J. Kim, "For Adoptees." *Harlow's Monkey*.

4 Singley, *Adopting America*, 21–22.

5 Ibid., 26.

6 In keeping with the preferred terminology used among adoption advocates, I retain the phrase "first parents," "first mother," and "first families" instead of "birth parents," "birth mother," or "birth families."

7 It perhaps goes without saying that matching happened among white families with white children; non-white children were neither sought after in great numbers nor available through private or state adoption agencies. For more see Ellen Herman, *Kinship by Design*, E. Wayne Carp, *Family Matters*, and Julie Berebitsky, *Like Our Very Own*.

8 Given the white supremacy of the first half of the twentieth century, placing non-white children in adoptive families was never a priority, whether those families matched their race or not, which means that transracial adoptions were virtually unheard of.

9 Berebitsky, *Like Our Very Own*, 138.

10 Herman, *Kinship by Design*, 123.

11 Carp, *Family Matters*, 35.

12 Herman, *Kinship by Design*, 251. In 1972 the NABSW issued a statement condemning the placement of black children with white families, using strongly worded language equating such transracial adoptions to genocide and slavery. For a nuanced understanding of how the NABSW arrived at this statement and their later declarations that they did not want children needlessly staying in the foster care system, see Sandra Patton's *Birthmarks: Transracial Adoption in Contemporary America*, particularly chapter 4.

13 Transnational adoption of Amerasian children actually began in Japan but did not receive much public notice. See E. Kim, *Adopted Territory*, 46.

14 In keeping with the language and phraseology used within histories and accounts of adoption from the period of the Korean War, I use the term "Korean war baby." For more on the role of pictures and images of orphans as part of Cold War ideology see chapter 4 in Laura Briggs's *Somebody's Children: The Politics of Transracial and Transnational Adoption*.

15 Herman, *Kinship by Design*, 216.

16 E. Kim, *Adopted Territory*, 45.

17 Ibid., 44. The Holts were inspired to adopt children from Korea after seeing the film *Lost Sheep*, which was produced by the Christian evangelical organization World Vision.

18 Ibid., 72.

19 Briggs and Marre, *International Adoption*, 6.

20 J. Kim, "Scattered Seeds," 157.

21 For more on a critique of the Holts' lax practices regarding adoption placement see Ellen Herman and JaeRan Kim.

22 J. Kim, "Scattered Seeds," 156.

23 For more on the specific details of the Holt agency go to their website, www.holtinternational.org/.

24 For more specific details and statistics about adoptions from China to the US see Karin Evans and the Evan B. Donaldson website, www.adoptioninstitute.org.

25 Herman, *Kinship by Design*, 239.

26 Jacobson, *Culture Keeping*, 33.

27 Louie, "Pandas, Lions, and Dragons," 297.

28 Ibid., 257.

29 For more on Bordieu's notion of "habitus" see *Distinction: A Social Critique of the Judgment of Taste*.

30 For more on theories of intersectionality, see works by Trina Grillo and Kimberle Crenshaw.

31 Brian, *Reframing Transracial Adoption*, 14.

32 For more on a nuanced examination of the complexities surrounding gender preferences and China's population control policy, see Kay Johnson's *Wanting a Daughter, Needing a Son: Abandonment, Adoption, and Orphanage Care in China*.

33 Volkman, "Embodying Chinese Culture," 83.

34 Dorow, *Transnational Adoption*, 44.

35 Ibid., 48.

36 For more on the particular details of these scholars' works, please refer to their texts in the bibliography.

37 Jacobson, *Culture Keeping*, 19. According to a recent Pew Report, "The Rise of Intermarriage," 36 percent of Asian American women married outside their race, as opposed to 17 percent of Asian American men; furthermore, Asian American female–white male pairings constitute the highest percentage of intermarriage in the study. The Pew Report only lists white-Asian American pairings as interracial couples (there is no mention of African American/Latino/American Indian and Asian American intermarriage). For more on the report go to www.pewsocialtrends.org/2012/02/16/the-rise-of-intermarriage/.

38 Dorow recounts an anecdote by social worker Rita Jasper, who describes prospective adoptive parents who express discomfort with adopting an African American child domestically because of the hierarchy of skin color privilege (*Transnational Adoption*, 46).

39 Dorow, *Transnational Adoption*, 47.

40 Collier, "Performing Childhood," 212.

41 Eng, *Feeling of Kinship*, 117. For more analysis of racial passing, particularly as a form of racial ambiguity, see chapter 4, "Ambiguous Movements and Mobile Subjectivity: Passing in between Autobiography and Fiction with Paisley Rekdal and Ruth Ozeki." I also discuss passing with respect to multiracial identities in chapter 3, "Cablinasian Dreams, Amerasian Realities: Transcending Race in the Twenty-First Century and Other Myths Broken by Tiger Woods."

42 Eng, *Feeling of Kinship*, 117.

43 Ibid.

44 All quotes related to *First Person Plural* come directly from the documentary.

45 Louie, "Pandas, Lions, and Dragons," 297. This adoptive parent admits that the reality of her daughter's identity turned out to be more complex than what she and her husband originally thought.

46 Dorow, *Transnational Adoption*, 218.

47 Trenka, *Language of Blood*, 129.

48 E. Kim, *Adopted Territory*, 93–94.

49 Singley, *Adopting America*, 3.

50 Shirley Temple is not truly orphaned in *The Little Princess* because her father has mistakenly been listed as dead when, in fact, he had been wounded in action during the war, but for a significant portion of the film she is treated like an orphan. Also, out

of twenty films that she starred in within a six-year period, she played an orphan in eleven of them.

51 Indeed, Little Orphan Annie as a concept first came to life as a novel and then evolved into a popular comic strip before finding life in musical and movie form.

52 Singley, *Adopting America*, 3.

53 This is the plot of *Heidi* and *Annie* and to a certain extent *The Secret Garden* and *Oliver!*, as well as countless Shirley Temple films and the *Anne of Green Gables* series.

54 The orphan as symbolic or literal emotional healer is seen in the resolutions of the films mentioned at the beginning of this chapter, *Then She Found Me* and *Have You Heard about the Morgans?* and in classic orphan narratives. The parentless protagonists Heidi, Oliver, and Mary in *Heidi, Oliver!*, and *The Secret Garden* all heal the emotional wounds of their adoptive parents/guardians.

55 Hood, *Red Thread*, epigraph.

56 Jacobson, *Culture Keeping*, 50. Stories associated with the Chinese proverb use the red thread not simply to describe those you are fated to meet but the heterosexual partner you are destined to marry. See Karin Evans, *The Lost Daughters of China*, 149. Furthermore, though there are adopted sons from China, daughters are placed out and abandoned at far greater rates than boys. Furthermore, boys who are placed for adoption are often disabled, either physically or developmentally/intellectually. For more on the specifics of Chinese adoption see Sara Dorow, Karin Evans, and Kay Johnson.

57 Ellis, *Politics of Sensibility*, 19.

58 Bell, *Sentimentalism, Ethics*, 2.

59 Hood, *Red Thread*, 297.

60 Ibid., 302.

61 For the remainder of this chapter, I refer to Asian American adult adoptees as simply adult adoptees—I will not be highlighting their racial category in order to prevent me from repeating "Asian American adult adoptee" throughout, a locution that can be cumbersome to read repeatedly.

62 Barlow, *Rise of the Blogosphere*, 37.

63 Ibid., 50.

64 Although legally I did not have to gain permission to quote from the blogs in this chapter, ethically I thought it was important to write each blogger and gain permission for the citations in this monograph, and I am grateful for their permissions.

65 E. Kim recounts one such KAD, Thomas Clement, doing just this (*Adopted Territory*, 84).

66 Although many blog accounts may be free, blogging still requires time and effort, which signals a socioeconomic status where people have the means for such leisure.

67 E. Kim, *Adopted Territory*, 104.

68 Ibid., 87.

69 Kolko, et al., *Race in Cyberspace*, 9.

70 All quotations from JaeRan Kim's blog are taken from *Harlow's Monkey*, http://harlowmonkey.typepad.com/harlows_monkey/.

71 All quotations from Paula O's blog are taken from *Heart, Mind and Seoul*, http://heartmindandseoul.typepad.com/weblog/.

72 All quotations from Jane Jeong Trenka's blog are taken from *Jane's Blog: Bitter Angry Ajumma*, http://jjtrenka.wordpress.com/.

73 All quotations from Sume's blog are taken from *Ethnically Incorrect Daughter*, http://ethnicallyincorrect.wordpress.com/.

74 All quotations from Mei-Ling's blog are taken from *The Original Heping*, http://littlewing04.wordpress.com/.

75 The blogger Mei-Ling should not be confused for the journalist and author of the memoir *Lucky Girl*, Mei-Ling Hopgood, although both are TRA/TN adoptees from Taiwan. Furthermore, the addresses for all these blogs can be found in the bibliography.

76 I refer to bloggers by their first names since there are some, like Mei-Ling and Paula, who do not disclose their last names on their blogs.

77 Jo, "Making of KAD Nation," 288.

78 Hopgood, *Lucky Girl*, 178.

79 Mei-Ling was raised in Canada, Sume was raised in Texas, and the rest of the bloggers were raised in the Midwest.

80 JaeRan has a professional blog that she periodically updates, and Mei-Ling has two additional blogs, the latest one is password protected. Both JaeRan and Mei-Ling have talked about their adoption blogs as being "closed," but Sume and Jane are still active on their sites, and Paula has not had a "last post," which signals that she may simply be taking a blogging hiatus.

81 Williams, "About Sumeia Williams," *Ethnically Incorrect Daughter*.

82 J. Kim, "For Adoptive Parents," *Harlow's Monkey*.

83 Barlow, *Rise of the Blogosphere*, 50.

84 Truthfully, there are not many mainstream narratives, either fiction or nonfiction, that feature Asian–white TRA/TN adoption; however, there are the *Sex and the City* films, I and II, documentaries like *Found in China* and *China's Lost Girls*, and the celebrity examples of Angelina Jolie and Katherine Heigl, as well as the novel *The Red Thread*, which is discussed earlier in this chapter.

85 The documentary *Somewhere Between* does feature the voices and perspectives of teenage Chinese adopted girls who reflect on their feelings and experiences being adopted from China and raised in the United States; however, the filmmaker is not an adoptee but an adoptive mother. Later in this chapter I return to a discussion of an adult adoptee filmmaker, Deann Borshay Liem.

86 It should also be noted that the voices and perspectives of first parents, particularly first mothers, are nearly nonexistent.

87 Of course, from the point of view of seeing these children as sons and daughters of celebrities, protecting them from the media can be regarded as a good thing.

88 J. Kim, "For Adoptive Parents."

89 Ibid., March 11, 2007.

90 Brian, *Reframing Transracial Adoption*, 18.

91 Shame and lower socioeconomic status also contribute to the lack of first-parent narratives on adoption.

92 J. Kim, *Harlow's Monkey*, May 6, 2007.

93 Anzaldúa, *Making Face, Making Soul*, xvi.

94 Paula O., *Heart, Mind and Seoul*, June 23, 2010.

95 Ibid., May 30, 2007.

96 Williams, *Ethnically Incorrect Daughter*, April 11, 2009.

97 Sume's analysis of her adoption, and the practices of TRA/TN adoption in general, are very much in line with the kinds of analyses one finds in postcolonial studies and critical race theory, thinking through Cold War ideologies that connect war in Asian nations and the exploitation of Asian bodies in service to US imperialism that allows

for the commodification of Asian infants within white American families. See Ethnically Incorrect Daughter for a flavor of Sume's critical commentary.

98 Anzaldúa, *Making Face, Making Soul* xxv.

99 Trenka, *Bitter Angry Ajumma*, December 31, 2010.

100 Na, "Garlic and Salt," 22.

101 Trenka, *Bitter Angry Ajumma*, August 12, 2008.

102 Mei-ling, *The Original Heping*, March 25, 2008.

103 Paula O., *Heart, Mind and Seoul*, August 25, 2011.

104 Williams, *Ethnically Incorrect Daughter*, January 31, 2007.

105 Paula O., *Heart, Mind and Seoul*, August 25, 2011.

106 J. Kim, *Harlow's Monkey*, August 4, 2008.

107 Mei-ling, *The Original Heping*, July 25, 2007.

108 Williams, *Ethnically Incorrect Daughter*, August 28, 2008.

109 One example of Mei-Ling's commenting activity can be found on Paula O's August 9, 2011, post, "So If Your Child Went Missing What Would You Do?" Paula was discussing the case of a six-year-old Guatemalan girl who was discovered to have been kidnapped from her family, a fact unbeknownst to the US adoptive parents who believed her to be an orphan. In the lively thread that follows, Mei-Ling posted four comments, three of which were in response to other commenters (there were fifteen comments total). This type of exchange is common in the blogs of this chapter and is particularly common in terms of Mei-Ling's active presence on others' blogs.

110 Williams, *Ethnically Incorrect Daughter*, March 14, 2008.

111 Trenka, *Bitter Angry Ajumma*, September 5, 2011.

112 E. Kim, *Adopted Territory*, 105.

113 Jo, "Making of KAD Nation," 288.

114 Specifically, Borshay Liem's Korean brother says to her, "We have been apart from each other for thirty years. It would be easier to close the gap between us if we spoke the same language. However, our cultural differences are also difficult to overcome."

115 Trenka, *Language of Blood*, 252.

3: CABLINASIAN DREAMS, AMERASIAN REALITIES

1 This quote by Roberts has been widely circulated among golf journalists and, according to Alan Shipnuck, was first cited by the African American professional golfer Charlie Sifford in his memoir *Just Let Me Play*. Shipnuck says that there is dispute among Roberts's supporters that he actually said this, but given the description of Roberts's attitude toward African Americans, it doesn't seem beyond the pale. See Shipnuck, *The Battle for Augusta National*, 22–23.

2 Among the prizes a golfer receives upon achieving a win at the Masters is a green sports coat, one that only past Masters winners and members of Augusta National are allowed to possess. Rather than holding aloft a trophy during the televised award's ceremony, a Masters champion is ceremoniously fitted into the green jacket by the previous year's champion.

3 Qtd. in Smith, "The Chosen One," 54.

4 Qtd. in ibid., 61.

5 I say ostensibly for sex addiction with respect to Tiger's entry into a rehabilitation facility because he has never publicly described the type of therapeutic counseling he received during his stay at a rehabilitation facility. However, it was widely known

that the clinic he attended, Pine Grove Behavioral Health and Addiction Services in Hattiesburg, Mississippi, treated sex addiction. Additionally, Woods's former swing coach, Hank Haney, confirms in his tell-all memoir that Tiger was in treatment for sex addiction (*The Big Miss*, 227).

6 As noted throughout this book, although the conventional wisdom in the United States is to refer to the global conflict in Southeast Asia that occurred in the 1960s through early 1970s as the "Vietnam war," scholars who research this conflict and the Vietnamese people who lived through it refer to it as the American war. In general, I will refer to the country as "Viet Nam" and the war as "Vietnam."

7 One minor incident that is told in nearly every biography about Woods and on his first visit to Oprah Winfrey's show is that Tiger was tied to a tree by a group of sixth-grade boys after his first day of kindergarten, where he was pelted with rocks and called a "nigger." Both Earl and Tiger have recited this story throughout the years. Biographer Howard Sounes is one of the first to raise doubts as to whether this incident actually happened; his interviews with Tiger's kindergarten teacher and elementary school principal reject that this story is true (127–128), and subsequent stories published post–sex scandal have also questioned the veracity of this story.

Additionally, Tiger has talked about "the look" that he would receive at white country clubs, a look that signaled that the gazer was not pleased at the intrusion of the dark-skinned Woods into the bastion of white privilege, which Haney confirms: "I knew that during Tiger's junior golf days, he and Earl had called the unwelcoming glances they'd received at some country clubs 'the look,' and that since turning pro, Tiger had received hate mail and even death threats that were racially tinged. I have no doubt Tiger felt racial vibes in what he read and heard on and off the course" (90).

8 Titleist, a premiere golf equipment company, paid Woods $20 million over three years for Tiger to use its balls and clubs and Nike paid $40 million over five years for Tiger's endorsement of its shoes and clothing line—a line that Nike would specifically create to highlight Tiger Woods.

9 Yu, "Stripes," 224.

10 Although I believe that golf courses and the game itself perpetuates white male privilege, I would be remiss in noting that there have certainly been many elite golfers, both male and female, who originated in working-class families or non-white households. Lee Trevino's humble background, for example, is evidence that neither class nor race (Trevino is Mexican American) nor education (Trevino was forced to leave school at fourteen to help with his family's finances) are absolute barriers to achieving success in golf. And the many women on the LPGA would point to the refutation of golf as an all-male sport; indeed, golf is one of the few games where both men and women can play as equals because of the handicap system.

11 Chambers, *Unplayable Lie*, 7.

12 Orin Starn cites St. Andrews in Yonkers, New York, as the first golf course built (1888), but other sources claim Oakhurst Links in White Sulphur Springs, West Virginia (1884) as the first course constructed in the United States. See Starn's "Caddying for the Dalai Lama: Golf, Heritage Tourism, and the Pinehurst Resort" and Charles McGrath's "America's First Golf Course." Van Cortlandt golf course in New York City first opened to the public in July 1895 and is still in operation today. See the New York City website, "On the Links in Parks," www.nycgovparks.org/about/history/golf.

13 It should be noted that quite a few public courses also prevented African Americans from playing; Atlanta barred African Americans from playing on municipal courses

until a lawsuit in 1955 forced them to desegregate. In this way, golf courses, like swimming pools and other public recreational centers, discriminated on the basis of race until civil rights legislation in the 1950s and 1960s forced desegregation. See John Kennedy's *A Course of Their Own: A History of African American Golfers*. For a thorough accounting of the sexism and prejudice that female golfers face see Chambers's *The Unplayable Lie: The Untold Story of Women and Discrimination in American Golf*.

14 For more on the story of Lawrence Otis Graham and the experiment he did working for two weeks as a busboy at the Greenwich Country Club (taking a temporary leave of absence from his Manhattan law firm) see "Act II: Deceiving Others" in the *This American Life* episode #173 "Three Kinds of Deception" (original air date December 15, 2000) and Graham's book, *A Member of the Club: Reflections on Life in a Racially Polarized World*. The amount of racist language and conversations that Graham encounters reinforces the institutional racism perpetuated in these settings.

15 Owen, *Chosen One*, 182.

16 Sounes, *Wicked Game*, 22. Although the PGA is the preeminent association and tour for professional golfers, then as now the PGA is only one of several organizations that represent the sport, such as the United States Golf Association (USGA) and the United Golf Association (UGA), which many African American golfers belonged to in the era of the Caucasian clause.

17 See Article III, section 1—it is also reprinted in Sounes's book *The Wicked Game* (22).

18 Kennedy, *Course of Their Own*, 24.

19 In the waning days of the Caucasian clause, sponsors could invite African American golfers to play in PGA tour events, although this was a rare occurrence.

20 See Chambers, *Unplayable Lie*, 179 and McDaniel, *Uneven Lies*, 90.

21 For a full accounting of Sifford's incident see Kennedy, *A Course of Their Own*, 90–91.

22 Callahan, *In Search of Tiger*, 57.

23 Joo, *Transnational Sport*, 70.

24 Feinstein, *The First Coming*, 22.

25 Kindred, "So Young to Have the Master's Touch," 85.

26 Reilly, "Strokes of Genius."

27 Sounes, *Wicked Game*, 205.

28 Several sources have noted that the galleries at golf events have become more diverse in race, age, gender after the advent of Tiger Woods's professional career, and others have noted the increase in African Americans playing golf. For Donna Barbie, Tiger's impact on golf is encapsulated in an anecdote she shares in "Faithful Fandom" of an African American girl exclaiming to her mother "'Momma—he looks like *us!*'" [emphasis in original] (69).

29 Perez, "Hello World."

30 It is worth noting that while this ad celebrates many forms of diversity, it's questionable whether professional golf at this time, or in our present moment, would be so welcoming of openly gay male golfers, since homophobic jokes and comments are a regular feature of casual golf culture, and unlike the LPGA, there are no openly queer PGA members.

31 Perez, "Hello World."

32 Rodriguez and Trevino each came from working-class backgrounds where they learned to play and become professionals through caddying.

33 I write "golfers of Korean descent" because there are notable Korean American golfers, like Cristina Kim and Michelle Wie, who were born and raised in the United States.

However, the majority of golfers on the LPGA are from South Korea. For an excellent analysis of Korean/Korean American athletes in a transnational context, particularly those on the LPGA see Joo's *Transnational Sport: Gender, Media, and Global Korea.*

34 Joo, *Transnational Sport*, 74.

35 As the reigning US Amateur, Woods qualified to play in the US Open even though he had not yet become a professional golfer.

36 Woods, "Media Statement." Though it is true that most published accounts of Woods refer to him as African American or black, I cannot recall seeing any news accounts that refer to him solely as Asian American or Asian; in other words, his monoracial identification is most squarely linked to his blackness rather than his Asianness.

37 Chang, *Disoriented*, 134.

38 Wong, *Yellow Journalist*, 251. Wong is not technically correct if by "first person of Asian descent to break the Masters color barrier" he means the first professional to play at the Masters. That distinction is held by another player of Thai descent, Sukree Onsham, a Thai national who played in 1970 and 1971 at the Masters tournament.

39 Yu, "Center of History," 334.

40 Haney, *The Big Miss*, 9.

41 Ibid., 91.

42 There is a common belief that Tida Woods is responsible for Tiger's uber-competitive instinct, perhaps deriving from the many interviews that Earl Woods has given over the years in which he said that Tida was the disciplinarian in the family. Hank Haney, Howard Sounes, Jaime Diaz, and Tom Callahan are among the biographers and writers who have repeated this belief.

43 Callahan, *In Search of Tiger*, 151.

44 Joo, *Transnational Sport*, 143.

45 The following transcript was recorded and typed, by me, on December 14, 2012, after viewing an online version of Woods's April 1997 interview with Oprah Winfrey. The ellipses in the extended quote/transcript reflect verbal tics and placeholders "um, ugh, hmmm, and, but" that were taken out for clarity. It was during this interview that Woods told Winfrey that "growing up, I came up with this name 'Cablinasian' . . . 'ca,' caucasian, 'bl,' black, 'in,' Indian, and 'Asian.'"

46 Rockquemore, "Deconstructing Tiger Woods," 136.

47 See Maureen Dowd's "Tiger Woods Goes for the Green."

48 Tiger was asked by the NAACP not to participate in a golf tournament in South Carolina because the state still flew the Confederate flag, but Tiger refused to boycott the event. See Jay Nordlinger's *National Review* essay "Hunting Tiger" (September 6, 2002).

49 Martha Burk, the director of the National Council of Women's Organizations, upon learning that Augusta National had no female members, began lobbying for the elite country club to open up its membership. Hootie Johnson, Augusta National's chairman at the time, released a media statement infamously saying that "there may well come a day when women will be invited to join our membership, but not at the point of a bayonet." Woods was asked, multiple times, to weigh in on this issue, but he remained neutral on the affair (at one point he said that both Hootie and Burk were right) and did not take up Burk's suggestion to boycott the 2003 Masters in protest of its all-male membership policy. It is worth noting that even though as biographer Steve Helling observes, Tiger's "barrier-breaking made him the go-to spokesperson for all issues of equality" (142), no other prominent golfer (such as Phil Mickelson, Ernie Els, or Mark O'Meara) was asked to weigh in and join Burk's protest. In other

words, Woods bears additional pressures for shouldering the burden of fighting against inequality when in reality all members of the PGA should be equally accountable for ending oppression. For more on the Augusta-Burk episode see Alan Shipnuck's *The Battle for Augusta National: Hootie, Martha, and the Masters of the Universe.*

50 Eng, *Kinship*, 117. For more on the concept of "new passing" as it relates to transracial and transnational adoptees see chapter 2, "Anti-Sentimental Loss: Stories of Transracial and Transnational Asian American Adult Adoptees in the Blogosphere."

51 McCaroll, "Claiming," 219.

52 Starn, *Passion*, 93. Tigergate refers to the cluster of events that were first brought to public attention in November 2009 in which the *National Inquirer* reported that Tiger Woods was having an affair with a New York event planner, and then the news that he had crashed his Escalade into a neighbor's tree, the revelations of Woods's many sexual indiscretions, and culminating in the public apology he issued in February 2010.

53 Ibid., 94.

54 Ibid.

55 Izrael, "Ten Things You Could Learn from Tiger Woods."

56 Although one could argue that no one escapes being interpellated by ideology—just as no one escapes hegemony—one could also argue that Tiger Woods is rejecting the hail of monoraciality and rejecting the interpellation of himself as a monoracial African American in favor of a different ideology that would acknowledge the complexity of race and racial identities. In fact, Woods may have succeeded, partially, in changing the way that others see him, so while he is consistently referred to primarily through his African American ancestry (when people choose to talk about his racial identity) there has been an attempt by the public to acknowledge his multiraciality.

57 Lim, "100% Cablinasian."

58 Dr. Root's "Bill of Rights for People of Mixed Heritage" can be found on her website, www.drmariaroot.com/doc/BillOfRights.pdf.

59 Among those who have repeated this story are David Owen in his biography *The Chosen One* (187–188) and Tim Rosaforte in *Raising the Bar: The Championship Years of Tiger Woods* (64).

60 Qtd. in Callahan, *In Search of Tiger*, 199.

61 Qtd. in Smith, "The Chosen One," 73. In various interviews Earl has often attributed Tiger's success as directly related to his bicultural identity, noting his wife's Thai influences on Tiger's upbringing. Callahan quotes Tida as saying "'I raised him as an Asian child'" (202), although Callahan says that she is not forthcoming with details, a characteristic typical of the media-shy mother.

62 T. Woods, "Tiger Woods's Apology."

63 This image can be found in Starn, *Passion of Tiger Woods*, 35.

64 Reporters and journalists have noted that Tida is notoriously private; Lawrence Londino writes in *Tiger Woods: A Biography* that "Kultida Woods is certainly the least publicized member of what has become known as team Tiger" (21); Charles Pierce, reporting on Woods's apology for *Esquire* magazine, notes that "Kultida Woods has been a largely invisible presence since her son exploded as an athletic celebrity" ("Tiger Woods: Mama's Boy?"); and Jaime Diaz, in a unique extended interview with Tida for *Golf Digest*, the longest interview and essay devoted to Woods's mother to date, explains her reticence to be interviewed as stemming from being "loath to do or say anything publicly that will further complicate her son's hyper-scrutinized life" ("Tida in Thailand"). Indeed, it would appear that Tida agreed to the lengthy piece

in *Golf Digest*, one in which Diaz traveled with her for a week in Thailand in order to shed light on her charitable work involving two schools: one devoted to helping girls rescued from the Thai sex trade and the other helping intellectually disabled children. Both foundations are listed on the Tiger Woods Foundation website, with the link displayed at the end of the article.

65 Bass, *Vietnamerica*, 3. I am indebted to Matthew Briones for helping me see the connection of Tiger and Tida as part of the Amerasian discourse.

66 In my discussion of Amerasians in this section, I often refer to Vietnamese and Viet Nam as the primary ethnicity and site for discussing Amerasians. However, this is largely due to the available resources, almost all of which focus on Vietnamese Amerasians. Nonetheless, as even these researchers have shown, Amerasians born during the American war in Viet Nam came not only from Viet Nam but also from Cambodia and Thailand—all locations in which US military men were stationed. Jan Weisman, citing the Pearl Buck Foundation in one of her footnotes, estimates that 5,000–7,000 Amerasian children were born in Thailand during the war (241).

67 Trin Yarborough cites the figure of 100,000 Amerasians being born during the war in Viet Nam, and subsequent authors have also repeated this number, most notably Thomas Bass, who credits James Reston (34) with providing this estimate. Neither Yarborough nor Bass lists their sources; thus, it is unclear whether "Reston" refers to James Reston Sr., *New York Times* columnist and editor, or his son, James Reston Jr., a former Army soldier and journalist who has also written about the war in Viet Nam in *Sherman's March and Vietnam*.

68 In keeping with the nomenclature used by scholars who study Viet Nam and the way that people in Viet Nam reference this city, I divide the name of this city into two words, Sai Gon; however, I refer to "Saigon" when quoting from others and when referencing the musical *Miss Saigon*.

69 McKelvey, *The Dust of Life*, 3.

70 Steven DeBonis, Thomas Bass, Trin Yarborough, and Robert McKelvey have interviewed Amerasians who describe the verbal harassment that followed them from the time they were young children through to their adult lives. The taunts of *my lai, my den,* and *con lai* appear to be on the order of serious racial and sexual epithets, damaging to the mental and emotional well-being of the Amerasians who endured this verbal abuse. These authors also describe numerous physical abuses that Amerasians suffer from, as well as mental and emotional anguish that oftentimes manifests as extreme depression, self-mutilation, and suicide.

71 For more on the plight of Amerasians in Viet Nam see Robert McKelvey's chapter, "Prejudice and Discrimination" in *The Dust of Life: America's Children Abandoned in Vietnam*. McKelvey, like other journalists and researchers who have interviewed Amerasians, has noted that "while many Amerasians experienced prejudice and discrimination in Vietnam, black Amerasians appear to have experienced more than others" (47).

72 Bass, *Vietnamerica*, 54.

73 The 1987 Amerasian Homecoming Act allowed for the immigration of Amerasians born in Viet Nam from January 1, 1962, to January 1, 1976, to come to the United States as war refugees. These "children" were predominantly adults between the ages of fourteen and twenty-six (some of them had families of their own); Trin Yarborough cites approximately 30,000 Amerasians who came to the United States (123) and

Susan Zeiger states that 69,000 men and women had taken part in this program (233). Neither Yarborough nor Zeiger notes the source for their statistics.

74 Bass, *Vietnamerica*, 40.

75 Klein, *Cold War Orientalism*, 163.

76 Zeiger, *Entangling Alliances*, 2. Zeiger does note that the American war in Viet Nam marked a change in US policy toward war brides; no longer were marriages between US military men and foreign women regarded in an official capacity requiring special immigration status, which therefore created more hurdles for US soldiers bringing their wives to the United States. See chapter 6, "The Demise of the War Bride," in *Entangling Alliances: Foreign War Brides and American Soldiers in the Twentieth Century.*

77 I thank Robert Ku for helping me arrive at this astute observation.

78 The most accepted definition for those identified (by self or by others) as Amerasian is that they are the product of the union between a US soldier and an Asian woman, although there have been US civilian contractors who have fathered Amerasian children. Some definitions of Amerasian are looser (encompassing any mixed race child who has an Asian mother and US father) and some are more stringent (Kieu Linh Caroline Valverde discusses three types of mixed race Vietnamese; for her, Amerasians must be born in Viet Nam and raised without their American fathers, whereas a person such as Tiger Woods she would count as a multiracial Vietnamese, someone whose parents met as a result of the war in Viet Nam but whose children either migrated at an early age with them or were born and raised in the United States). With the rise of women in the US military stationed in combat zones in the Middle East, it will be interesting to see whether the definition of Amerasian will expand to think about Asian men and US women producing Amerasian children out of global conflicts involving the US and Asian nations.

79 A number of Amerasian children were abandoned in orphanages, especially when the United States pulled out of Viet Nam, because the rumor at the time was that the Viet Cong would target anyone with ties to the United States; with their visible racial difference, Amerasian children were often thought to be among the groups that would suffer from this policy. In reality, no formal edicts to harm Amerasians were ever enacted, although the social stigma that Amerasians experienced (and the discrimination and prejudice that they suffered from, including being denied access to education, housing, jobs, and being targeted by police) certainly made them feel persecuted due to their mixed race status and connection to the United States. Also, orphaned Amerasian children were among those who were taken out of Viet Nam during Operation Babylift. One such account is told in the documentary *Daughter from Danang* and is fictionalized in Aimee Phan's short story collection, *We Should Never Meet.*

80 Several biographers of Woods have described the enthusiastic reception the golfer receives whenever he visits Thailand; news footage of Tiger landing in Bangkok shows him being showered with flower garlands, with throngs of journalists and crowds following him during his stay.

81 Poe, "Woods Spotlights Multiracial Identity."

82 Weisman, "The Tiger and His Stripes," 236.

83 I have written about the stereotype of Vietnamese female prostitutes featured in Hollywood cinema in chapter 3 of my first book, *Consumption and Identity in Asian American Coming-of-Age Novels.* Renny Christopher and Eben Muse have similarly commented on this stereotype in films depicting the war in Viet Nam. Also, though there is much to commend journalist Trin Yarborough's work, *Surviving Twice: Amerasian*

Children of the Vietnam War (most notably her in-depth interviews with several Amerasian subjects over the period of several years), her own biases are on display through this work, as she persists in perpetuating the stereotype that the Vietnamese mothers of Amerasians were predominantly prostitutes and, most troubling and puzzling, that Amerasians, by virtue of their mixed race nature, are also bisexual. Yarborough presents no statistics or evidence to support either claim.

84 Zeiger, *Entangling Alliances*, 205.

85 Weisman, "The Tiger and His Stripes," 233.

86 It is a commonplace convention to describe the multiracial children born to African American soldiers and Asian women as black Amerasian. Yet this description reinforces the unspoken assumptions linking American nationality to whiteness, with the term "Amerasian" implying that the child must be half white and half Asian, since the appendage of the racial adjective "black" is used to differentiate between these racial mixings. This eliding of race and nation is similar to what I describe in chapter 1 with the US government's rationale of the Mixed-Marriage Policy of 1942, since the archives show the conflation of American nationality and white racial qualities. For further analysis see chapter 1: "From Enemy Alien to Assimilating American: Yoshiko deLeon and the Mixed-Marriage Policy of the Japanese American Incarceration."

87 Weisman, "The Tiger and His Stripes," 234. Though there are varying debates about the roots of Southeast Asian prejudice against darker phenotypes, both Weisman and McKelvey point to European influences: to Thai elites studying in Europe and inheriting the view that attractiveness is equated with lighter skin and moral worth and darker skin associated with black abjection and low morality and to the influence of French values of whiteness inculcated in Vietnamese of an earlier era.

88 McKelvey, *The Dust of Life*, 47.

89 Yarborough, *Surviving Twice*, 125.

90 Qtd. in Bass's *Vietnamerica: The War Comes Home*, (158). Ahn Dung is the Vietnamese name of Clarence Taylor, whose name is taken from a father figure (a black Korean war veteran married to a Korean woman) who befriended him in Utica, New York.

91 Bass, *Vietnamerica*, 157.

92 Yarborough also describes the prejudice that Vietnamese immigrants carried over from Viet Nam to the United States in their belief that Amerasians were second-class citizens, criminals, and people of low moral values (150).

93 Yarborough, *Surviving Twice*, 1–2.

94 Zeiger, *Entangling Alliances*, 229.

95 Ibid., 231.

96 *South Pacific* is another musical that readily comes to mind in this genre, as does the film *Sayonara*.

97 According to Yarborough "only 2 percent of all US fathers were ever found, and many of them refused any contact with their Amerasian children" (140). Other researchers of Amerasians have also noted the difficulty that Amerasian adults have had in locating their fathers and the rejection that many of them faced when they were able to find them.

98 While it's hard to determine whether this is a completely accurate depiction of Tida and Earl's marriage, certainly the fact that Tida remained married to Earl, even after separating physically from him by moving into a home purchased for her by Tiger, seems to signal her loyalty to the idea of her marriage to Earl if not to Earl himself.

99 Perhaps it's worth also exploring whether Tiger could, perhaps, claim an American Indian or white identity because he can trace both white and American Indian ancestors. Beyond the problem of seeing such a move as an appropriation of a heritage or identity that Woods would be using to eschew blackness or a more visible position as a person of color, from the statements he has made about how he is influenced by his parents and their cultures, it would seem that Woods would reject such monoraciality based on the fact that neither of his parents identifies with these racial subjectivities and that the culture in his home was distinctly African American and Asian influenced.

100 Yu, "Center of History," 330–331.

4: AMBIGUOUS MOVEMENTS AND MOBILE SUBJECTIVITY

1 Although it is an indisputable fact that Maxine Hong Kingston was not the first Asian American writer to be published in the United States (her predecessors include Sui Sin Far, Carlos Bulosan, John Okada, and Hisaye Yamamoto, to name a few), the enormous success of The Woman Warrior created an awareness and a market for other Asian American writings and placed The Woman Warrior (and by extension Kingston) in the canon of American literature. This, in turn, yielded the turn-into-the-twenty-first-century surge in Asian American writings, particularly after the publication of Amy Tan's The Joy Luck Club in 1989, a novel that enjoyed phenomenal publishing success, as evidenced by being on the New York Times bestseller's list more than six months, the translation of The Joy Luck Club into several languages, and its development into a major motion picture directed by Oliver Stone.

2 The decision to brand the work as "autobiography/nonfiction" in its first-run publication was made by Random House and not Kingston, as noted by Sau-ling Cynthia Wong in an interview with Kingston: "The only correspondence I had with the published [sic] concerning the classification of my books was that he said that Non-fiction would be the most accurate category; Non-fiction is such a catch-all that even 'poetry is considered non-fiction'" (Kingston qtd in Wong "Autobiography" 30). Although the latest imprint of The Woman Warrior no longer lists it as "autobiography" it is still classified as "Non-fiction/Literature."

3 For more on the authenticity debates over The Woman Warrior, see "Part I: Setting Forth Issues and Debates" in Maxine Hong Kingston's "The Woman Warrior": A Casebook, edited by Sau-ling Cynthia Wong.

4 The charge of Orientalism and pandering to white audiences is one that various critics of Kingston have made from the time of The Woman Warrior's publication; among her most notable and notorious critics is Frank Chin.

5 Both Frank Chin and Ya-Jie Zhang have written about the inaccuracies of Chinese myths and legends within The Woman Warrior. For their particular take on Kingston's inconsistent portrayal of Chinese life see their essays in Wong's edited collection Maxine Hong Kingston's "The Woman Warrior": A Casebook.

6 Chen, Double Agency, 17.

7 Williams, "Race-ing and Being Raced," 62–63.

8 Caughie, Passing and Pedagogy, 2.

9 Although it is certainly true that there is not more discourse surrounding mixed race identity, the most recent census (2010) allowed people to mark off more than one racial category—which is a promising step. However, various ethnic and racial communities have contested the idea of multiple racial categories out of fear that such

accounting will result in the loss of representation and hence resources allocated for various ethnic groups and organizations, which highlights the real financial and power issues at stake in defining people according to "race," as Michael Omi observes: "At issue here is not only Census enumeration but its impact on federal voting rights and civil rights" (*The Sum of Our Parts*, xi).

10 Salgado, "Misceg-narrations," 53–54.

11 On the power of the visual to define subjects by race see Frantz Fanon's *Black Skin, White Masks*, Ann Laura Stoler's *Race and the Education of Desire: Foucault's History of Sexuality and the Colonial Order of Things*, and Frank Wu's *Yellow: Race in America beyond Black and White*.

12 I am aware that by invoking the word "gaze" and, in the remainder of the paragraph, to also call attention to the scopic and the mirror is to remind readers of the language of psychoanalytic theory, particularly the works of Jacques Lacan. However, I am neither trying to invoke this tradition nor am I making an argument utilizing psychoanalytic theory; rather, I refer to "gaze" and "mirror" as literal states confronting people in their raced lives. After all, sometimes a mirror is simply a mirror: a reflecting surface.

13 Chen, *Double Agency*, 9.

14 Taken from *Woman Warrior*, 5–6.

15 Two particularly cogent volumes are James Phelan and Peter J. Rabinowitz's edited collection *A Companion to Narrative Theory* and Sidonie Smith and Julia Watson's coauthored *Reading Autobiography: A Guide for Interpreting Life Narratives*.

16 Lanser, "The 'I' of the Beholder," 206.

17 As noted previously, Kingston is not the first Asian American or Chinese American writer to be published in the United States; however, the marginalization as well as scarcity of such literature would make it difficult if not impossible for Kingston to have access or even knowledge of such Chinese American works during her childhood, works such as Sui Sin Far's "Leaves from a Mental Portfolio of an Eurasian" (1909), Pardee Lowe's *Father and Glorious Descendant* (1944), and Jade Snow Wong's *Fifth Chinese Daughter* (1945).

18 Smith and Watson, *Reading Autobiography*, 13.

19 Murdock, *Unreliable Truth*, 16.

20 I also note that Ishiguro's ethnic and racial difference from the characters of his novel are another element that does not limit or detract from the novel's believability. For more on "transgressive texts" (a term borrowed from the literary scholar Shelley Fisher Fishkin) see chapter 5, "Transgressive Texts and Ambiguous Authors: Racial Ambiguity in Asian American Literature."

21 Reviewers who have commented on the loose structure of Rekdal's work include Roland Kelts, "Baggage Check," *Village Voice* (November 15–21, 2000), and Ann Marlowe, "Hyphenated Life: Essays by a Chinese-American-Norwegian on the Difficulties of Assimilation," *New York Times*, October 15, 2000.

22 Rekdal's most recent book *Intimate: An American Family Photo Album* (2012) returns to the themes of *The Night My Mother Met Bruce Lee* through its multi-generic invocations of memoir, poetry, ethnography, and photography.

23 Rekdal has four published poetry collections: *A Crash of Rhinos* (2000), *Six Girls without Pants* (2002), *The Invention of the Kaleidoscope* (2007), and *Animal Eye* (2012).

24 Hogan, "Paisley Rekdal."

25 Redkal, *Bruce Lee*, 159.

26 For more on the specifics of the Tasaday tribe hoax, see Eliot Marshall's "Anthropolo-
    gists Debate Tasaday Hoax Evidence," *Science* 246:4934 (December 1, 1989): 1113(2) and
    the BBC website *The Tasaday Tribe Hoax.*

27 Redkal, *Bruce Lee*, 175–176.

28 Ibid., 29.

29 Ibid.

30 Ibid., 46.

31 Butler, *Gender Trouble*, 19.

32 Indeed, a compulsory racial identity governs many aspects of US culture, most nota-
    bly in newscasts and newspaper reports in which race is almost always only invoked
    to suggest non-white persons: the "black" judge, the "Asian" suspect, the "Latino"
    students.

33 Rekdal, *Bruce Lee*, 46.

34 Ibid., 36–37.

35 Ibid., 37.

36 Ibid., 42.

37 Ibid., 43.

38 Ibid.

39 Ibid., 42.

40 Ibid., 48.

41 Ibid.

42 Ibid., 49. When the ex-pat observes to Rekdal that he had watched her dancing, Rek-
    dal asks him if he witnessed her harassment by the photographer, and his response
    makes clear his lack of empathy over her situation: "'Could you blame him?' he
    replied, smiling at my costume" (49).

43 Cho, "Asian Pacific American Women," 166.

44 Commenting on the link between media stereotypes of Asian/Asian American women
    and cultural perceptions of Asian American female subjectivity, Espiritu argues that
    "through connoting two extremes [the Dragon Lady and the Lotus Blossom], these
    stereotypes are interrelated: Both eroticize Asian women as exotic 'others'—sensuous,
    promiscuous, but untrustworthy . . . [endowing] Asian women with an excess of 'wom-
    anhood,' sexualizing them but also impugning their sexuality" (*Women and Men*, 93).

45 Espiritu, *Asian American Women and Men*, 94.

46 Rekdal, *Bruce Lee*, 49.

47 Lowe, *Immigrant Acts*, 5.

48 Rekdal, *Bruce Lee*, 49.

49 Ibid., 49.

50 Butler, *Gender Trouble*, 136.

51 Ibid., 3.

52 Omi and Winant, *Racial Formation*, 62.

53 Ozeki, *My Year of Meats*, 15.

54 DES, or diethylstilbestrol, is an engineered estrogen first used in animal husbandry in
    the 1940s and 1950s (to fatten up chickens and cattle) and subsequently used as an aid
    to prevent miscarriages and premature birth for women. By the 1970s, researchers were
    discovering links between DES with cancer for both women who ingested this hor-
    mone as well as people eating meat from animals given this substance, so that by 1979
    the US government banned use of DES in livestock production. For more on the dan-
    gers of DES (beyond what is referred to in Ozeki's book), see Julie Sze's cogent analysis

of both DES and Ozeki's use of this trope in her novel in "Boundaries and Border Wars: DES, Technology, and Environmental Justice," and a Cornell University website, http://envirocancer.cornell.edu/Bibliography/diet/bib.hormones.cfm#zeranol that lists medical articles specifically related to DES and cancer.

55 The didactic qualities of the novel include educating readers about the links among DES, consumption of meat, and cancer, as well as a general warning about eating US mass-produced beef and chicken.

56 Lanser, "The 'I' of the Beholder," 210–211.

57 In various interviews Ozeki has admitted to her compromised sense of ethics in producing television episodes sponsored by Phillip-Morris. For more on specific interviews in which Ozeki refers to this conflict see the Penguin Reader's guide in the paperback edition of *My Year of Meats* as well as her interview with *Mother Jones.*

58 I return to this slippage later in the chapter; it is also addressed in chapter 5 of this book.

59 Ozeki, *My Year of Meats*, 363. *My Year of Meats* will be abbreviated to *MYOM* in all future notes.

60 Fish, "The Toxic Body Politics," 52.

61 Critics like Julie Sze, Nina Cornyetz, Monica Chiu, Cheryl Fish, and Emily Cheng point to Jane's mixed race status in their analyses of the novel. Other scholars, like Shameen Black, fail to acknowledge Jane's or Ozeki's biraciality and, instead, refer to both character and author as simply Japanese American.

62 Ozeki, *MYOM*, 51.

63 Chiu, *Filthy Fictions*, 142.

64 Creef, *Imaging Japanese America*, 179.

65 Ozeki, *MYOM*, 15.

66 Ibid., 9.

67 Ibid.

68 Ibid., 27.

69 Like the concept of identity, "authenticity" is a mutable term, and I am not arguing for a pure or correct notion of what constitutes authenticity. I develop the notion of questionable "authenticity" further in this chapter. For a work that provocatively and productively troubles notions of authenticity see Robert Ku's *Dubious Gastronomy: The Cultural Politics of Eating Asian in the USA.*

70 Lowe, *Immigrant Acts*, 146.

71 Ozeki, *MYOM*, 102.

72 Bow, *Partly Colored*, 42.

73 For more on the indeterminate and ambiguous racial status of Asian Americans, see the Introduction.

74 Bow, *Partly Colored*, 137.

75 As a mixed race person, Jane is simultaneously white, Japanese, and more than all of these categories—she passes in between terms and embodies all of these identities in her hybridity and her multiracial status.

76 Ozeki, *MYOM*, 104–5.

77 Ibid., 105.

78 Ibid., 106.

79 Cornyetz, "The Meat Manifesto," 212.

80 Ozeki, *MYOM*, 314.

81 Ibid., 360.

82 Williams, "Race-ing and Being Raced," 61.

83 A few examples of passing narratives that depict the act of passing as betrayal and/or where tragedy strikes the passer include James Weldon Johnson's *Autobiography of an Ex-Colored Man* (1912), Nella Larsen's *Quicksand* (1928) and *Passing* (1929), and both film versions of *Imitation of Life* (1934 and 1959).

84 Wald, *Crossing the Line*, 189.

85 Caughie, *Passing and Pedagogy*, 180.

86 Rekdal, *Bruce Lee*, 183.

87 Ibid., 188.

88 Ibid., 189.

89 Ibid., 199.

90 Ibid., 195.

91 Ibid., 198–199.

92 Ibid., 200–201.

93 The name and address on the back of the photos belong to Marianne Wang, Aunt Opal's eldest daughter who lives in Seattle. She had, apparently, donated the photos to the Natchez historical society.

94 Opal's first name is listed in parentheses next to her husband's in the phone book, as was the custom of that time.

95 Rekdal, *Bruce Lee*, 206.

96 Ibid., 208.

97 Chuh, *Imagine Otherwise*, 19.

5: TRANSGRESSIVE TEXTS AND AMBIGUOUS AUTHORS

1 All books honored at the 2008 awards banquet were works published in 2006, which is the custom of AAAS, to acknowledge works that had been published two years previous to the conference. Additionally, for the remainder of this article, I abbreviate Association of Asian American Studies, the official academic association for students and scholars of Asian American studies (nationally as well as internationally), to its commonly used abbreviation, AAAS.

2 The controversy over Chinese American author Bill Cheng's book, *Southern Cross the Dog*, which focuses on black southerners, had critics wondering whether an Asian American non-southerner can create a legitimate southern literary text.

3 Fishkin, "Desegregating American Literary Studies," 121.

4 See fn. 1 in Fishkin's essay.

5 C. Lee, "Asian American Literature and the Resistances of Theory," 37. Nam Le's *The Boat* is another transgressive text; its author is a Vietnamese Australian writer who studied at the famed Iowa Writers Workshop and whose collection of short stories feature settings and protagonists that range from Columbian teenage assassins to Japanese children finding refuge in the countryside during World War II to a dying white American artist in New York City. It also includes stories about Vietnamese fleeing Viet Nam in the aftermath of the fall of Sai Gon and one about a writer who, similar to the author, is a Vietnamese Australian studying for his MFA.

6 Wong, "Denationalization Reconsidered," 16.

7 Koshy, "The Fiction of Asian American Literature," 315.

8 The coinage of "Asian American" is credited to two graduate students, Emma Gee and Yuji Ichioka, who wanted a label that would replace "Oriental" and that would capture

the centrality of Asian ethnicities as well as political action. As Ichioka explains, an Asian American "gives a damn about his life, his work, his beliefs, and is willing to do almost anything to help Orientals become Asian Americans" (qtd. in Kwong and Miscevic, *Chinese America: The Untold Story of America's Oldest New Community*, 267–268). For more on the history of the Asian American movement see William Wei's *The Asian American Movement*.

9 For a longer description of Frank Chin's role as a founding figure in Asian American literature and for the controversy surrounding this essay as well as the very public debate between Chin and Maxine Hong Kingston that preceded and escalated from this introduction, please see Edward Iwata's "Word Warriors," King-kok Cheung's "The Woman Warrior Versus the Chinaman Pacific: Must a Chinese American Critic Choose between Feminism and Heroism?," and selections from Sau-ling Cynthia Wong's *Maxine Hong Kingston's "The Woman Warrior": A Casebook*.

10 In a 1989 interview with Maxine Hong Kingston, Bill Moyers observes that *Woman Warrior* is the most widely taught book on US college campuses.

11 See Han Ong's *Fixer Chao*.

12 See Chieh Chieng's *Long Stay in a Distant Land*.

13 See Don Lee's *Yellow: Stories*.

14 See Betsy Huang's *Contesting Genres in Asian American Fiction*, Allan Isaac's *American Tropics: Articulating Filipino America*, and erin Khue Ninh's *Ingratitude: The Debt-Bound Daughter in Asian American Literature* as a few examples of this trend.

15 Lauter, *From Jurassic Park to Walden Pond*, 137.

16 I recognize that the fifteen faculty members and twenty-seven syllabi I collected from my single call for course information cannot be seen as a complete representative sampling; however, as a regular attendee of the annual AAAS conference, as well as other American literature conferences with panels dedicated to Asian American literature (MELUS: Multiethnic Literatures of the United States, and ALA: American Literature Association), I believe that I have seen only one panel devoted to David Guterson's novel. For the most part, papers on Asian American literature focus on US writers of Asian descent.

17 Among a small sample of monographs written in the last decade, works by Victor Bascara, Anita Mannur, and Juliana Chang all rely on close readings of Asian American literature written by Asian American authors.

18 Jin's most recent novels are the exceptions: *A Free Life* takes place entirely in the contemporary United States and *Nanjing Requiem* is set during the late 1930s in China.

19 Additionally, because Lee's first two novels feature Asian American protagonists, his reputation as an Asian American writer was solidified prior to *Aloft*'s publication.

20 See works by Colleen Lye, Robert G. Lee, and James S. Moy for confirmation of the racist portrayals of Asian Americans in the late nineteenth and early twentieth centuries.

21 Buck, the daughter of Chinese missionaries, was born and raised in China, was fluent in Mandarin, wrote predominantly about China and Chinese issues (both fiction and nonfiction), and dedicated her life to humanitarian work, such as founding Welcome Home, an orphanage devoted to placing mixed race Asian children into homes in the United States. For more on Buck's life see the website Pearl S. Buck International (www.pbsi.org).

22 According to Colleen Lye, "In 1958 Harold Isaac's study of American opinions about Asia found that a majority of interviewees still identified Buck as the source of their images of China" (204). For more on Buck and her role in American conceptions of Chinese, see *America's Asia*.

23 Asian American literary critics are not only examining issues that move beyond race but that also extend our definition of texts; Cathy Schlund-Vials's *War, Genocide, and Justice: Cambodian American Memory Work* and Cynthia Wu's *Chang and Eng Reconnected: The Original Siamese Twins in American Culture* are two such examples. For recent examples of works that look at the intersection of sexuality, gender, and class see Martin Joseph Ponce's *Beyond the Nation: Diasporic Filipino Literature and Queer Reading* and Yoonmee Chang's *Writing the Ghetto: Class, Authorship, and the Asian American Enclave*.

24 I discuss notions of authenticity in chapter 4, "Ambiguous Movements and Mobile Subjectivity: Passing in between Autobiography and Fiction with Paisley Rekdal and Ruth Ozeki." For more on an examination of authenticity related to ethnicity see Vincent Cheng's *Inauthentic: The Anxiety over Culture and Identity* and Robert Ku's *Dubious Gastronomy: The Cultural Politics of Eating Asian in the USA*.

25 For two very astute analyses of this phenomenon see Stephen Sohn's *Racial Asymmetries: Asian American Fictional Worlds* and Min Song's *The Children of 1965: On Writing, and Not Writing as an Asian American*.

26 Vikram Seth's *The Golden Gate* is written in verse, specifically in the onegin sonnet form. Although there is a third-generation Japanese American character, Jan, the main plotlines center on twin love affairs between two different white American couples (one gay, one straight) taking place in San Francisco during the 1980s.

27 Hahn, "Sigrid Nunez."

28 Chee, "An Interview with Sigrid Nunez."

29 Nunez's latest work, *Sempre Susan: A Memoir of Susan Sontag*, is also not focused on issues of her mixed race heritage but is, as its title suggests, an account of her friendship with the famous writer.

30 Conventional wisdom suggests that when writers do not indicate a racial or ethnic identity for their characters, readers assume that the fictional characters are white, because the default in fiction in the United States seems to be to white normativity when reading about racially or ethnically unmarked characters. Interestingly, Philip D. Beidler, who reviews *For Rouenna* in the *Michigan Quarterly Review*, does just this when he fails to mention the race of any of the characters, save for a high school classmate, Luther, whom Beidler consistently refers to as black in his review, for no apparent reason other than to highlight his racial difference from the other, assumably white characters. In terms of the similarities between the narrator in *For Rouenna* and the one from her first novel are the number and gender of her siblings as well as her birth order, growing up in housing projects in Staten Island, being former ballet dancers in their youth, being the author of an autobiographical first novel, and having her mother's brother bring home a Vietnamese war bride after his stint fighting in the war in Viet Nam.

31 Nunez, *For Rouenna*, 87.

32 Ibid., 133.

33 Ibid., 84.

34 Ibid.

35 Ibid., 85.

36 Ibid., 183.

37 Ibid., 184.

38 The phrase "chop-chop" is generally associated with a command that white patrons would say to their Asian (Chinese/Korean/Filipino/Japanese) servants, meant to encourage them to act with speed or swiftness in carrying out their orders. It is typically

understood as an offensive and racist phrase, especially when directed at someone of Asian ancestry, and in popular and public discourse of the early twentieth century this phrase was almost always associated as a command given to Asians by whites.

39 Immediately after graduating from college the unnamed narrator engages in an affair with a married British journalist who has spent a considerable amount of time covering the war in Viet Nam. The journalist insists that if the narrator really wants to understand Viet Nam she should read *The Quiet American*, a novel by British author Graham Greene about the French-Indochinese conflict in Viet Nam of the 1950s told through the perspective of a love triangle involving an older British ex-pat, an idealistic young American Harvard grad, and the Vietnamese woman both men desire. Needless to say, the Vietnamese love interest, Phuong, is portrayed as a passive, shallow, largely silent woman whose existence seems to be predicated on pleasing the men in her life.

40 Beidler says that *For Rouenna* "is a PTSD narrative. It is a book about Vietnam as a class war and a race war. It is surely, in particular, a novel about Vietnam as a gender war, and by extension, in the narrator's relationship with Rouenna, a novel of the imprisoning violence, physical and emotional, that remains a daily fact of life for women, ranging from rapes and beatings to career pigeonholings and the cultural tyrannies of aging and body image"; notably, among the many ways in which Beidler defines *For Rouenna*, he does not call this an Asian American novel.

41 Ruta, "Veteran's Day," 8.

42 For a different perspective on Sigrid Nunez as an Asian American writer see chapter 3, "The Incomplete Biography in the Post–Civil Rights Era: Narrating Imagined Lives in Sigrid Nunez's Fiction," in Stephen Sohn's *Racial Asymmetries*.

43 Murphy, "The Nature of Inheritance."

44 Chee, "An Interview with Sigrid Nunez."

45 Murphy, "The Nature of Inheritance."

46 Alfonso-Ferero, "A Whole New Race," 1.

47 In addition to the ambiguity of her racial and sexual identity, Chen Fang also crossed borders of gender in the first sixteen years of her life when her mother, distraught over the birth of a third daughter, falsely announces that she has birthed a son. The local villagers are acquiescent in the collusion because Lorenzo Chen, Chen Fang's father, was a wealthy merchant and would spend more money on the family (and subsequently the village) for a first son rather than a third daughter. Cheng Fang, thus, does not have her feet bound as her two older sisters do, and she is sent away to Shanghai to be educated, passing as a boy until the age of sixteen when her mother calls her home because the money her father had been sending from Cuba stopped. Chen Fang is then subsequently married off to a family from a distant village.

48 Garcia, *Monkey Hunting*, 232.

49 Ibid., 233.

50 I deliberately hyphenate "Chinese-American" and later "Asian-American" to emphasize the truly hyphenated nature of Garcia's work.

51 I put "rescues" in quotation marks because the misogynist trope of a Western man saving a woman (often non-Western or brown-skinned women) from a life of prostitution is troubling. Yet Domingo does, indeed, seem to defend Tham Thanh Lan, who is having sex with men for money, from the attention of other male customers and to provide her with both material and emotional comforts that, while problematic within the context of the war and his position as a US American GI, nonetheless seems to signal a romantic relationship rather than a prostitute-client relationship.

52 Garcia, *Monkey Hunting*, 209.

53 Ibid., 209.

54 Caminero-Santangelo, *On Latinidad*, 104. Although other Asian American writers have taken up non-US and non-Asian settings (Monique Truong's *Book of Salt* is set in Paris, and Karen Tei Yamashita's *Through the Arc of the Rainforest* takes place in Brazil) and other Asian American writers have concentrated on themes of hybridity and inter-raciality (Don Lee's *Country of Origin* features a mixed race Korean-black protagonist), I argue that Garcia's work is unique in its sustained attention to Chinese-Cuban diasporic characters across a range of continents, cultures, languages and through an attention to hybridity that does not diminish either the Chinese nor Cuban elements and characters in her fiction. No other work pays attention to such a diversity and multiplicity of influences, although Margaret Cezair-Thompson's *The True History of Paradise*, does contain Asian characters in its sprawling portrait of a multi-ethnic Jamaican family, and Patricia Powell's *The Pagoda* also depicts a multiethnic mix of characters in late nineteenth-century Jamaica. However, the Asian elements in Cezair-Thompson's works are muted and used more as background flavor rather than foregrounded as a crucial element within the novel, and Powell's work, I argue, focuses more centrally on issues of gender and sexuality than race and ethnicity.

55 Garcia, *Monkey Hunting*, 245.

56 Moiles, "Search for Utopia," 177.

57 Another work that looks at Asian American figures in works of canonical American literature in the twentieth century is Heidi Kim's manuscript-in-progress *Invisible Subjects: Asian America in Postwar US Fiction*.

58 Lye, *America's Asia*, 5.

59 Srikanth, *The World Next Door*, 153.

60 R. Lee, "Gish Jen Interview," 223.

61 *The Laughing Sutra* is white American Mark Salzman's second book and first novel. Told in the third-person restricted narration, it follows the foibles and fortunes of a Chinese orphan, Hsun-ching, who embarks on a journey in the 1970s that takes him from Yunnan province in southern China to San Francisco, California, on a quest to retrieve a Buddhist sutra. Given Salzman's fluency with Chinese language and knowledge of Chinese history, culture, and customs, the work is rendered both authentically and sensitively, giving agency and voice to Hsun-ching in an entirely respectful way, including a potential love interest for him in the guise of white American museum assistant, Alison Weber.

62 Chuh, *Imagine Otherwise*, 10–11.

63 I argue that all scholarly research and all college syllabi have ideological components; in the case of Asian American literary studies (like other ethnic studies fields), the politics and ideologies of our scholarship and coursework seem more obviously pronounced because the study of race is tied to ideas of exceptionalism rather than universalism. In other words, a course on Shakespeare may be deemed apolitical, yet anyone who has read and studied his plays understands that he was deeply invested in politics, power, and ideology.

64 Chua's recent and controversial works (*Battle Hymn of the Tiger Mother* and *Triple Package*) have been soundly critiqued by scholars of Asian American studies, most notably by literary scholar erin Khue Ninh and journalist Jeff Yang. I, myself, have written a piece deeply critical of Chua for the blog The Good Men Project, "Why I Am Not Reading Amy Chua's 'The Triple Package.'"

65 Goellnicht, "Blurring Boundaries," 341.

66 Srikanth, *The World Next Door*, 153. Anecdotally, I have heard from colleagues that they do not teach the novels of Amy Tan or Lisa See because they find their works to be self-Orientalizing, particularly in their focus on pre-Communist Chinese female characters who seem to satisfy a desire by mainstream American (largely white) audiences for Asian exotica.

67 In an effort at full disclosure, I must note that I delivered a version of this chapter in the form of a conference paper, "Who Passes for What? Questions of Embodiment in Asian American Literature," at the 2008 AAAS conference (the same conference in which Janko won the fiction prize), and my conclusion then was that the time was not right to consider works by non–Asian American writers, like Cristina Garcia, as Asian American literature. My thinking around this issue changed after the 2008 conference, in no small part because of Janko's winning the Asian American fiction award. In an odd coincidence, my conference paper as well as Janko's award is charted in an essay by music scholar Eric Hung, "Introduction: Music and the Asian Diaspora."

68 I am thinking of any number of nameless, underdeveloped, and stereotyped Vietnamese characters who populate the films of the late 1970s through early 1990s depicting the US American military's perspective on the war in Viet Nam, films like *The Deer Hunter, Apocalypse Now, Platoon*, and *Full Metal Jacket*, to name but a few.

69 Information about Janko's writing process and biography came from comments on my blog *Mixed Race America* when I wrote about Janko's book winning the 2008 Asian American fiction award; specifically Janko's friend Mike Wong and Janko himself were kind enough to write and explain how he developed his novel. For more, see "What Does It Mean to Win an Asian American Book Award" (April 28, 2008) and "Thoughts on *Buffalo Boy and Geronimo*" (June 27, 2008) on www.mixedraceamerica.blogspot.com.

70 Indeed, Rajini Srikanth makes this argument for teaching Robert Olen Butler's *A Good Scent from a Strange Mountain* alongside works of Vietnamese American writers, for it "enables a discussion of responsibility, sensitivity, and skill in the deployment of the imagination" (166). My only departure from Srikanth is my belief that one need not always teach transgressive texts alongside works by writers from that particular ethnicity because I do not believe in setting up a juxtaposition between writers from a supposedly authentic culture and authors who are deemed inauthentic. Though there are those who may feel strongly about Butler's inappropriate appropriation of Vietnamese exilic voices, his Vietnamese language skills, his work with exiled Vietnamese immigrants, and his acceptance by this community as a "friend" to the Vietnamese complicates simple repudiation of his text as inauthentic or inappropriately appropriating a subject to which he has no firsthand knowledge.

71 Taken from an anonymous student writing exercise, April 28, 2005.

CODA: ENDING WITH ORIGINS

1 Truong, *Bitter in the Mouth*, 169.

2 For a very astute analysis of the anomalous position of Asian Americans in the US South see Leslie Bow's *Partly Colored*.

3 My paternal family's story of fleeing Communist China during the late 1940s and early 1950s and coming to the United States is a more common immigration tale, one that mirrors the plot of many Amy Tan novels.

4   Gung Gung is the name in Chinese culture given to one's maternal grandfather; its paternal counterpart is Ye Ye.

5   Po Po is the name in Chinese culture given to one's maternal grandmother; its paternal counterpart is Nai Nai.

6   I emphasize the various modes of transportation and distances that my grandmother traveled to demonstrate that cross continental travel in the first few decades of the twentieth century was a fairly arduous endeavor, which is one reason my grandmother did not want to travel with her infant daughter.

7   My grandmother did return to Hong Kong to reclaim my eldest aunt; however, by the time she arrived my aunt was an eight-year-old girl who had no memories of my Po Po and who didn't want to leave the family who had been raising her all along. She remained in Hong Kong and my grandmother returned to Kingston.

8   The earliest wave of Chinese came to Jamaica when the transatlantic slave trade ended; they were recruited as a replacement cheap labor force. However, many Chinese either escaped or bought themselves out of their indentured servitude and opened up shops. For more on this history see *The Shopkeepers: Commemorating 150 Years of the Chinese in Jamaica, 1854–2004*.

9   For more on the Mixed-Marriage Policy of 1942, see chapter 1.

10 In my first book *Consumption and Identity in Asian American Coming-of-Age Novels*, I open my introduction with a similar anecdote over the nature of how I identified as Chinese Jamaican as a youth and the ways that both Chinese and Jamaican food contributed to my ethnic identifications.

BIBLIOGRAPHY

Alfonso-Ferero, Ann Marie. "A Whole New Race: Chinese Cubans and Hybrid Identities in Cristina Garcia's *Monkey Hunting.*" *Anthurium: A Caribbean Studies Journal* 7.1 (2010): 1–8.

Ancheta, Angelo. *Race, Rights, and the Asian American Experience.* 2nd ed. New Brunswick, NJ: Rutgers University Press, 2006.

Anderson, Benedict R. *Imagined Communities: Reflections on the Origin and Spread of Nationalism.* London: Verso, 1983.

Anzaldúa, Gloria. *Making Face, Making Soul Haciendo Caras: Creative and Critical Perspectives by Feminists of Color.* San Francisco: Aunt Lute Books, 1990.

———, ed. *Borderlands/La Frontera: The New Mestiza.* 25th anniv. 4th ed. San Francisco: Aunt Lute Books, 2012.

Apocalypse Now. VHS. Directed by Francis Ford Coppola. 1977. Hollywood: Paramount Home Entertainment, 1992.

Asian American Federation of New York. "Census Study Shows Severe Poverty among New York City's Asian American Children." www.aafny.org/proom/pr/pr20030610.asp.

Balibar, Etienne, and Immanuel Wallerstein. *Race, Nation, Class: Ambiguous Identities.* London: Verso, 2002.

Barbie, Donna, ed. *The Tiger Woods Phenomenon: Essays on the Cultural Impact of Golf's Fallible Superman.* Jefferson, NC: McFarland, 2012.

Barkley, Charles. *Who's Afraid of a Large Black Man?* New York: Penguin, 2005.

Barlow, Aaron. *The Rise of the Blogosphere.* Westport, CT: Praeger, 2007.

Bascara, Victor. *Model-Minority Imperialism.* Minneapolis: University of Minnesota Press, 2006.

Bass, Thomas. *Vietnamerica: The War Comes Home.* New York: Soho Press, 1996.

Bataan. VHS. Directed by Tay Garnett. 1943. Warner Home Video, 1999.

Beidler, Philip D. "Enlarging the Vietnam Canon: Sigrid Nunez's *For Rouenna.*" *Michigan Quarterly Review* 42:4 (2004). http://hdl.handle.net/2027/spo.act2080.0043.426.

Bell, Michael. *Sentimentalism, Ethics, and the Culture of Feeling.* New York: Palgrave Macmillan, 2000.

Bendetsen, Karl. Transcript. File 291.1. Records of the Western Defense Command and 4th Army and Wartime Civil Control Administration General Correspondence, Record Group 499. College Park, MD: National Archives II. May 24, 1943.

Bennett, Juda. *The Passing Figure: Racial Confusion in Modern American Literature.* New York: Peter Lang, 1998.

Berebitsky, Julie. *Like Our Very Own: Adoption and the Changing Culture of Motherhood, 1851–1950.* Lawrence: University Press of Kansas, 2000.

Bhabha, Homi K. *The Location of Culture*. London and New York: Routledge, 1994.

The Blind Side. Directed by John Lee Hancock. Burbank, CA: Warner Bros. Pictures, 2009.

Boekel, William. Correspondence. File 291.1. Records of the Western Defense Command and 4th Army and Wartime Civil Control Administration General Correspondence, Record Group 499. College Park, MD: National Archives II. April 3, 1942.

Bourdieu, Pierre. *Distinction: A Social Critique of the Judgment of Taste*. Cambridge, MA: Harvard University Press, 1984.

Bow, Leslie. *Betrayal and Other Acts of Subversion: Feminism, Sexual Politics, Asian American Women's Literature*. Princeton, NJ: Princeton University Press, 2001.

——. *Partly Colored: Asian Americans and Racial Anomaly in the Segregated South*. New York: New York University Press, 2010.

Brian, Kristi. *Reframing Transracial Adoption: Adopted Koreans, White Parents, and the Politics of Kinship*. Philadelphia: Temple University Press, 2012.

Briggs, Laura. *Somebody's Children: The Politics of Transracial and Transnational Adoption*. Durham, NC: Duke University Press, 2012.

Briggs, Laura, and Diana Marre. *International Adoption: Global Inequalities and the Circulation of Children*. New York: New York University Press, 2009.

Buck, Pearl. *The Good Earth*. 1931. Rpt. New York: Washington Square Press, 2004.

Butler, Judith. *Gender Trouble: Feminism and the Subversion of Identity*. London and New York: Routledge, 1999.

Butler, Robert Olen. *A Good Scent from a Strange Mountain: Stories*. New York: H. Holt, 1992.

Callahan, Tom. *In Search of Tiger: A Journey through Golf with Tiger Woods*. New York: Three Rivers, 2003.

Caminero-Santangelo, Marta. *On Latinidad: US Latino Literature and the Construction of Identity*. Gainesville: University Press of Florida, 2009.

Caputo, Philip. *A Rumor of War*. New York: Holt Paperbacks, 1996.

Carp, E. Wayne. *Family Matters: Secrecy and Disclosure in the History of Adoption*. Cambridge, MA: Harvard University Press, 1998.

Caughie, Pamela. *Passing and Pedagogy: The Dynamics of Responsibility*. Chicago: University of Illinois Press, 1999.

Cezair-Thompson, Margaret. *The True History of Paradise*. New York: Plume, 2000.

Chambers, Marcia. *The Unplayable Lie: The Untold Story of Women and Discrimination in American Golf*. New York: Pocket Books, 1995.

Chan, J. Paul, Frank Chin, Lawson Fusao Inada, and Shawn Wong. *The Big Aiiieeeee!* New York: Penguin Books, 1991.

Chan, Sucheng. *Asian Americans: An Interpretive History*. Boston: Twayne, 1991.

——. *In Defense of Asian American Studies: The Politics of Teaching and Program Building*. Urbana and Chicago: University of Illinois Press, 2005.

Chang, Juliana. *Inhuman Citizenship: Traumatic Citizenship and Asian American Enjoyment*. Minneapolis: University of Minnesota Press, 2012.

Chang, Robert. *Disoriented: Asian Americans, Law, and the Nation-State*. New York: New York University Press, 1999.

Chang, Yoonmee. *Writing the Ghetto: Class, Authorship and the Asian American Enclave*. New Brunswick, NJ: Rutgers University Press, 2011.

Charles, John. *Abandoning the Black Hero: Sympathy and Privacy in the Postwar African American White-Life Novel*. New Brunswick, NJ: Rutgers University Press, 2012.

Chee, Alexander. "An Interview with Sigrid Nunez." *Memorious* 11. www.memorious.org/?id=264.

Chen, Ray, ed. *The Shopkeepers: Commemorating 150 Years of the Chinese in Jamaica, 1854–2004.* Kingston, Jamaica: Periwinkle Publishers, 2005.

Chen, Tina. *Double Agency: Acts of Impersonation in Asian American Literature and Culture.* Stanford, CA: Stanford University Press, 2005.

Cheng, Bill. *Southern Cross the Dog.* New York: HarperCollins, 2013.

Cheng, Emily. "Meat and the Millennium: Transnational Politics of Race and Gender in Ruth Ozeki's *My Year of Meats.*" *Journal of Asian American Studies* 12:2 (June 2009): 191–220.

Cheng, Vincent. *Inauthentic: The Anxiety over Culture and Identity.* New Brunswick, NJ: Rutgers University Press, 2004.

Cheung, King-Kok. *Articulate Silences: Hisaye Yamamoto, Maxine Hong Kingston, and Joy Kogawa.* Ithaca, NY: Cornell University Press, 1993.

——. "The Woman Warrior versus the Chinaman Pacific: Must a Chinese American Critic Choose between Feminism and Heroism?" In *Asian American Studies: A Reader*, ed. Jean Yu-wen Shen Wu and Min Song, 307–323. New Brunswick, NJ: Rutgers University Press, 2000.

Chiang, Mark. *The Cultural Capital of Asian American Studies: Autonomy and Representation in the University.* New York: New York University Press, 2009.

Chieng, Chieh. *Long Stay in a Distant Land.* New York: Bloomsbury USA, 2005.

Chin, Frank. "Come All Ye Asians of the Real and the Fake." In *The Big Aiiieeeee!*, ed. Frank Chin, J. Paul Chan, Lawson Fusao Inada, and Shawn Wong, 1–92. New York: Penguin, 1991.

China's Lost Girls. DVD. Directed by David Royle. Washington, DC: National Geographic Television & Film, 2005.

Chiu, Monica. *Filthy Fictions: Asian American Literature by Women.* Lanham, MD: AltaMira, 2004.

Cho, Sumi. "Asian Pacific American Women and Racialized Sexual Harassment." In *Making More Waves: New Writing by Asian American Women*, ed. Elaine H. Kim, Lilia V. Villanueva, and Asian Women United of California, 164–173. Boston: Beacon Press, 1997.

Chou, Rosalind. *Asian American Sexual Politics: The Construction of Race, Gender, and Sexuality.* Lanham, MD: Rowman & Littlefield, 2012.

Christian, Barbara. *Black Feminist Criticism: Perspectives on Black Women Writers.* New York: Pergamon, 1985.

Christopher, Renny. "Sigrid Nunez." In *Dictionary of Literary Biography: Asian American Writers.* Detroit: Gale, 2005.

——. *The Viet Nam War/the American War: Images and Representations in Euro-American and Vietnamese Exile Narratives.* Amherst: University of Massachusetts Press, 1995.

Chu, Patricia P. *Assimilating Asians: Gendered Strategies of Authorship in Asian America.* Durham, NC: Duke University Press, 2000.

Chua, Amy. *Battle Hymn of the Tiger Mother.* New York: Penguin, 2011.

Chua, Amy, and Jed Rubenfeld. *The Triple Package: How Three Unlikely Traits Explain the Rise and Fall of Cultural Groups in the United States.* New York: Penguin, 2014.

Chuh, Kandice. *Imagine Otherwise: On Asian Americanist Critique.* Durham, NC: Duke University Press, 2003.

Clark, Thomas A. Correspondence. File 291.1. Records of the Western Defense Command and 4th Army and Wartime Civil Control Administration General Correspondence, Record Group 499. College Park, MD: National Archives II. March 31, 1942.

Clark de Nevers, Klancy. *The Colonel and the Pacifist: Karl Bendetsen, Perry Saito, and the Incarceration of Japanese Americans during World War II*. Salt Lake City: University of Utah Press, 2004.

Collier, Rachel Quy. "Performing Childhood." In *Outsiders Within: Writing on Transracial Adoption*, ed. Jane Jeong Trenka, Julia Cinyere Oparah, and Sun Yung Shin, 207–213. Cambridge, MA: South End Press, 2006.

Cornyetz, Nina. "The Meat Manifesto: Ruth Ozeki's Performative Poetics." *Women & Performance: A Journal of Feminist Theory* 12:1 (2001): 207–224.

Creef, Elena Tajima. *Imaging Japanese America: The Visual Construction of Citizenship, Nation, and the Body*. New York: New York University Press, 2004.

Crenshaw, Kimberle. "Mapping the Margins: Intersectionality, Identity Politics, and Violence against Women of Color." *Stanford Law Review* 43:6 (July 1991): 1241–1299.

Crosby, Peter J. Correspondence. File 291.1. Records of the Western Defense Command and 4th Army and Wartime Civil Control Administration General Correspondence, Record Group 499. College Park, MD: National Archives II. Sept. 1, 1943.

Daniels, Roger. *Concentration Camps USA: Japanese Americans and World War II*. New York: Henry Holt, 1972.

Daniels, Roger, Sandra Taylor, and Harry Kitano, eds. *Japanese Americans: From Relocation to Redress*. Salt Lake City: University of Utah Press, 1986.

Dariotis, Wei-ming. "Hapa: The Word of Power." Mixed Heritage Center. www.mixedheritage center.org/index.php?option=com_content&task=view&id=1259&Itemid=34.

Daughter from Danang. DVD. Directed by Gail Dolgin and Vincente Franco. Arlington, VA: Public Broadcasting System, 2002.

Davis, Mike. "Uprising and Repression in L.A." In *Reading Rodney King/Reading Urban Uprising*, ed. Robert Gooding-Williams, 142–155. New York and London: Routledge, 1993.

Days of Waiting. DVD. Directed by Steven Okazaki. 1990. San Francisco: NAATA, 2003.

de Beauvoir, Simone. *The Ethics of Ambiguity*. New York: Citadel, 1964.

DeBonis, Steven. *Children of the Enemy: Oral Histories of Vietnamese Amerasians and Their Mothers*. Jefferson, NC: McFarland, 1995.

The Deer Hunter. VHS. Directed by Michael Cimino. 1978. Burbank, CA: Multi-Channel Access Home Video, 1991.

Defoe, Daniel. *Moll Flanders*. 1722. Rpt. New York: Penguin Classics. 1989.

Densho: The Japanese American Legacy Project. www.densho.org/densho.asp.

Deutsch, Monroe. Correspondence. File 291.1. Records of the Western Defense Command and 4th Army and Wartime Civil Control Administration General Correspondence, Record Group 499. College Park, MD: National Archives II. March 19, 1942.

DeWitt, John L. Correspondence. File 291.1. Records of the Western Defense Command and 4th Army and Wartime Civil Control Administration General Correspondence, Record Group 499. College Park, MD: National Archives II. June 16, 1943.

———. *The Final Report: Japanese Evacuation from the West Coast 1942*. Washington, DC: US Government Printing Office, 1943.

Diaz, Jamie. "Tida in Thailand." *Golf Digest* (May 2009). www.golfdigest.com/magazine/ 2009–05/tida.

Did You Hear about the Morgans? Directed by Marc Lawrence. Culver City, CA: Columbia Pictures, 2009.

Dorow, Sara K. *Transnational Adoption: A Cultural Economy of Race, Gender, and Kinship*. New York: New York University Press, 2006.

Dowd, Maureen. "Tiger Woods Goes for the Green." In *Chasing Tiger: The Tigers Woods Reader*, ed. Glenn Stout, 89–92. Cambridge, MA: Da Capo, 2002.

Easy A. Directed by Will Gluck. Culver City, CA: Sony Pictures. 2010.

Edwards, Brent Hayes. *The Practice of Diaspora: Literature, Translation, and the Rise of Black Internationalism*. Cambridge, MA: Harvard University Press, 2003.

Elliot, Emory, Louis Freitas Caton, and Jeffrey Rhyne, eds. *Aesthetics in a Multicultural Age*. Oxford: Oxford University Press, 2002.

Ellis, Markman. *The Politics of Sensibility: Race, Gender, and Commerce in the Sentimental Novel*. Cambridge: Cambridge University Press, 2004.

Empson, William. *Seven Types of Ambiguity*. New York: New Directions, 1966.

Eng, David L. *The Feeling of Kinship: Queer Liberalism and the Racialization of Intimacy*. Durham, NC: Duke University Press, 2010.

———. *Racial Castration: Managing Masculinity in Asian America*. Durham, NC: Duke University Press, 2001.

Espiritu, Yen Le. *Asian American Panethnicity: Bridging Institutions and Identities*. Philadelphia: Temple University Press, 1992.

———. *Asian American Women and Men: Labor, Laws, and Love*. Thousand Oaks, CA: Sage Publications, 1997.

Evans, Karin. *The Lost Daughters of China*. New York: Penguin, 2000.

"Exempted Persons of Japanese Ancestry Now Resident in Evacuated Areas." File 291.1. Records of the Western Defense Command and 4th Army and Wartime Civil Control Administration General Correspondence, Record Group 499. College Park, MD: National Archives II. September 1, 1943.

Fanon, Frantz. *Black Skin, White Masks*. New York: Grove, 1967.

Feinstein, John. *The First Coming. Tiger Woods: Master or Martyr?* New York: Ballantine, 1998.

———. *The Majors*. Boston: Little, Brown, 1999.

First Person Plural. DVD. Directed by Deann Borshay Liem. Berkley: Mu Films. 2000.

Fish, Cheryl. "The Toxic Body Politics: Ethnicity, Gender, and Corrective Eco-Justice in Ruth Ozeki's *My Year of Meats* and Judith Helfand and Daniel Gold's *Blue Vinyl*." *MELUS: Multiethnic Literatures of the United States* 34:2 (2009): 43–62.

Fishkin, Shelly Fisher. "Desegregating American Literary Studies." In *Aesthetics in a Multicultural Age*, ed. Emory Elliot, Louis Freitas Caton, and Jeffrey Rhyne, 121–134. Oxford: Oxford University Press, 2002.

Foley, Barbara. "The Documentary Novel and the Problem of Borders." In *Essentials of the Theory of Fiction*, ed. Michael J. Hoffman and Patrick D. Murphy, 392–408. Durham, NC: Duke University Press, 1996.

Foucault, Michel. *"Society Must Be Defended": Lectures at the College de France 1975–1976*. New York: Picador, 1997.

Found in China. DVD. Directed by Carolyn Stanek. Hinsdale, IL: Tai-Kai Productions. 2007.

Fulbeck, Kip. *Paper Bullets: A Fictional Autobiography*. Seattle: University of Washington Press, 2001.

———. *Part Asian*100% Hapa*. San Francisco: Chronicle, 2006.

Full Metal Jacket. VHS. Directed by Stanley Kubrick.1987. Burbank, CA: Warner Bros. Home Video, 1988.

Garcia, Cristina. *The Aguerro Sisters*. New York: Knopf, 1997.

———. *Dreaming in Cuban*. New York: Knopf, 1992.

———. *A Handbook to Luck*. New York: Vintage, 2008.

———. *I Wanna Be Your Shoebox*. New York: Simon and Schuster, 2009.

——. *King of Cuba*. New York: Scribner, 2013.

——. *The Lady Matador Hotel*. New York: Scribner, 2012.

——. *Monkey Hunting*. New York: Ballantine Books, 2004.

Gilroy, Paul. *Postcolonial Melancholia*. New York: Columbia University Press, 2005.

Glasser, Jeffrey D. *The Secret Vietnam War: The United States Air Force in Thailand, 1961–1975*. Jefferson, NC: McFarland, 1995.

Glenn, Evelyn Nakano. *Issei, Nisei, Warbride: Three Generations of Japanese American Women in Domestic Service*. Philadelphia: Temple University Press, 1988.

Goebel, Herman P. Jr. Correspondence. File 291.1. Records of the Western Defense Command and 4th Army and Wartime Civil Control Administration General Correspondence, Record Group 499. College Park, MD: National Archives II. July 12, 1943.

Goellnicht, Donald. "Blurring Boundaries: Asian American Literature as Theory." In *An Interethnic Companion to Asian American Literature*, ed. King-kok Cheung, 338–361. Cambridge: Cambridge University Press, 1997.

Graham, Lawrence Otis. *A Member of the Club: Reflections on Life in a Racially Polarized World*. New York: Harper Perennial, 1996.

Greene, Graham. *The Quiet American*. 1955. Rpt. New York: Penguin, 2004.

Grice, Helena. *Maxine Hong Kingston*. Manchester: Manchester University Press, 2006.

Griffiths, Austin E. Correspondence. File 291.1. Records of the Western Defense Command and 4th Army and Wartime Civil Control Administration General Correspondence, Record Group 499. College Park, MD: National Archives II. March 27, 1942.

Grillo, Trina. "Anti-Essentialism and Intersectionality: Tools to Dismantle the Master's House." *Berkeley Women's Law Journal* 10 (1995): 16–30.

Guterl, Matthew Pratt. "After Slavery: Asian Labor, the American South, and the Age of Emancipation." *Journal of World History* 14:2 (2003): 209–241.

Guterson, David. *Snow Falling on Cedars*. New York: Random House, 1995.

Hagedorn, Jessica. *Dogeaters*. New York: Penguin, 1991.

Hahn, Kimiko. "Sigrid Nunez." *Bomb: Artists in Conversation* 50 (Winter 1995). http://bombmagazine.org/article/1840/sigrid-nunez.

Haney, Hank. *The Big Miss: My Years Coaching Tiger Woods*. New York: Crown Archetype, 2012.

Harris, David R., and Jeremiah Joseph Sim. "Who Is Multiracial? Assessing the Complexity of Lived Race." *American Sociological Review* 67:4 (2002): 614–627.

Harrison, Ralph. Correspondence. File 291.1. Records of the Western Defense Command and 4th Army and Wartime Civil Control Administration General Correspondence, Record Group 499. College Park, MD: National Archives II. March 30, 1942.

Hawley, Charles. "You're a Better Filipino Than I Am, John Wayne: World War II, Hollywood, and U.S.–Philippines Relations." *Pacific Historical Review* 71 (2002): 389–414.

Herman, Ellen. *Kinship by Design: A History of Adoption in the Modern United States*. Chicago: University of Chicago Press, 2008.

Ho, Jennifer. *Consumption and Identity in Asian American Coming-of-Age Novels*. New York and London: Routledge, 2003.

——. "Thoughts on Buffalo Boy and Geronimo." *Mixed Race America*. Last modified June 27, 2008. http://mixedraceamerica.blogspot.com/2008/06/thoughts-on-buffalo-boy-and-geronimo.html.

——. "What Does It Mean to Win an Asian American Book Award?" *Mixed Race America*. Last modified April 28, 2008. http://mixedraceamerica.blogspot.com/2008/04/what-does-it-mean-to-win-asian-american.html.

——. "Why I Am Not Reading Amy Chua's Book, *The Triple Package*." The Good Men Project. Last modified January 13, 2014. http://goodmenproject.com/opeds/why-i-am-not-reading-amy-chuas-triple-package-shesaid/.

Hoffman Michael J., and Patrick D. Murphy, eds. *Essentials of the Theory of Fiction*. Durham, NC: Duke University Press, 1996.

Hogan, Ron. "Paisley Rekdal." Beatrice Interview. www.beatrice.com/interviews/rekdal/.

Hood, Ann. *The Red Thread*. New York: Norton, 2010.

Hopgood, Mei-ling. *Lucky Girl: A Memoir*. Chapel Hill, NC: Algonquin, 2009.

"Hormones in Food and the Risk of Breast Cancer." Ithaca, NY: Cornell University. Last modified June 8, 2008. http://envirocancer.cornell.edu/Bibliography/diet/bib/hormones.cfm#zeranol.

Hosseini, Khaled. *The Kite Runner*. New York: Riverhead, 2003.

Houston, Jeanne Wakatsuki. *Farewell to Manzanar: A True Story of Japanese American Experience during and after the World War II Internment*. New York: Bantam Books, 1973.

Houston, Velina Hasu, and Teresa K. Williams, eds. No Passing Zone: The Artistic and Discursive Voices of Asian-Descent Multiracials. Special Issue, *Amerasia* 23:1 (1997).

Howard, John. *Concentration Camps on the Home Front: Japanese Americans in the House of Jim Crow*. Chicago: University of Chicago Press, 2008.

"How to Tell Japs from Chinese." *Life*, December 22, 1941, 81–82.

Huang, Betsy. *Contesting Genres in Contemporary Asian American Fiction*. New York: Palgrave Macmillan, 2010.

Iida, Deborah. *Middle Son*. New York: Berkeley Books, 2000.

Ikeda, Stewart David. *What the Scarecrow Said: A Novel*. New York: Regan Books, 1997.

Imitation of Life. DVD. Directed by John Stahl. 1934. Universal City, CA: Universal Home Entertainment. 2003.

Imitation of Life. DVD. Directed by Douglas Sirk. 1959. Universal City, CA: Universal Home Entertainment. 2003.

Inada, Lawson Fusao, ed. *Only What We Could Carry: The Japanese American Internment Experience*. Berkeley, CA: Heyday, 2000.

In the Matter of Cha Jung Hee. DVD. Directed by Deann Borshay Liem. Berkeley: Mu Films. 2010.

Isaac, Allan. *American Tropics: Articulating Filipino America*. Minneapolis: University of Minnesota Press, 2006.

Ishiguro, Kazuo. *Remains of the Day*. New York: Vintage International, 1989.

Izrael, Jimi. "Ten Things You Could Learn from Tiger Woods." *The Root*. Last modified December 2, 2009. www.theroot.com/blogs/the_hardline/2009/12/10_things_you_could_learn_from_tiger_woods.html.

Jacobson, Heather. *Culture Keeping: White Mothers, International Adoption, and the Negotiation of Family Difference*. Nashville: Vanderbilt University Press, 2008.

Janko, James. *Buffalo Boy and Geronimo: a Novel*. Willimantic, CT: Curbstone, 2006.

Jarrett, Gene Andrew. *African American Literature beyond Race: An Alternative Reader*. New York: New York University Press, 2006.

——. *Deans and Truants: Race and Realism in African American Literature*. Philadelphia: University of Pennsylvania Press, 2007.

Jenkins, Dan. *Jenkins at the Majors: Sixty Years of the World's Best Golf Writing, from Hogan to Tiger*. New York: Doubleday, 2009.

Jerng, Mark C. *Claiming Others: Transracial Adoption and National Belonging*. Minneapolis: University of Minnesota Press, 2010.

Jin, C. D. *The Rest Is History*. New York: CMM Ruff Ryders, 2004.

Jin, Ha. *The Bridegroom*. New York: Pantheon, 2000.

——. *A Free Life*. New York: Pantheon, 2007.

——. *Ocean of Words: Army Stories*. Cambridge, MA: Zoland, 1996.

——. *Waiting*. New York: Pantheon, 1999.

Jo, Sunny. "The Making of KAD Nation." In *Outsiders Within: Writing on Transracial Adoption*, ed. Jane Jeong Trenka, Julia Cinyere Oparah, and Sun Yung Shin, 285–290. Cambridge, MA: South End Press, 2006.

Johnson, James Weldon. *The Autobiography of an Ex-Colored Man*. 1912. Rpt. Mineola, NY: Dover, 1995.

Johnson, Kay. *Wanting a Daughter, Needing a Son: Abandonment, Adoption, and Orphanage Care in China*. St. Paul, MN: Yeong & Yeong, 2004.

Joo, Rachel Miyung. *Transnational Sport: Gender, Media, and Global Korea*. Durham, NC: Duke University Press, 2012.

Jung, Moon-Ho. *Coolies and Cane: Race, Labor, and Sugar in the Age of Emancipation*. Baltimore: Johns Hopkins University Press, 2006.

Kashima, Tetsuden. *Judgment without Trial: Japanese American Imprisonment during World War II*. Seattle: University of Washington Press, 2003.

Kelts, Roland. "Baggage Check." *Village Voice*. Last modified November 14, 2000. www.villagevoice.com/2000–11–14/books/baggage-check/.

Kennedy, John H. *A Course of Their Own: A History of African American Golfers*. Lincoln: University of Nebraska Press, 2000.

Kennedy, Randall. *Interrracial Intimacies: Sex, Marriage, Identity, and Adoption*. New York: Pantheon, 2003.

Kim, Claire Jean. *Bitter Fruit: The Politics of Black-Korean Conflict in New York City*. New Haven, CT: Yale University Press, 2003.

Kim, Daniel. *Writing Manhood in Black and Yellow: Ralph Ellison, Frank Chin, and the Literary Politics of Identity*. Stanford, CA: Stanford University Press, 2005.

Kim, Elaine H. *Asian American Literature: An Introduction to the Writings and Their Social Context*. Philadelphia: Temple University Press, 1982.

Kim, Eleana. *Adopted Territory: Transnational Korean Adoptees and the Politics of Belonging*. Durham, NC: Duke University Press, 2010.

Kim, Heidi. *Invisible Subjects: Asian America in Postwar US Fiction*. Forthcoming.

Kim, Jae Ran. Blog. *Harlow's Monkey*. http://harlowmonkey.typepad.com/harlows_monkey/.

——. "Scattered Seeds." In *Outsiders Within: Writing on Transracial Adoption*, ed. Jane Jeong Trenka, Julia Cinyere Oparah, and Sun Yung Shin, 151–162. Cambridge, MA: South End Press, 2006.

Kina, Laura, and Wei Ming Dariotis, eds. *War Baby/Love Child: Mixed Race Asian American Art*. Seattle: University of Washington Press, 2013.

Kindred, David. "So Young to Have the Master's Touch." In *Chasing Tiger: The Tigers Woods Reader*, ed. Glenn Stout, 83–87. Cambridge, MA: Da Capo, 2002.

Kingston, Maxine Hong. *China Men*. New York: Knopf, 1980.

——. *Tripmaster Monkey: His Fake Book*. New York: Random House, 1989.

——. *The Woman Warrior: Memoirs of a Girlhood among Ghosts*. New York: Vintage Books, 1977.

Klein, Christina. *Cold War Orientalism: Asia in the Middlebrow Imagination, 1945–1961*. Berkeley: University of California Press, 2003.

Kogawa, Joy. *Obasan*. New York: Anchor, 1993.

Kolko, Beth, Lisa Nakamura, and Gilbert B. Rodman, eds. *Race in Cyberspace.* New York and London: Routledge, 2000.

Koshy, Susan. "The Fiction of Asian American Literature." *Yale Journal of Criticism* 9 (1996): 315–346.

———. *Sexual Naturalization: Asian Americans and Miscegenation.* Stanford, CA: Stanford University Press, 2004.

Ku, Robert. *Dubious Gastronomy: The Cultural Politics of Eating Asian in the USA.* Honolulu: University of Hawaii Press, 2014.

Kwan, SanSan, and Kenneth Speirs. *Mixing It Up: Multiracial Subject.* Austin: University of Texas Press, 2004.

Kwong, Peter, and Dusanka Miscevic. *Chinese America: The Untold Story of America's Oldest New Community.* New York: New Press, 2005.

Lahiri, Jhumpa. *Interpreter of Maladies.* Boston: Houghton Mifflin Mariner, 1999.

Lai, Eric, and Dennis Arguelles. *The New Face of Asian Pacific America: Numbers, Diversity, and Change in the 21st Century.* Los Angeles: UCLA Asian American Studies Center Press, 2003.

Lanser, Susan. "The 'I' of the Beholder: Equivocal Attachments and the Limits of Structuralist Narratology." In *Blackwell Companion to Narrative Theory*, ed. Jim Phelan and Peter Rabinowitz, 206–219. Malden: Blackwell, 2005.

Larsen, Nella. *Passing.* 1929. Rpt. New York: Penguin Books, 2003.

———. *Quicksand.* 1928. Rpt. Mineola, NY: Dover, 2006.

Lauter, Paul. *From Jurassic Park to Walden Pond: Activism, Culture, and American Studies.* Durham, NC: Duke University Press, 2004.

Le, Nam. *The Boat: Stories.* New York: Knopf, 2008.

Lee, Chang-rae. *Aloft.* New York: Riverhead, 2004.

———. *Gesture Life.* New York: Riverhead, 1999.

———. *Native Speaker.* New York: Riverhead, 1995.

Lee, Christopher. "Asian American Literature and the Resistances of Theory." *Modern Fiction Studies* 56.1 (2010): 19–39.

Lee, Don. *Yellow: Stories.* New York: Norton, 2001.

Lee, Rachel. "Gish Jen Interview." In *Words Matter: Conversations with Asian American Writers*, ed. King-Kok Cheung, 213–232. Honolulu: University of Hawaii Press, 2000.

Lee, Robert G. *Orientals: Asian Americans in Popular Culture.* Philadelphia: Temple University Press, 1999.

Lee-Loy, Anne-Marie. *Searching for Mr. Chin: Constructions of the Nation and Chinese in West Indian Literature.* Philadelphia: Temple University Press, 2010.

Leonard, David J., and C. Richard King, eds. *Commodified and Criminalized: New Racism and African Americans in Contemporary Sports.* Lanham, MD: Rowman & Littlefield, 2011.

Lim, Shirley. "The Ambivalent American: Asian American Literature on the Cusp." In *Reading the Literatures of Asian America*, ed. Shirley Geok-lin Lim and Amy Ling, 13–32. Philadelphia: Temple University Press, 1992.

———. *Approaches to Teaching Maxine Hong Kingston's "The Woman Warrior."* New York: Modern Language Association, 1991.

Lim, Thea. "100% Cablinasian: Getting the Race Facts Right about Tiger Woods." *Racialicious.* Last modified December 8, 2009. www.racialicious.com/2009/12/08/100-cablinasian -getting-the-race-facts-right-on-tiger-woods/.

Ling, Huping. *Surviving on the Gold Mountain: A History of Chinese American Women and Their Lives.* Albany: State University of New York Press, 1998.

Lipman, Jana K. "'The Face Is the Roadmap': Vietnamese Amerasians in U.S. Political and Popular Culture, 1980–1988." *Journal of Asian American Studies* 14:1 (2011): 33–68.

"List of Exempted Persons of Japanese Ancestry Now Resident in Evacuated Areas." File 291.1. Records of the Western Defense Command and 4th Army and Wartime Civil Control Administration General Correspondence, Record Group 499. College Park, MD: National Archives II. September 1, 1943.

The Little Princess. DVD. Directed by Walter Lang. 1939. Los Angeles: 20th Century Fox, 2007.

Londino, Lawrence. *Tiger Woods: A Biography.* Westport, CT: Greenwood, 2008.

Lopez, Ian Haney. *White by Law: The Legal Construction of Race.* Rev. and upd. ed. New York: New York University Press, 2006.

Lott, Juanita Tamayo. *Common Destiny: Filipino American Generations.* New York: Rowman & Littlefield, 2006.

Louie, Andrea. "'Pandas, Lions, and Dragons, Oh My!': How White Adoptive Parents Construct Chineseness." *Journal of Asian American Studies* 12:3. (2009): 285–320.

Lovink, Geert. "Talking Race and Cyberspace: An Interview with Lisa Nakamura." *Frontiers: A Journal of Women Studies* 26:1 (2005): 60–65.

——. *Zero Comments: Blogging and Critical Internet Culture.* New York and London: Routledge, 2008.

Lowe, Lisa. *Immigrant Acts: On Asian American Cultural Politics.* Durham, NC: Duke University Press, 1996.

Lye, Colleen. *America's Asia: Racial Form and American Literature, 1893–1945.* Princeton, NJ: Princeton University Press, 2005.

Ma, Sheng-mei. "The Politics of Teaching Asian American Literature amidst Middle-Class Caucasian Students 'East of California.'" In *Teaching Asian America: Diversity and the Problem of Community*, ed. Lane Ryo Hirabayashi, 243–247. Lanham, MD: Rowman & Littlefield, 1998.

Maki, Mitchell T., Harry H. L. Kitano, and S. Megan Berthold. *Achieving the Impossible Dream: How Japanese Americans Obtained Redress.* Chicago: University of Illinois Press, 1999.

Malkin, Michelle. *In Defense of Internment: The Case for "Racial Profiling" during World War II and the War on Terror.* Washington, DC: Regnery, 2004.

Mannur, Anita. *Culinary Fictions: Food in South Asian Diasporic Cultures.* Philadelphia: Temple University Press, 2009.

Marlowe, Ann. "Hyphenated Life." *New York Times*, October 15, 2000. www.nytimes.com/books/00/10/15/reviews/001015.15marlowt.html.

Marre, Diana, and Laura Briggs, eds. *International Adoption: Global Inequalities and the Circulation of Children.* New York: New York University Press, 2009.

Marshall, Eliot. "Anthropologists Debate Tasaday Hoax Evidence." *Science* 246:4934 (December 1, 1989): 1113–1114.

Martin, Wallace. *Recent Theories of Narrative.* Ithaca, NY: Cornell University Press, 1986.

McCarroll, Meredith. "'Claiming': White Ambition, Multiracial Identity, and the New American Racial Passing." In *At Home and Abroad*, ed. La Vinia Delois Jennings. Knoxville: University of Tennessee Press, 2009. www.nytimes.com/books/00/10/15/reviews/001015.15marlowt.html.

McDaniel, Pete. *Uneven Lies: The Heroic Story of African-Americans in Golf.* Greenwich, CT: American Golfer, 2000.

McGrath, Charles. "America's First Golf Course." *Travel + Leisure.* Last modified March 1998. www.travelandleisure.com/articles/americas-first-golf-course.

McKelvey, Robert S. *The Dust of Life: America's Children Abandoned in Vietnam.* Seattle: University of Washington Press, 1999.

Mei-ling. Blog. *The Original Heping.* http://littlewing04.wordpress.com/.

Miller, Nancy K. *Getting Personal: Feminist Occasions and Other Autobiographical Acts.* New York: Routledge, 1991.

Modern Family. Television series. New York: American Broadcasting Company. 2009–2014.

Moiles, Sean. "Search for Utopia, Desire for the Sublime: Cristina Garcia's *Monkey Hunting.*" *MELUS: Multiethnic Literatures of the United States* 34:4 (2009): 167–186.

Morrison, Toni. *Beloved: A Novel.* New York: Knopf, 1998.

Moy, James. *Marginal Sights: Staging the Chinese in America.* Iowa City: University of Iowa Press, 1993.

Moyers, Bill. "Maxine Hong Kingston." *World of Ideas.* PBS. February 25, 1990.

Muller, Eric L. *American Inquisition: The Hunt for Japanese American Disloyalty in World War II.* Chapel Hill: University of North Carolina Press, 2007.

Mura, David. "A Shift in Power, a Sea Change in the Arts: Asian American Constructions." In *The State of Asian America: Activism and Resisance in the 1990s,* ed. K. Aguilar-San Juan, 183–204. Boston: South End Press, 1994.

Murdock, Maureen. *Unreliable Truth: On Memoir and Memory.* Berkeley, CA: Seal Press, 2003.

Murphy, Jessica. "The Nature of Inheritance." *Atlantic,* April 11, 2003. www.theatlantic.com/magazine/archive/2003/04/the-nature-of- inheritance/303087/.

Muse, Eben, J. *The Land of Nam: The Vietnam War in American Film.* Lanham, MD: Scarecrow Press, 1995.

Na, Soo. "Garlic and Salt." In *Outsiders Within: Writing on Transracial Adoption,* ed. Jane Jeong Trenka, Julia Cinyere Oparah, and Sun Yung Shin. Cambridge, MA: South End Press, 2006, 19–26.

Nakamura, Lisa. *Cybertypes: Race, Ethnicity, and Identity on the Internet.* New York and London: Routledge, 2002.

———. *Digitizing Race: Visual Cultures of the Internet.* Minneapolis: University of Minnesota Press, 2007.

Ng, Wendy. *Japanese American Internment during World War II: A History and Reference Guide.* Westport, CT: Greenwood, 2001.

Nguyen, Mimi Thi, and Thuy Linh Nguyen Tu, eds. *Alien Encounters: Popular Culture in Asian America.* Durham, NC: Duke University Press, 2007.

Nguyen, Viet Thanh. *Race and Resistance: Literature and Politics in Asian America.* New York: Oxford University Press, 2002.

Ninh, erin Khue. *Ingratitude: The Debt-Bound Daughter in Asian American Literature.* New York: New York University Press, 2011.

Nordlinger, Jay. "Hunting Tiger." *National Review,* September 6, 2002. www.freerepublic.com/focus/news/745722/posts.

Nunez, Sigrid. *A Feather on the Breath of God.* New York: HarperCollins, 1995.

———. *For Rouenna.* New York: Picador, 2002.

———. *The Last of Her Kind.* New York: Picador, 2006.

———. *Mitz: The Marmoset of Bloomsbury.* New York: Soft Skull Press, 2007.

———. *Naked Sleeper.* New York: Perennial, 1997.

———. *Salvation City.* New York: Riverhead Trade, 2011.

———. *Sempre Susan: A Memoir of Susan Sontag.* New York: Atlas & Co., 2011.

O., Paula. Blog. *Heart, Mind and Seoul.* http://heartmindandseoul.typepad.com/weblog/.

O'Hearn, Claudine Chiawei. *Half and Half: Writers Growing up Biracial and Bicultural.* New York: Pantheon, 1998.

Okihiro, Gary. *The Columbia Guide to Asian American History.* New York: Columbia University Press, 2001.

———. *Margins and Mainstreams: Asians in American History and Culture.* Seattle: University of Washington Press, 1994.

Okubo, Miné. *Citizen 13660.* Seattle: University of Washington Press, 1983.

Old Man River. DVD. Directed by Allan Holzman. New York: Old Man River Productions, 1999.

Omi, Michael, and Howard Winant. "Foreword." In *The Sum of Our Parts*, ed. Teresa Williams-Leon and Cynthia L. Nakashima, ix–xiii. Philadelphia: Temple University Press, 2001.

———. *Racial Formation in the United States: From the 1960s to the 1980s.* New York and London: Routledge & Kegan Paul, 1986.

Ondaatje, Michael. *The English Patient.* New York: Vintage, 1993.

Ong, Han. *Fixer Chao.* New York: Farrar Straus and Giroux, 2001.

"On the Links in Parks." New York City Department of Parks and Recreation. Last modified December 2, 2013. www.nycgovparks.org/about/history/golf.

"Outline of Mixed-Marriage Policy." File 291.1. Records of the Western Defense Command and 4th Army and Wartime Civil Control Administration General Correspondence, Record Group 499. College Park, MD: National Archives II. September 24, 1943.

Owen, David. *The Chosen One: Tiger Woods and the Dilemma of Greatness.* New York: Simon & Schuster, 2001.

Oxford English Dictionary. Oxford: Oxford University Press, 1989.

Ozeki, Ruth L. *My Year of Meats.* New York: Viking, 1998.

Park, Ed. *Personal Days.* New York: Random House, 2008.

Patton, Sandra. *Birthmarks: Transracial Adoption in Contemporary America.* New York: New York University Press, 2000.

Perez, Hiram. "Hello World: How Nike Sold Tiger Woods." Asian American Writers' Workshop. Last modified August 2, 2012. http://aaww.org/hello-world-how-nike-sold-tiger-woods/.

Pertman, Adam. *Adoption Nation: How the Adoption Revolution Is Transforming America.* New York: Basic Books, 2000.

Pfaelzer, Jean. *Driven Out!: The Forgotten War against Chinese Americans.* Berkeley: University of California Press, 2008.

Phan, Aimee. *We Should Never Meet.* New York: Picador, 2005.

Phelan, James, and Peter J. Rabinowitz, eds. *A Companion to Narrative Theory.* Malden, MA: Blackwell, 2005.

Pierce, Charles P. "Tiger Woods: Mama's Boy?" *Esquire*, February 19, 2010. www.esquire.com/the-side/opinion/tiger-woods-buddhist-statement-021910

Platoon. VHS. Directed by Oliver Stone. 1986. New York: Home Box Office Video, 1990.

Poblete-Cross, JoAnna. *Islanders in the Empire: Filipino and Puerto Rican Laborers in Hawaii.* Chicago: University of Illinois Press, 2014.

Poe, Janita. "Woods Spotlights Multiracial Identity." *Chicago Tribune.* Last modified April 21, 1997. http://articles.chicagotribune.com/1997–04–21/news/9704210122_1_multiracial-category-multi-ethnic-americans-african-american.

Ponce, Martin Joseph. *Beyond the Nation: Diasporic Filipino Literature and Queer Reading.* New York: New York University Press, 2012.

Powell, Patricia. *The Pagoda.* New York: Knopf, 1998.

Prince, Gerald. *Dictionary of Narratology*. Lincoln: University of Nebraska Press, 2003.

Raphael-Hernandez, Heike, and Shannon Steen, eds. *AfroAsian Encounters: Culture, History, Politics*. New York: New York University Press, 2006.

Regret to Inform. DVD. Directed by Barbara Sonneborn. San Francisco: Sun Fountain Productions, 2000.

Reilly, Rick. "Strokes of Genius." *Sports Illustrated*. Last modified February 22, 2008. www.golf.com/special-features/strokes-genius.

Rekdal, Paisley. *Animal Eye*. Pittsburgh: University of Pittsburgh Press, Pitt Poetry Series, 2012.

——. *A Crash of Rhinos*. New York: Contemporary Poetry Series, 2000.

——. *Intimate: An American Family Photo Album*. North Adams, MA: Tupelo, 2012.

——. *The Invention of the Kaleidoscope*. Pittsburgh: University of Pittsburgh Press, Pitt Poetry Series, 2007.

——. *The Night My Mother Met Bruce Lee: Observations on Not Fitting In*. New York: Pantheon, 2000.

——. *Six Girls without Pants*. Cheney: Eastern Washington University Press, 2002.

Robinson, Greg. *By Order of the President: FDR and the Internment of Japanese Americans*. Cambridge, MA: Harvard University Press, 2001.

Robinson, Katy. *A Single Square Picture: A Korean Adoptee's Search for Her Roots*. New York: Berkeley Books, 2002.

Rockquemore, Kerry Ann. "Deconstructing Tiger Woods: The Promise and the Pitfalls of Multiracial Identity." In *The Politics of Multiracialism: Challenging Racial Thinking*, ed. Heather M. Dalmadge, 125–141. Albany: State University of New York Press, 2004.

Root, Maria. *Love's Revolution: Interracial Marriage*. Philadelphia: Temple University Press, 2001.

——. "Multiracial Asians: Models of Ethnic Identity." *Amerasia* 23:1 (1997): 29–41.

Rosaforte, Tim. *Raising the Bar: The Championship Years of Tiger Woods*. New York: St. Martin's Griffin, 2002.

Rosenberg, Scott. *Say Everything: How Blogging Began, What It's Becoming, and Why It Matters*. New York: Crown, 2009.

Rowe, John Carlos. "The Resistance to Cultural Studies." In *Aesthetics in a Multicultural Age*, ed. Emory Elliot, Louis Freitas Caton, and Jeffrey Rhyne, 105–117. Oxford: Oxford University Press, 2002.

Ruta, Susanne. "Veteran's Day." *Women's Review of Books* 19:7 (2002): 8.

Ruth, Richard A. *In Buddha's Company: Thai Soldiers in the Vietnam War*. Honolulu: University of Hawaii Press, 2011.

Salgado, Raquel Scherr. "Misceg-narrations." In *Mixing It Up: Multiracial Subjects*, ed. SanSan Kwan and Kenneth Spiers, 31–70. Austin: University of Texas Press, 2004.

Salzman, Mark. *The Laughing Sutra*. New York: Vintage, 1992.

Sang-Shil. *Land of the Not-So-Calm*. Blog. http://notsocalm.wordpress.com/.

Sayonara. VHS. Directed by Joshua Logan. 1957. Beverly Hills, CA: Metro-Goldwyn Mayer/ United Artists Home Video. 1990.

Schlund-Vials, Cathy. *War, Genocide, and Justice: Cambodian American Memory Work*. Minneapolis: University of Minnesota Press, 2012.

Seth, Vikram. *The Golden Gate*. New York: Vintage, 1991.

Sex and the City. Television series. New York: Home Box Office. 1998–2004.

Sex and the City I. Directed by Michael Patrick King. Los Angeles: New Line Cinema, 2008.

Sex and the City II. Directed by Michael Patrick King. Burbank, CA: Warner Bros. Pictures, 2010.

Shelby, Tommie. *We Who Are Dark: The Philosophical Foundations of Black Solidarity.* Cambridge, MA: Harvard University Press, 2005.

Shipnuck, Alan. *The Battle for Augusta National: Hootie, Martha, and the Masters of the Universe.* New York: Simon & Schuster, 2004.

Simon, Rita J., and Howard Alstein. *Adoption, Race, and Identity: From Infancy to Young Adulthood.* 2nd ed. New Brunswick, NJ: Transaction, 2002.

Simon, Scott. *Baby, We Were Meant for Each Other: In Praise of Adoption.* New York: Random House, 2010.

Simpson, Caroline Chung. *An Absent Presence: Japanese Americans in Postwar American Culture, 1945–1960.* Durham, NC: Duke University Press, 2001.

Singley, Carol. *Adopting America: Childhood, Kinship, and National Identity in Literature.* New York: Oxford University Press, 2011.

Smith, Anna Deveare. *Twilight: Los Angeles, 1992.* New York: Anchor, 1994.

Smith, Gary. "The Chosen One." In *Chasing Tiger: The Tigers Woods Reader,* ed. Glenn Stout, 51–81. Cambridge, MA: Da Capo, 2002.

Smith, Sidonie, and Julia Watson. *Reading Autobiography: a Guide for Interpreting Life Narratives.* Minneapolis: University of Minnesota Press, 2001.

Smith, Zadie. *The Autograph Man.* New York: Vintage, 2003.

——. *On Beauty.* New York: Penguin, 2006.

Sohn, Stephen. *Racial Asymmetries: Asian American Fictional Worlds.* New York: New York University Press, 2014.

Somewhere Between. DVD. Directed by Linda Goldstein Knowlton. New York: Ladylike Films, 2012.

Sone, Monica Itoi. *Nisei Daughter.* Seattle: University of Washington Press, 1979.

Song, Min. *The Children of 1965: On Writing and Not-Writing as an Asian American.* Durham, NC: Duke University Press, 2013.

So Proudly We Hail. VHS. Directed by Mark Sandrich. 1943. Los Angeles: Universal Studios, 2001.

Sounes, Howard. *The Wicked Game: Arnold Palmer, Jack Nicklaus, Tiger Woods, and the Business of Modern Golf.* New York: Perennial Currents, 2004.

Spickard, Paul. "Injustice Compounded: Amerasians and Non-Japanese Americans in World War II Concentration Camps." *Journal of American Ethnic History* 5:2 (1986): 5–22.

——. *Japanese Americans: The Formation and Transformations of an Ethnic Group.* New York: Twayne, 1996.

——. "What Must I Be? Asian Americans and the Question of Multiethnic Identity." *Amerasia Journal* 23:1 (1997): 43–60.

Spickard, Paul, and W. Jeffrey Burroughs. *We Are a People: Narrative and Multiplicity in Constructing Ethnic Identity.* Philadelphia: Temple University Press, 2000.

Srikanth, Rajini. *The World Next Door: South Asian American Literature and the Idea of America.* Philadelphia: Temple University Press, 2004.

Starn, Orin. "Caddying for the Dalai Lama: Golf, Heritage Tourism, and the Pinehurst Resort." *South Atlantic Quarterly* 105:2 (2006): 447–463.

——. *The Passion of Tiger Woods: An Anthropologist Reports on Golf, Race, and Celebrity Scandal.* Durham, NC: Duke University Press, 2011.

Stevick, Philip. *The Theory of the Novel.* New York: Free Press, 1967.

Stoler, Ann Laura. *Race and the Education of Desire: Foucault's History of Sexuality and the Colonial Order of Things.* Durham, NC: Duke University Press, 1995.

Stout, Glenn, ed. *Chasing Tiger: The Tiger Woods Reader.* Cambridge, MA: DaCapo, 2002.

Strege, John. *A Biography of Tiger Woods.* New York: Broadway Books, 1997.

Sze, Julie. "Boundaries and Border Wars: DES, Technology, and Environmental Justice." *American Quarterly* 58:3 (2006): 791–814.

Takaki, Ronald T. *Strangers from a Different Shore: A History of Asian Americans.* New York: Penguin, 1990.

Tan, Amy. *The Bonesetter's Daughter.* New York: Putnam, 2001.

———. *The Hundred Secret Senses.* New York: Putnam, 1995.

———. *The Joy Luck Club.* New York: Putnam, 1989.

———. *The Kitchen God's Wife.* New York: Putnam, 1991.

Tasady Tribe Hoax. BBC. www.bbc.co.uk/dna/ h2g2/A750944.

Tessler, Richard, Gail Gamache, and Liming Liu. *West Meets East: Americans Adopt Chinese Children.* Westport, CT: Bergin & Garvey, 1999.

Then She Found Me. Directed by Helen Hunt. Los Angeles: Think Films. 2007.

This American Life. "Three Kinds of Deception." Radio program. December 15, 2000.

Transracial Adoption. Cambridge, MA: South End Press, 2006.

Trenka, Jane Jeong. *Bitter Angry Ajumma.* Blog. http://jjtrenka.wordpress.com/.

———. *Fugitive Visions: An Adoptee's Return to Korea.* Saint Paul, MN: Graywolf, 2009.

———. *The Language of Blood: A Memoir.* Saint Paul, MN: Graywolf, 2003.

Trenka, Jane Jeong, Julia Cinyere Oparah, and Sun Yung Shin. *Outsiders Within: Writing on Transracial Adoption.* Cambridge, MA: South End Press, 2006.

Trophy Wife. Television Series. New York: American Broadcasting Company, 2013–2014.

Truong, Monique. *Bitter in the Mouth.* New York: Random House, 2010.

———. *The Book of Salt.* New York: Mariner Books, 2004.

Tuan, Mia. *Forever Foreigners or Honorary Whites?: The Asian Ethnic Experience Today.* New Brunswick, NJ: Rutgers University Press, 1998.

Valverde, Caroline Kieu Linh. "Doing the Mixed Race Dance: A Multiracial Vietnamese American Class Typology." In *The Sum of Our Parts: Mixed Heritage Asian Americans*, ed. Teresa Williams-Leon and Cynthia L. Nakashima, 131–143. Philadelphia: Temple University Press, 2001.

Veblen, Thorstein. *Theory of the Leisure Class.* New York: Viking, 1967.

Volkman, Toby Alice. "Embodying Chinese Culture: Transnational Adoption in North America." In *Cultures of Transnational Adoption*, ed. Toby Alice Volkman, Kay Johnson, and Barbara Yngvesson, 81–114. Durham, NC: Duke University Press, 2005.

Volkman, Toby Alice, Kay Johnson, and Barbara Yngvesson, eds. *Cultures of Transnational Adoption.* Durham, NC: Duke University Press, 2005.

Wald, Gayle. *Crossing the Line: Racial Passing in Twentieth-Century US Literature and Culture.* Durham, NC: Duke University Press, 2000.

Wang, Wendy. "The Rise of Intermarriage." Pew Research Social & Demographic Trends. Last Modified February 16, 2012. www.pewsocialtrends.org/2012/02/16/the-rise-of -intermarriage/.

Weglyn, Michi. *Years of Infamy: The Untold Story of America's Concentration Camps.* New York: Morrow, 1976.

Wei, William. *The Asian American Movement.* Philadelphia: Temple University Press, 1993.

Weisman, Jan. "The Tiger and His Stripes: Thai and American Reactions to Tiger Woods's (Multi) 'Racial Self.'" In *The Sum of Our Parts: Mixed Heritage Asian Americans*, ed. Teresa

Williams-Leon and Cynthia L. Nakashima, 231–243. Philadelphia: Temple University Press, 2001.

Williams, Sumeia. *Ethnically Incorrect Daughter.* Blog. http://ethnicallyincorrect.wordpress.com.

Williams, Teresa Kay. "Race-ing and Being Raced: The Critical Interrogation of 'Passing.'" *Amerasia* 23:1 (1997): 61–65.

Williams-Leon, Teresa, and Cynthia L. Nakashima. *The Sum of Our Parts: Mixed Heritage Asian Americans.* Philadelphia: Temple University Press, 2001.

Winfrey, Oprah. "Interview with Tiger Woods." *Oprah Winfrey Show,* April 24, 1997.

Wong, Sau-ling Cynthia. "Autobiography as Guided Chinatown Tour? Maxine Hong Kingston's *The Woman Warrior* and the Chinese American Autobiography Controversy." In *Maxine Hong Kingston's "The Woman Warrior": A Casebook,* ed. Sau-ling Cynthia Wong, 29–53. New York and Oxford: Oxford University Press. 1999.

——. "Denationalization Reconsidered: Asian American Cultural Criticism at Theoretical Crossroads." *Amerasia* 21:1–2 (1995): 1–27.

——. *Reading Asian American Literature: From Necessity to Extravagance.* Princeton, NJ: Princeton University Press, 1993.

——, ed. *Maxine Hong Kingston's "The Woman Warrior": A Casebook.* New York and Oxford: Oxford University Press, 1999.

Wong, William. *Yellow Journalist (Mapping Racisms).* Philadelphia: Temple University Press, 2001.

Woods, Earl, and Pete McDaniel. *Training a Tiger: A Father's Guide to Raising a Winner in Both Golf and Life.* New York: HarperCollins, 1997.

Woods, Earl, and Fred Mitchell. *Playing Through: Straight Talk on Hard Work, Big Dreams, and Adventures with Tiger.* New York: HarperCollins, 1998.

Woods, Tiger. "Tiger Woods's Apology: Full Transcript." CNN. Last modified February 19, 2010. www.cnn.com/2010/US/02/19/tiger.woods.transcript/.

Wu, Cynthia. *Chang and Eng Reconnected: The Original Siamese Twins in American Culture.* Philadelphia: Temple University Press, 2012.

Wu, Frank. *Yellow: Race in America beyond Black and White.* New York: Basic Books, 2002.

Wu, Jean Yu-wen Shen, and Thomas Chen, eds. *Asian American Studies Now.* New Brunswick, NJ: Rutgers University Press, 2010.

Wu, Jean Yu-wen Shen, and Min Song, eds. *Asian American Studies: A Reader.* New Brunswick, NJ: Rutgers University Press, 2000.

Yamada, Mitsuye. *Camp Notes and Other Writings.* New Brunswick, NJ: Rutgers University Press, 1992.

Yamamoto, Hisaye. "Wilshire Bus." In *Seventeen Syllables and Other Stories,* 34–38. Latham, NY: Kitchen Table: Women of Color Press, 1988.

Yamamoto, Traise. *Masking Selves, Making Subjects: Japanese American Women, Identity, and the Body.* Berkeley: University of California Press, 1999.

Yamanaka, Lois-Ann. *Blu's Hanging.* New York: Farrar Straus & Giroux, 1997.

——. *Wild Meat and the Bully Burgers.* San Diego: Harcourt Brace, 1997.

Yamashita, Karen Tei. *Through the Arc of the Rainforest.* Minneapolis: Coffee House Press, 1990.

Yarborough, Trin. *Surviving Twice: Amerasian Children of the Vietnam War.* Washington, DC: Potomac Books, 2005.

Yu, Henry. "How Tiger Lost His Stripes: Post-Nationalist American Studies as a History of Race, Migration, and the Commodification of Culture." In *Post-Nationalist American Studies*, ed. John Carlos Rowe, 223–245. Berkeley: University of California Press, 2000.

——. *Thinking Orientals: Migration, Contact, and Exoticism in Modern America*. Oxford: Oxford University Press, 2001.

——. "Tiger Woods at the Center of History: Looking Back at the Twentieth Century through the Lenses of Race, Sports, and Mass Consumption." In *Sports Matters: Race, Recreation, and Culture*, ed. John Bloom and Michael Williard, 320–353. New York: New York University Press, 2002.

——. "Tiger Woods Is Not the End of History; or, Why Sex across the Color Line Won't Save Us All." *American Historical Review* 108:5 (2003): 1406–1414.

Yu, Timothy. "Has Asian American Studies Failed?" *tympan*. Last modified December 20, 2011. http://tympan.blogspot.com/2011/12/has-asian-american-studies-failed.html.

Yun, Lisa. *The Coolie Speaks: Chinese Indentured Laborers and African Slaves in Cuba*. Philadelphia: Temple University Press, 2008.

Yung, Judy. *Unbound Voices: A Documentary History of Chinese Women in San Francisco*. Berkeley: University of California Press, 1999.

Zack, Naomi. "Preface." In *Mixing It Up: Multiracial Subject*, ed. SanSan Kwan and Kenneth Speirs, ix–xii. Austin: University of Texas Press, 2004.

Zeiger, Susan. *Entangling Alliances: Foreign War Brides and American Soldiers in the Twentieth Century*. New York: New York University Press, 2010.

Zia, Helen. *Asian American Dreams: The Emergence of an American People*. New York: Farrar Strauss & Giroux, 2000.

INDEX

Adams, Ansel, 161n31

adoptees, Asian American, 6, 44–45, 47–70; adoption narratives of, 55–57; and anti-sentimentalism, 62; blogs of, 19, 57–68; and Christianity, 48; first parents of, 46, 62, 63, 169n86; honorary white status of, 50, 52–53, 54, 60, 67; identity formation of, 60, 69–70; as "the only one," 59; and race, 67; racial ambiguity of, 19, 45, 47, 51, 54, 66; and red thread trope, 55–56; and sentimentalism, 56; silencing of, 64; visibility of, 64–65; and war, 47–48, 65. *See also* adoption; adoption, transnational/transracial; adoption narratives

adoption: of African American children, 50, 51, 165n2, 167n38; and Christianity, 45–46, 48; institutionalization of, 46; and kinship, 45; of Korean children, 47–48, 58–59, 65; of Latino children, 50; matching paradigm of, 46–47, 48, 52–53, 166n7; and sentimentalism, 6, 19, 45, 54, 55–56, 62–63; terminology of, 166n6. *See also* adoptees, Asian American; adoption, transnational/transracial; adoption narratives

adoption, transnational/transracial, 166n13; advertising for, 48; of Chinese children, 49, 50–51, 57, 62, 168n56; and colorblindness, 52–53, 54, 66; gender imbalance of, 50–51; of Koreans, 47–50; and one-drop rule, 48; and passing, 53; and race matching, 49; and racial ambiguity, 50; rescue narratives of, 45–46, 48–49, 57, 63; and white supremacy, 166n8; and whiteness, 52–53, 166n8. *See also* adoptees, Asian American; adoption; adoption narratives; Amerasians

adoption narratives: and colorblindness, 57; and sentimentalism, 57, 62. *See also* adoption; orphan narratives

African Americans, 11; adoption of, 50, 51, 165n2, and Asian Americans, 3, 167n38; in golf, 76, 77–78, 172n28; and model minority myth, 13; stereotypes of, 84. *See also* blackness; Woods, Tiger

Ahn Dung (Clarence Taylor III), 91, 177n90

Aiiieeee! An Anthology of Asian-American Writers, 126, 157n46. See also *Big Aiiieeee!, The*

Alfonso-Forero, Ann Marie, 137

Aloft (Chang-rae Lee), 130

Amerasia (journal), 9

Amerasians, 87–93, 175n66; and American war in Viet Nam, 73, 87–89; black, 90–91, 175n71, 177n86; children, 87–93, 175n67, 177n97; and citizenship, 88, 91, 92; defined, 176n78; prejudice against, 88, 175n70, 176n79, 177n92; racial ambiguity of, 88. *See also* adoption, transnational/transracial; Asian Americans

American studies, 16; non-white authors, marginalization of, 128. *See also* Asian American studies

antiracism: and Asian American literature, 128; and canonization, 20–21; and colorblindness, 83; and racial ambiguity, 7

Anzaldúa, Gloria, 64, 65

Asian Americans: activism of, 155n34; African Americans, relations with, 3; alienation of, 1; and assimilation, 43; and authenticity, 6; and black-white axis, 148; as category, 12, 13–14; census categories of, 12; and citizenship, 1, 14; and epistemology, 5, 6; and gender, 51; interracial marriage among, 51, 167n37; and knowledge production, 8, 15; as mixed race, 72, 86–87; as model minorities, 19, 72; and multiracialism, 2, 9; and narrative, 6–7; as national in-between, 1–2; and passing, 99, 119; as perpetual foreigners, 125; as privileged group, 13; racial ambiguity of, 1–10, 12–14, 19, 45, 51, 54, 66, 72, 116, 140, 150, 152, 153n1, 153n3, 181n73; racialization of, 12–14; as racially anonymous, 8–9; silencing of, 123; stereotypes of, 3, 84; subjectivity of, 148, 155n34; as term, 125, 140, 154n10, 155n34, 182n8; and whiteness, 13, 18. *See also* adoptees, Asian American; Asian American studies; Asianness; Asians; literature, Asian American

Asian American studies, 9–10, 14–16, 125, 156n43, 157n48; as ambiguous field, 15; as anti-essentialist, 127, 142–43, 144;

Asian American studies (*continued*)
  and Asian studies, 16, 157n49; and authenticity, 141–142; diversity of, 15, 156nn44–45;
  and epistemology, 147; history of, 125–126;
  and identity politics, 141; and mixed race
  people, 141; and racial ambiguity, 10, 14,
  141; and social justice, 142, 143–144. *See
  also* Asian American literature; Asian
  Americans
Asianness: erasure of, 95; and phenotype,
  86–87, 98–99, 177n87; in Rekdal, 105–106;
  of Tida Woods, 77; of Tiger Woods, 74, 77,
  83, 173n36; and whiteness, 19
Asians: categorization of, 161n38; citizenship of, 162n46; and interracial marriage,
  163n62; as racially ambiguous, 72, 79,
  86; and whiteness, 86. *See also* Asian
  Americans
Asian studies, 16, 157n49. *See also* Asian
  American studies
assimilation, 18; and Asian Americans, 43; of
  Japanese Americans, 24, 29, 30, 32, 34, 39;
  and Mixed-Marriage Policy, 18, 22,
  23–24, 30, 33, 37–38, 43, 162n51; and racial
  ambiguity, 23; and whiteness, 30–31, 39;
  and Yoshiko Nakamura deLeon, 41–42
assimilation theory, Chicago school, 30–31,
  162n51
Association of Asian American studies
  (AAAS), 123–124, 128, 129–130, 146, 157n47,
  182n1; annual conference, 123, 129, 145,
  183n16. *See also* Asian American studies;
  literature, Asian American
Augusta National Golf Club, 71, 81, 170n2;
  racial exclusion at, 76, 77, 173n49; women,
  exclusion of, 173n49
authenticity, 181n69; in Asian American
  literature, 96, 99, 107, 115, 117–118, 126, 128,
  130, 136, 144, 147, 178n5, 187n70; and Asian
  Americans, 6; and Asian American studies, 141–142; and ethnic literature, 20; and
  Monkey Hunting, 136; and passing, 117, 119
autobiography: and fiction, 99–100, 103; and
  passing, 96; and truth, 100
Ayeesha, 3

Baby, We Were Meant for Each Other (Simon), 63
Balibar, Etienne, 10
Barbie, Donna, 172n28
Barlow, Aaron, 58, 59; on blogging, 61–62
Bascara, Victor, 183n17
Bass, Thomas, 87, 90, 175n67
Beidler, Philip D., 184n30
Bell, Michael, 56
Bendetsen, Karl, 25, 32–34
Berebitsky, Julie, 46
Biddle, Francis, 25–26
Big Aiiieeee!, The, 126, 183n8. See also *Aiiieeee!
  An Anthology of Asian-American Writers*;
  Chin, Frank
Bitter in the Mouth (Truong), 148
blackness: and one-drop rule, 95; in *My Year
  of Meats*, 115–116; and professional sports,

79; and Tiger Woods, 78, 81–83, 94, 173n36.
  See also African Americans
Black Power movement, 14
Blind Side, The (film), 44, 165n2
blogs, 6, 168n66; and ambiguity, 70; of Asian
  American adoptees, 19, 57–68; as communal space, 58, 67; and community building, 59–60, 61–62; as counter-narrative,
  58, 65
Boas, Franz, 162n51
Boat, The (Le), 125; as transgressive text,
  182n5
bodies: of Asian Americans, 98; and black-
  ness, 74; hybrid, 113–114; of mixed race
  people, 104, 110–111; and place, 4; and race,
  72; and racial ambiguity, 2; of writers,
  127–128, 130
Boekel, William A., 26
Borshay Liem, Deann, 68–70, 170n114; *First
  Person Plural*, 52, 68–69; *In the Matter of
  Cha Jung Hee*, 69; and racial ambiguity,
  69–70
Bourdieu, Pierre, 50
Bow, Leslie, 1–2, 8, 116
Brian, Kristi, 50
Briggs, Laura, 48
Brown, James, 3
Buck, Pearl, 130, 140, 183nn21–22
Buffalo Boy and Geronimo (Janko), 123, 145–
  146; American war in Vietnam in, 145–146;
  as Asian American literature, 146. *See also*
  Janko, James
Bullock, Sandra, 62
Bulosan, Carlos, 178n1
Burk, Martha, 173n49
Butler, Judith, 106, 110
Butler, Robert Olen, 129, 187n70

Callahan, Tom, 76, 173n42
Caminero-Santangelo, Marta, 138
Campbell, Michael, 79
Carp, E. Wayne, 47
Caughie, Pamela, 97
Cezair-Thompson, Margaret, 186n54
Chambers, Marcia, 75
Chan, Jeffrey Paul, 126
Chang, Yoonmee, 184n23
Chang, Juliana, 183n17
Chang, Robert, 80
Chen, Tina, 97, 98
Cheng, Bill, 182n2
Cheng, Emily, 181n61
Cheng, Vincent, 184n24
Chin, Frank, 126, 178nn4–5; introduction to
  The Big Aiiieeee!, 126, 183n8
China's Lost Girls (documentary), 63, 169n84
Chinese Americans, 11
Chinese diaspora, 21, 149, 151–152, 188n8
Chinese Jamaicans, 149–152
Chiu, Monica, 114, 181n61
Cho, Sumi, 108
Chou, Rosalind, 51
Christian, Barbara, 6

Christopher, Renny, 176n83

Chua, Amy, 186n64; *Battle Hymn of the Tiger Mother*, 143; model minority myth and, 143

Chuh, Kandice, 8, 122, 142–143

citizenship: and Amerasians, 88, 91, 92; and Asian Americans, 1, 14, 29, 40, 160n14; of Asians, 162n46; and incarceration, 40; and interracial marriage, 163n63; of Japanese Americans, 29, 40, 160n14; and whiteness, 29–30, 106

Clark, Thomas A., 26

Clement, Thomas, 168n65

Coleman, Gary, 165n2

Collier, Rachel Quy, 51–52

colorblindness: and adoption narratives, 57; as antiracist, 83; and meritocracy, 78; and multiculturalism, 78, 80–81; and racial ambiguity, 18; rhetoric of, 5; and Tiger Woods, 19, 81

Consumption and Identity in Asian American Coming-of-Age Novels (Ho), 176n83, 188n10

Cornyetz, Nina, 117–118, 181n61

Creef, Elena Tajima, 2, 114

Critical Mixed Race Studies, 9, 10, 155n25. *See also* mixed race people

critical race theory, 65, 94, 151, 169n97

Crosby, Peter, 158nn1–2

cultural studies, 15, 16–17

Daniels, Roger, 25, 160n19

Das EFX, 3

Davis, Mike, 154n7

Day, Jason, 79

de Beauvoir, Simone, 106

DeBonis, Steven, 90

Defoe, Daniel, 99–100

deLeon, Gabriel, 22, 36, 37, 164n75, 165n83

deLeon, Martin, 36, 42

deLeon, Yoshiko Nakamura, 18, 22, 35–38, 95, 163n69; and assimilation, 41–42; incarceration, exemption from, 23–24, 36–37, 40–43, 159n12, 165n83; interracial marriage of, 148; and racial ambiguity, 24, 37, 95

deNevers, Klancy Clark, 23, 159n4

Deutsch, Monroe, 161n31

deWitt, John, 22–23, 25, 31–32, 158n4, 160n20

Diaz, Jaime, 173n42, 174n64

Did You Hear about the Morgans? (film), 44, 165n1, 168n54

Different Strokes (television series), 165n2

Dogeaters (Hagedorn), 129

Dorow, Sara, 51, 167n38

Dorr, Patricia, 36, 37, 42, 164n78

Dorr, Trish, 42, 159n12

Du, Soon Ja, 154n7

East Asian Americans, 15

Easy A (film), 44

Ebony magazine, 48

Edwards, Brent Hayes, 16

Elder, Lee, 77, 79

Ellis, Markman, 56

Eng, David, 52, 83

English Patient, The (film), 129

Ennis, Edward, 160n15

epistemology, 8; Asian American, 7, 10, 123, 127, 135, 140–141, 143, 147; and Asian American literature, 124–125, 130, 140, 143, 147; and Asian Americans, 5, 6; and Asian American studies, 147; and fiction, 100–101; and transgressive texts, 146

Espiritu, Yen Le, 51, 108–110, 180n44

Ethnically Incorrect Daughter (blog), 60, 65; as counter-narrative, 65–66

ethnic studies, 8, 14–15, 151, 186n63. *See also* Asian American studies

eugenics, 13, 28; and Amy Chua, 143; and white supremacy, 30, 141

Evans, Karin, 63

Feather on the Breath of God (Nunez), 131–133, 134–135. *See also* Nunez, Sigrid

Feinstein, John, 77

fiction: and epistemology, 100–101; and facticity, 100–101

Filipino Americans, 37–38, 165n81; and interracial marriage, 164n76; and Japanese incarceration, 27–28. *See also* deLeon, Gabriel; deLeon, Yoshiko Nakamura

First Person Plural (Borshay Liem), 52, 68–69

Fish, Cheryl, 113, 181n61

Fishkin, Shelley Fisher, 124

For Rouenna (Nunez), 132–135, 146, 184n30, 185n39; and Asian American epistemology, 135; as Asian American literature, 133, 135; American war in Viet Nam in, 133–134, 135; reviews of, 185n40; Vietnamese, representations of, 133–134. *See also* Nunez, Sigrid

Foucault, Michel, on subjugated knowledges, 7

Found in China (documentary), 169n84

Fowler, Rickie, 79

Free Life, A (Ha Jin), 129

Frost, Masako Nakamura, 36–37, 38, 164n74

Fujikawa, Jerry, 163n67

Fulbeck, Kip, 2, 155n24; *Part Asian*100% Hapa*, 2–3

Garcia, Cristina, 20, 135–136; as Cuban American writer, 136–137. See also *Monkey Hunting*

Gee, Emma, 182n8

Gibbs, Althea, 79

Gilroy, Paul, 7–8

Glenn, Evelyn Nakano, 35

Goebel, Herman P., 27

Goellnicht, Donald, 144

Golden Gate, The (Seth), 131, 184n26

golf: and African Americans, 172n28; Asians in, 172n33; caddies, African American, 76, 77–78; desegregation of, 76, 172n13; golfers of color, 79; growth of, 171n12, 184n23;

golf (*continued*)
and power, 74–75; public courses, 75, 76, 171n13; and racial exclusion, 75; and racism, 74, 75, 77–78; spectatorship of, 172n28; and white male privilege, 74–75, 171n10; and whiteness, 74. *See also* PGA (Professional Golfers' Association) of America; Woods, Tiger
Good Earth, The (Buck), 130
Good Scent from a Strange Mountain, A (R. O. Butler), 129, 142, 187n70; exoticization in, 142
Graham, Lawrence Otis, 172n14
Greene, Graham, 134, 185n39
Griffiths, Austin, 26
Guterson, David, 131, 183n16

Hagedorn, Jessica, 129, 130, 145
Hall, Denise, 57
Hall, John, 32–33
Hall, Marissa, 56–57
Haney, Hank, 81, 171n5, 173n42
hapas, 2; as term, 153n5
Harlins, Latasha, 154n7
Harlow's Monkey (blog), 45, 58, 61–62, 67; antisentimentalism of, 63–64; as counternarrative, 60. *See also* Kim, Jae Ran
Harrison, Ralph, 26
Harry Potter series (Rowling), 44, 54, 62
Heart, Mind and Seoul (blog), 60, 61
Herman, Ellen, 46
Hoa, Alan "Tiger," 91
Hogan, Ron, 102–103
Holt, Bertha, 47–48, 166n17
Holt, Harry, 47–48, 166n17
Holt Adoption Agency, 48–49
Holt International Children's Services, 49
Hood, Ann, 55, 63
Hopgood, Mei-Ling, 60, 169n75
Hosseini, Khaled, 130
Houston, Velina Hasu, 9
Huang, Betsy, 183n14
Hume, Brit, 86
hybridity: in Asian American literature, 20, 111, 112–114, 138, 186n54; and bodies, 113–114; in *Monkey Hunting*, 138
hypodescent. *See* one-drop rule

Ichioka, Yuji, 182n8
Iida, Deborah, 142
immigration policies, US: Amerasian Homecoming Act, 88, 92, 175n73; Chinese Exclusion Act (1882), 162n46; Gentlemen's Agreement (1908), 164n71; Immigration Act of 1917, 161n38; Immigration Act of 1924, 35, 162n46, 164n71; McCarran-Walter Immigration and Naturalization Act (1952), 162n46; and whiteness, 162n47
imperialism, US, 88, 89, 156n39
Inada, Lawson, 126
incarceration, Japanese American, 17, 18, 22; and citizenship, 40; Executive Order 9066, 25–26, 39, 159n9, 160n14; exemptions from, 23–24, 26–27, 33, 35–38, 95,

159n5, 161n37, 163n69; and Filipino Americans, 27–28; *The Final Report: Japanese Evacuation from the West Coast 1942*, 26, 31, 39; issei, 29, 35, 159n8; *Korematsu v. United States*, 165n86; military necessity, myth of, 39, 43, 159n6, 160n20; and mixed race people, 27–28, 160n21, 163n67; and race, 17, 39; and racial ambiguity, 43; in Rekdal, 103; and silence, 41, 164n79; and split families, 27, 161nn29–30; terminology of, 158n1; War Relocation Authority, 158n1. *See also* Japanese Americans
integration, and capitalism, 76
internment, Japanese American. *See* incarceration, Japanese American
interracial marriage, 33, 51; antimiscegenation laws, 13; among Asian Americans, 51, 167n37; and Asians, 163n62; and citizenship, 163n63; and Filipino Americans, 164n76; Mixed-Marriage Policy, 16, 148; pre-WWII, 164n76; and racial ambiguity, 24, 37, 95
In the Matter of Cha Jung Hee (Borshay Liem), 69
Isaac, Allan, 183n14
Ishiguro, Kazuo, 101, 179n20
Izrael, Jimi, 83–84

Jacobson, Heather, 50, 51
Jamaica, 149–150
Jane's Blog: Bitter Angry Ajumma (blog), 60, 67
Jang, Bong Ok, 154n7
Janko, James, 123, 132, 145, 187n69. See also *Buffalo Boy and Geronimo*
Japanese Americans: and anti-Japanese sentiment, 37; assimilability of, 24, 29, 32, 34, 39; and assimilation, 30, 32, 39; and citizenship, 29, 160n14; racial ambiguity of, 24–25, 43; US military service of, 33. *See also* incarceration, Japanese American
Jasper, Rita, 167n48
Jean, Wyclef, 3
Jen, Gish, 142
Jin (rapper): *The Rest Is History*, 3–4
Jin, Ha, 129, 130, 145, 183n18
Jo, Sunny, 60, 68
Johnson, Hootie, 173n49
Jolie, Angelina, 62
Joo, Rachel, 76, 79, 81–82
Jordan, Michael, 79
Journal of Asian American Studies, 157n47
Joy Luck Club, The (Tan), 178n1
Jung, Moon-Ho, 140

Kashima, Tetsuden, 23, 158n4, 160n15
Kennedy, John H., 75
Kim, Anthony, 79
Kim, Cristina, 172n33
Kim, Daniel, 17–18
Kim, Eleana, 68, 168n65; on adoptee identity, 59
Kim, Heidi, 186n57
Kim, Jae Ran, 45, 47, 58, 60, 61, 67–68, 169n80; on adoption and Christianity,

49; on whiteness, 66. *See also Harlow's Monkey* (blog)
Kindred, Dave, 77
Kingston, Maxine Hong, 96, 127, 128, 145, 178n1, 179n17, 183nn9–10. *See also Woman Warrior, The*
Klein, Christina, 88
Knox, Frank, 159n6
Korean Americans: adoptees, 60; as war babies, 47–48
Koreans, transnational adoption of, 47–50
Korean War, and adoption, 47–48, 65
Koshy, Susan, 125
Ku, Robert, 176n77, 181n69, 184n24
Kwan, SanSan, 11

Lacan, Jacques, 179n12
Lahiri, Jhumpa, 147
Land of the Not-So-Calm (blog), 58
Lanser, Susan, 99, 102; on narrative voice, 112
Latinos: adoption of, 50; and model minority myth, 13; and race, 153n3
Laughing Sutra, The (Salzman), 143, 186n61
Lauter, Paul, 128
Le, Nam, 125, 182n5
Lee, Bruce, 102
Lee, Chang-rae, 130, 183n19
Lee, Christopher, 125
Lee, Don, 186n54
Lee-Loy, Anne-Marie, 157n45
Lewis, Emmanuel, 165n2
Life magazine, 28–29
Lim, Thea, 84
Ling, Lisa, 56–57
literary theory: and Asian American literature, 127, 144, 146–147; and race, 6
literature, American: Asian American characters in, 140, 186n57; presumed whiteness in, 184n30. *See also* literature, Asian American
literature, Asian American, 96, 123–131, 157n46; activist origins of, 126; and aesthetics, 126, 127; as anti-essentialist, 141; and antiracism, 128; and authenticity, 96, 99, 126, 128, 130, 144, 147, 187n70; canon formation of, 17, 20–21, 96, 124, 127–28, 130–131, 140–146, 147, 187n67; and epistemology, 124–125, 130, 143, 147; as foreign, 128; and genre, 96; growth of, 126–127, 130; history of, 126; hybridity in, 20, 111, 112–114, 138, 186n54; and identity politics, 144; and ideology, 143–144, 186n63; and literary theory, 127, 144, 146–147; and multiculturalism, 122; ontology of, 125, 129; and pedagogy, 146–147; and power, 143; race of authors, 123; as race writing, 124; and racial ambiguity, 124; and social justice, 126, 128, 144, 145, 146; transgressive texts in, 123–125, 130–131, 138–142, 143, 144, 146, 186n54. *See also* Asian Americans; Asian American studies; literature, American
Little Orphan Annie (comic strip character), 62, 168n51

London, Jack, 130, 140
Lopez, Ian Haney, 155n30, 156n37, 162n47
Los Angeles uprising, 3, 154n7
Lost Daughters of China, The (Evans), 63, 168n56
Louie, Andrea, 50, 52
Lovink, Geert, 17
Lowe, Lisa, 8, 109; on interpellation, 115
Lowe, Pardee, 179n17
LPGA (Ladies Professional Golf Association), 171n10; Asian golfers in, 79
Lye, Colleen, 140
lynching, of Chinese, 13

Madame Butterfly (opera), 92, 93
Madonna, 62
Malkin, Michelle, 143
Mannur, Anita, 183n17
Marre, Diana, 48
Mather, Cotton, 45–46, 48
McCarroll, Meredith, 83, 85
McClatchy, V. S., 29
McCloy, John, 31–32
McKelvey, Robert, 88, 90, 175n71, 177n87
Mei-Ling (blogger), 60, 61, 66, 67–68, 169nn75–76, 169nn79–80, 170n109
memoir, meaning in, 100
miscegenation. *See* interracial marriage
Miss Saigon (musical), 92, 93
Mixed-Marriage Policy of 1942, 18, 22–23, 150, 158n2; as assimilation policy, 18, 22, 23–24, 30, 33, 37–38, 43, 162n51; exemptions from, 27–28, 159n10; and gender, 34, 40–41, 161n34, 163n65; and interracial marriage, 16, 148; and racial ambiguity, 34, 40; and whiteness, 177n86. *See also* mixed race people
Mixed-Marriage Program. *See* Mixed-Marriage Policy of 1942
Mixed Race America (blog), 58
mixed race people, 178n9; in Asian American literature, 97, 101, 102, 181n75; bodies of, 104; as census category, 178n9; concept of, 11; and Japanese American incarceration, 27–28, 160n21, 163n67; and passing, 82–83, 97, 99, 105, 119; scholarship on, 155n22, 155n24; self-identification of, 84–85; subjectivity of, 97; and Tiger Woods, 74, 79–80, 84, 89, 94, 148, 174n61, 178n99. *See also* Mixed Marriage Policy of 1942
model minority myth, 13, 16, 19, 50, 72, 156n40; and African Americans, 13; in Chua, 143; and Latinos, 13
Modern Family (television series), 44
Modern Language Association (MLA), 157n47
Moiles, Sean, 139
Moll Flanders (Defoe), 99–100
Monkey Hunting (Garcia), 135–139; and Asian American epistemology, 140; as Asian American literature, 138–139, 141, 142, 146, 186n54; and authenticity, 136; as Cuban American literature, 141; exile in, 138;

Monkey Hunting (Garcia) (*continued*)
gender passing in, 185n47; globalization
in, 136, 139; hybridity in, 138; racial ambiguity of, 136, 137–138, 139; rescue, trope of,
185n51. *See also* Garcia, Cristina
Morrison, Toni, 42
Mosk, Stanley, 76
Moyers, Bill, 183n10
multiculturalism: and Asian American
literature, 114–115, 122; and colorblindness, 78, 80–81; and race, 52; and Tiger
Woods, 78
Murakami, Haruki, 129
Murdock, Maureen, 100, 104
Muse, Eben, 176n83
My Year of Meats (Ozeki), 1, 4, 20, 96, 111–
118, 153n1; authenticity in, 115, 117–118;
biraciality in, 114–115; blackness in,
115–116; DES in, 112, 122, 180n54, 181n55;
as didactic, 111–112, 181n55; first person
narrative of, 112; and genre, 111–112; globalization in, 111, 113; mixed race identity
in, 181n75; mobile subjectivity in, 98;
movement in, 122; and multiculturalism,
114–115; narrative conventions in, 111,
112; passing in, 113, 115–116, 117, 118, 119,
122; racial ambiguity in, 113, 117; racial
hybridity in, 111, 112–114; travel in, 122;
white privilege in, 116. *See also* Ozeki,
Ruth

Na, Soon, 66
Nakamura, Heigo, 35–36
Nakamura, Lisa, 17
narrative: and Asian Americans, 6–7; and
subjugated knowledges, 7. *See also* litera-
ture, Asian American
National Association of Black Social Workers
(NABSW), 47, 166n12
Neher, Clark, 89
Ng, Wendy, 29
Nguyen, Mimi Thi, 157n45
Nguyen, Viet Thanh, 10
Night My Mother Met Bruce Lee, The (Rekdal),
96, 101–111; "American" identity in, 105–
107, 109; "Americans Abroad," 105–110,
119, 180n42; authenticity in, 107; "Bad
Vacation with Tasaday Tribe," 103–104;
biraciality in, 121; and genre, 98; mixed
race subjectivity in, 101, 102; movement in,
98, 122; and myth, 102; narrative conventions in, 103; passing in, 101, 108, 109–110,
121–122; performance in, 106–107; racial
ambiguity in, 105, 108–109, 120–121; as
racial bildungsroman, 102; travel in,
122; "Traveling to Opal," 102, 119–122,
182nn93–94; truth in, 103–104, 121–122;
whiteness in, 109–110. *See also* Rekdal,
Paisley
Nike, 78, 171n8
Ninh, erin Khue, 183n14, 186n64
Nordegren, Erin, 83
Norris, Frank, 130

Nunez, Sigrid, 20, 131–32, 136, 184n29; as
Asian American writer, 132, 134–135;
novels of, 132; racial ambiguity of, 135.
See also *Feather on the Breath of God; For
Rouenna*

Obata, Chiura, 161n31
Okada, John, 126, 178n1
Okihiro, Gary, 12
Omi, Michael, 10; on census categories,
178n10; on ethnicity and race, 28; on
racial identity, 110
one-drop rule, 19, 39, 157n55; and Asians, 86,
95; and passing, 119; and Tiger Woods, 72;
and transracial adoption, 48; and whiteness, 95
Onsham, Sukree, 173n38
ontology, 8; Asian American, 127; of Asian
American literature, 125, 129
Operation Babylift, 49, 176n79
Original Heping, The (blog), 60, 61
orphan narratives, 54–55; and emotional
healing, 168n54; rescue, trope of, 54, 55;
and sentimentalism, 44–45. See also adoption narratives
Owens, David, 75
Ozawa, Takao, 29, 162n47
Ozeki, Ruth, 96–98, 122; biraciality of, 112;
as documentarian, 111; ethics of, 181n57;
hybridity in, 20; as mixed race writer, 97;
passing in, 97, 112–113; racial ambiguity of,
20. See also *My Year of Meats*

Pacific Islanders, and terminology, 154n10
Pak, Se Ri, 81–82
Park, Ed, 131, 145
Park, Robert E., 31, 162n51
passing: and adoption, 53; as analytic, 101;
and Asian American identity, 99, 119; and
authenticity, 117, 119; in autobiography,
96; and honorary whiteness, 83; and identity, 113, 118; and mixed race identity, 82–
83, 97, 99, 105, 119; as mobile subjectivity,
105, 113, 120; as movement, 98, 118–119, 121;
and multiraciality, 85; in *My Year of Meats*,
97, 112–113, 115–116, 117, 118, 119, 122; narratives of, 97, 182n83; "new passing," 174n52;
in *The Night My Mother Met Bruce Lee*, 97,
101, 104, 106, 108, 109–110, 121–122; and
one-drop rule, 119; and performance, 110;
in post–civil rights era, 110, 118; and racial
ambiguity, 97, 117, 119, 167n41; and racial
categories, 118; as resistance, 119, 122; and
subjectivity, 97–98, 110–111; and tragedy,
182n83; and transnational adoptees, 53;
travel, as trope for, 104–105; trope of,
20, 97
Paula O., 60–61, 64–65, 67–68, 169n76,
169n80, 170n109; on racism, 66
Pearl Buck Foundation, 88
Perez, Hiram, 78
performance: and identity, and passing, 110,
106, 110; and subjectivity, 97–98

Personal Days (E. Park), 131
PGA (Professional Golfers' Association) of America, 75–76, 172n16; Caucasian clause of, 75–76, 172n19. *See also* golf; Woods, Tiger
Phelan, James, 29
Phong, Vuong Dang, 93
Pierce, Charles, 174n64
Pillow Book (Shonagon), 111
Ponce, Martin Joseph, 184n23
poststructuralism, 8
Powell, Patricia, 186n54

Quiet American, The (Greene), 134, 185n39

race: and adoption, 49, 167; and Asian American adoptees, 67; in Asian American literature, 97, 123–124; and compulsory identity, 180n32; as essentialist myth, 19, 21; and Latinos, 153n3; and literary theory, 6; and multiculturalism, 52; Omi and Winant on, 10, 28, 110; racial pentagram, 2, 153n3; and sexism, 108; as social construction, 10–11, 19, 21, 28, 30–31, 94–95, 110, 118, 144, 155n27; taxonomy of, 2, 153n3; during WWII. *See also* Asian Americans; literature, Asian American; mixed race people; racial ambiguity; racial formation; whiteness
racial ambiguity, 3–5, 11–12, 21–23, 148–149, 151; and adoption, 50; of Amerasians, 88; as analytic, 5, 21, 148; of Asian American adoptees, 19, 45, 47, 51, 54, 66; in Asian American literature, 124; of Asian Americans, 1–10, 12–14, 72, 116, 140, 150, 152, 153n1, 153n3, 181n73; in Asian American studies, 10, 14, 141; of Asians, 72, 79, 86; and assimilation, 23; and colorblindness, 18; as disruptive, 114; and excess, 4; and interracial marriage, 24, 37, 95; and Japanese American incarceration, 43; of Japanese Americans, 24–25, 43; and Mixed-Marriage Policy, 34, 40; of *Monkey Hunting*, 136, 137–138, 139; in *My Year of Meats*, 113, 117; in *The Night My Mother Met Bruce Lee*, 97, 117, 119, 167n41; of Paisley Rekdal, 20, 104; and passing, 97, 117, 119, 167n41; and racial formation, 3, 10; of Sigrid Nunez, 135; and subjectivity, 6; of Tida Woods, 93–94; of Tiger Woods, 19–20, 78–80, 84, 89, 91–92, 94–95; of transgressive texts, 141, 146; and transnational adoption, 50, 69–70. *See also* Amerasians; Asian Americans; mixed race people; race; racial formation
racial formation: and ambiguity, 10; and Asian American ambiguity, 3; and institutional racism, 7–8
racism: and golf, 74, 75, 77–78; and sexism, 108; against Tiger Woods, 73, 171n7. *See also* Yellow Peril stereotype
Raphael-Hernandez, Heike, 156n45
Red Apple boycott, 154n7

Red Thread, The (Hood), 55–56, 57, 62, 63, 169n84
Regasa, Hugo, 28, 161n37
Regasa, Matsuyo, 28, 161n37
Regasa, Miyoko, 28, 161n37
Reilly, Rick, 77
Rekdal, Paisley, 20, 96–98; Asianness in, 105–106; biraciality of, 101, 102, 121; genre, use of, 179n22; hybridity in, 20; as mixed race writer, 97; as movement, 104; passing in, 97, 104, 106; poetry, use of, 102–103; racial ambiguity of, 20, 104; truth in, 103–104; whiteness in, 106. See also *Night My Mother Met Bruce Lee, The*
Remains of the Day, The (Ishiguro), 101
Rhodes, Teddy, 79
Roberts, Clifford, 71, 170n1
Robinson, Greg, 160n19
Rockquemore, Kerry Ann, 82
Rodriguez, Chi Chi, 79, 172n32
Roosevelt, Franklin: anti-Japanese prejudice of, 160n19; and Japanese incarceration, 25, 158n1
Root, Maria, 9, 85

Salgado, Raquel Scherr, 98
Salzman, Mark, 143, 186n61
Sayonara (film), 93, 177n96
Schlund-Vials, Cathy, 157n45, 184n23
See, Lisa, 186n66
sentimentalism, 56; in adoption narratives, 57, 62; antisentimentalism, 62
Seth, Vikram, 131, 184n26
Sex in the City (television series), 44, 62, 169n84
Shade, John, 88
Shipnuck, Alan, 170n1
Shonagon, Sei, 111
Sifford, Charlie, 76, 77, 79, 170n1
Simon, Scott, 63
Singh, Vijay, 79
Singley, Carol J., 45, 54–55
Smith, Sidonie, 100, 102
Smith, Zadie, 127
Snow Falling on the Cedars (Guterson), 131, 142; exoticization in, 142
Sohn, Stephen, 155n19, 184n25
Somewhere Between (documentary), 169n85
Song, Min, 157n46, 184n25
Sounes, Howard, 75, 77, 171n7, 173n42
Southeast Asian Americans, 15. *See also* Asian Americans
Southeast Asian studies, 157n56
South Pacific (musical), 177n96
Speirs, Kenneth, 11
Spickard, Paul, 9, 23, 29, 158n1, 158n4; on gender, 34
Spillers, Bill, 79
Srikanth, Rajini, 142, 145, 187n70
Starn, Orin, 83, 171n12
Steen, Shannon, 156n45
Steinbeck, John, 140
Stimson, Henry, 25, 163n58

Stone, Oliver, 178n1
subjectivity: of Asian Americans, 148, 155n34; and compulsory racial identity, 180n32; and identity politics, 2; of mixed race people, 97, 101, 102; and passing, 97–98, 105, 110–111; and performance, 97–98; and racial ambiguity, 6. *See also* racial ambiguity; racial formation
Sui Sin Far, 179n17
Sze, Julie, 181n61

Takayashi, Theresa, 32–33
Tan, Amy, 127, 178n1, 187n66, 187n3 (Coda)
Tanaka, Eju, 35, 164n71
Tasaday hoax, 103–104
Temple, Shirley, 54, 167n50
Then She Found Me (film), 44, 62, 165n1, 168n54
Thind, Bhaghat Singh, 162nn47–48
Tojo, Hideki, 28–29
transgressive texts, 123–125, 140–141, 143; and Asian American epistemology, 146; and Asian American literary canon, 123–125, 144–145; and Asian American literary criticism, 130–131; racial ambiguity of, 141, 146. *See also* Asian American literature
travel, 188n6; and identity, 120
Trenka, Jane Jeong, 53, 60, 66, 67–68, 169n80; *Fugitive Visions*, 61; *The Language of Blood*, 53, 61, 70; on whiteness, 66
Trevino, Lee, 79, 171n10, 172n32
Trophy Wife (film), 44
Truong, Monique, 148, 186n54
Tu, Thuy Linh Nguyen, 157n45
Tuan, Mia, 155n35
Twain, Mark, 130

UGA (United Golf Association), 172n16
USGA (United States Golf Association), 172n16

Veblen, Thorstein, 117
Viet Nam: in American film, 187n68; American war in, 19, 49, 65, 72, 73, 87–89, 145–146, 171n6, 185n39
Vietnamese Americans, 51, 68, 134; Amerasians, 88, 90–92, 175n66, 176n78; in Asian American literature, 129, 133, 138–139, 145–146, 184n30; prejudice against, 177n92
Vietnamese people, 77, 92, 133–135, 187n68, 171n6; Saigon, fall of, 49, 88, 89, 182n5; and skin color, 177n87; women, 73, 87, 134, 176n83
Volkman, Toby Alice, 51

Wald, Gayle, 119
Watson, Julia, 100, 102
Webster (television series), 165n2
Weisman, Jan, 89, 90, 175n66; on Thai multiraciality, 90
West, Kanye, 3
West Coast Civil Authority (WCCA), 26, 158nn1–2; and assimilation, 34; exemption

policies of, 29, 158n2; and race, 39. *See also* incarceration, Japanese American; Mixed-Marriage Policy of 1942; Western Defense Command (WDC)
Western Defense Command (WDC), 26; and assimilation, 34, 38; exemption policies of, 26–27, 29, 34; and gender, 34; and race, 39. *See also* incarceration, Japanese American; Mixed-Marriage Policy of 1942; West Coast Civil Authority (WCCA)
whiteness: as "American," 31, 37–38, 106, 109, 177n86; and Asian American adoptees, 50, 52–53, 54, 60, 67; and Asian Americans, 13, 18; and Asianness, 19; and Asians, 86; and assimilation, 30–31, 39; and citizenship, 29–30, 106; and eugenics, 30, 141; and immigration policy, 162n47; and Mixed-Marriage Policy, 177n86; and multiraciality, 83, 85; in *The Night My Mother Met Bruce Lee*, 106, 109–110; and one-drop rule, 95; and privilege, 5, 12, 66; and Tiger Woods, 83; and transnational/transracial adoption, 52–53, 166n8; Trenka on, 66; and white superiority, 31
white supremacy, 11, 31, 86; and black abjection, 116; and silencing, 123; and transnational/transracial adoption, 166n8
Wie, Michelle, 172n33
Williams, Sumeia (Sume), 60, 61, 65–67, 68, 169n79, 169n97
Williams, Teresa Kay, 9, 97, 118
Winant, Howard, 10; on ethnicity and race, 28; on racial identity, 110
Winfrey, Oprah, 82, 171n7
Woman Warrior, The (Kingston), 96, 128–129, 178nn1–2; and authenticity, 99, 178n5; as Orientalist, 178n4; as postmodern text, 141; truth in, 100. *See also* Kingston, Maxine Hong
women, Asian: and American war in Viet Nam, 73, 87–95, 134, 176n78, 176n83; erasure of, 92–93; hypersexualization of, 108–109, 110, 180n44; as prostitutes, 90, 176n83; stereotypes of, 180n44; subjectivity of, 109–110
Wong, Jade Snow, 179n17
Wong, Mike, 187n69
Wong, Sau-ling Cynthia, 125, 147, 178n2
Wong, Shawn, 126
Wong, William, 81, 173n38
Woods, Earl, 71, 73, 93, 173n42, 177n98; infidelity of, 92; military service of, 89; racism against, 73. *See also* Woods, Tiger
Woods, Kultida (Tida), 72, 73, 87, 89–90; and Asianness, 77; erasure of, 81–82, 87, 92–93, 94, 174n64; racial ambiguity of, 93, 94; racism against, 73. *See also* Woods, Tiger
Woods, Tiger, 71–74, 76–87, 177n98; as African American, 72, 77, 78, 79–80, 81, 83, 84, 86–87, 94, 173n42, 174n56; as Amerasian, 89, 91–92, 94, 175n66; as "American," 80; as apolitical, 82–83, 84, 173n48; as Asian, 92, 174n61; as Asian American, 77, 78,

79–80, 83, 85, 86–87; and Asianness, 74, 77, 83, 173n36; and blackness, 78, 81–83, 94, 173n36; Buddhism of, 73, 85–86; as "Cablinasian," 6, 82, 83, 95; and color-blindness, 19, 81; as everyman, 78; as exceptional, 74, 91; golf success of, 73–74; marketing of, 78, 82, 85–86, 171n8, 172n30; as mixed race, 74, 79–80, 84, 89, 94, 148, 174n61, 178n99; as monoracial, 80–82, 84–87, 95; and multiculturalism, 78; naming of, 93–94; 1997 Masters victory, 71, 77, 81; and one-drop rule, 72; as race traitor, 83; racial ambiguity of, 19–20, 78–80, 84, 89, 91–92, 94–95; racism against, 73, 171n7; sex addiction of, 72, 170n5; as text, 72; Thailand, reception in, 89, 176n80; "Tigergate," 72, 83–84, 85–86, 174n52; and whiteness, 83
World Vision, 48, 166n17
Wu, Jean, 157n46

Xingjian, Gao, 129

Yamamoto, Hisaye, 126, 162n41, 178n1
Yamashita, Karen Tei, 186n54
Yang, Jeff, 186n64
Yang, YE, 79
Yarborough, Trin, 90, 175n67, 175n73, 176n83, 177n92
Yellow Peril stereotype, 13, 14, 156n39; and 9/11, 15
Yu, Henry, 81, 94
Yu, Timothy, 15, 157n47
Yun, Lisa, 140
Yung, Judy, 51

Zack, Naomi, 11
Zeiger, Susan, 88–89, 90, 175n73, 176n76; on Vietnamese women, 92
Zhang, Ya-Jie, 178n5

ABOUT THE AUTHOR

JENNIFER HO is an associate professor in the Department of English and Comparative Literature at the University of North Carolina Chapel Hill, where she teaches courses in Asian American literature, mulitethnic American literature, and contemporary American literature. Her first book, *Consumption and Identity in Asian American Coming-of-Age Novels* (2005), examines the intersection of coming-of-age, ethnic identity formation, and foodways in late twentieth-century Asian American coming-of-age narratives and American popular culture. She has published in *Modern Fiction Studies, Global South, Journal for Asian American Studies, Amerasia Journal*, among others, and she is broadly interested in critical race theory and antiracist activism.

How might Tiger's difficulty in asserting his multi-raciality be different if his father was asia + his mother black?

CPSIA information can be obtained at www.ICGtesting.com
Printed in the USA
LVOW06s1608211015

459180LV00002B/399/P